THE DISCIPLINE OF FREEDOM

SUNY Series in Buddhist Studies
Kenneth K. Inada, EDITOR

THE DISCIPLINE OF FREEDOM

A Kantian View of the Role of Moral Precepts in Zen Practice

Phillip Olson

STATE UNIVERSITY OF NEW YORK PRESS

In memory of
Dainin Katagiri, Daioshō

Published by
State University of New York Press, Albany

Printed in the United States of America

For information, address State University of New York

Press, State University Plaza, Albany, N.Y., 12246

Production by E. Moore
Marketing by Bernadette LaManna

Library of Congress Cataloging in Publication Data

Olson, Phillip, 1943-
The discipline of freedom : a Kantian view of the role of moral precepts in Zen practice / by Phillip Olson
p. cm. — (SUNY series in Buddhist studies)
Based on the author's thesis—Stanford University.
Includes bibliographical references and index.
ISBN 0-7914-1115-X (alk. paper). — ISBN 0-7914-1116-8 (pbk. : alk. paper)
1. Spiritual life (Zen Buddhism) 2. Kant, Immanuel, 1724-1804—Ethics. 3. Suzuki, Shunryū, 1904-1971. I. Title. II. Series.
BQ9288.0463 1992 91–26526
294.3'5—dc20 CIP

10 9 8 7 6 5 4 3 2 1

The T'ang poet and official Po Chu-i asked the Ch'an master 'Bird Nest' Tao-lin, "What is the great purport of the Buddha dharma?" The master answered, "To refrain from all evil and practice all good." Po said, "Even a child of three could say that." The master said, "Though a child of three may say it, an old man of eighty can't do it."

Ching-te ch'uan teng lu
(Transmission of the Lamp from the Ching-te era)

translated by Carl Bielefeldt

Contents

Abbreviations

Works of Immanuel Kant (all page numbers refer to the pagination of the Prussian Academy edition):

KV — *Critique of Pure Reason,* trans. Norman Kemp Smith (New York: St. Martin's Press, 1965). Page numbers prefaced with the capital letter *A* refer to the first edition of the *Critique of Pure Reason,* page numbers prefaced with the capital letter *B* refer to the second edition.

KP — *Critique of Practical Reason,* trans. Lewis White Beck (Indianapolis: Bobbs-Merrill, 1956).

GW — *Groundwork of the Metaphysic of Morals,* trans. H.J. Paton (New York: Harper & Row, 1964).

MM — *The Doctrine of Virtue: Part II of The Metaphysic of Morals,* trans. Mary J. Gregor (New York: Harper & Row, 1964).

Works of Shunryu Suzuki:

ZM — *Zen Mind, Beginner's Mind* (New York: John Weatherhill, 1970).

SL — *Sandōkai Lectures* (Zen Mountain Center Library, Tassajara, California). This title refers to the unpublished transcripts of a series of thirteen lectures on the Zen Buddhist text, *Sandōkai,* delivered by Suzuki at Tassajara Zen Mountain Center between May 27 and July 6, 1970. Page numbers for the *Sandōkai Lectures* are indicated as follows: first, in Roman numerals, the lecture number is indicated; second, in Arabic numerals, the page number of the typed transcript of that particular lecture is indicated.

WB *Wind Bell.* This is the title of the periodical published by Zen Center of San Francisco, the organization founded by Suzuki. Quotations from the texts of Suzuki published in this periodical are referenced as follows: first, in Roman numerals, the volume number of the issue is indicated; second, the date of the issue is given; and finally, the page number of the quotation is given (e.g., VII, Summer 1968:16).

Preface

In a 1910 paper entitled "Observations on 'Wild' Psycho-analysis," Freud warned that practitioners attempting to apply the techniques of psychoanalysis without understanding the fundamental principles underlying these techniques were in danger of "acting wrongly towards their patients"[1] as well as doing "harm to the cause of psycho-analysis."[2] Like the practice of psychoanalysis in Europe in the early decades of this century, the practice of Zen Buddhism in America today is a fairly recently introduced discipline whose fundamental principles are subject to misinterpretation, both by students and by beginning teachers of Zen. And like the relationship between analyst and analysand, in which the former may command "extraordinary powers"[3] over the latter, the teacher-student relationship in Zen is vulnerable to abuse—especially when the principles upon which that relationship should be based are obscured or distorted by misapprehension. Motivated by concerns similar to those expressed by Freud in regard to psychoanalytic practice, the present study attempts to develop a theoretical basis for criticizing the practice of "wild" Zen Buddhism in America by conducting a philosophical inquiry into the fundamental principles of Zen practice.

On another level, this study is an attempt to interpret the practice of Zen Buddhist meditation from the perspective of Kant's critical philosophy—especially as this philosophy, as expressed in the *Critique of Practical Reason*, depicts the practice of religion as a necessary outgrowth of the effort human beings make to live their lives in morally praiseworthy ways (see, e.g., *KP*, 130). By arguing in support of a Kantian interpretation of Zen practice I will be trying to persuade the reader both that the fundamental principles informing the practice of Zen Buddhism are ethical principles, and that Zen practice loses its validity as a religious practice when its students and teachers lose sight of the central role of such principles. It is my hope that in the course of presenting a plausible argument for the fundamental role of ethical principles in Zen practice I will also be providing a sound philosophical basis from which to criticize the practice of "wild" Zen Buddhism.

In choosing to conduct an inquiry into the fundamental principles of Zen practice by the comparative method of interpreting Zen Buddhist texts from a Western philosophical perspective, I do not mean to imply that Buddhist texts by themselves fail to provide a sufficient basis for demonstrating the ethical foundations of Zen practice. However, in the introductory and concluding chapters of this study I do suggest that the connection between Zen teachings and moral/ethical concerns is often not easily perceived by Western students of Zen—and that a Kantian interpretation of Zen practice may be of some help in discrediting the view, held by some, that moral rules and Zen practice have nothing to do with each other. The following passage from Masao Abe's *Zen and Western Thought* supports the view that a confrontation with Kant's ethical philosophy may help alert students of Zen to the special vulnerability of this religious practice to nonethical or even anti-ethical interpretations. Although Professor Abe insists that "Zen and Kant completely part company" in some important respects, he goes on to acknowledge:

> The Zen [philosophical] position . . . did not necessarily experience a self-conscious confrontation with the moral and ethical 'Ought' so keenly realized in the intellectual tradition of the West. The fact that, as a result, Zen often harboured the danger of losing its own authentic freedom, of falling into a non-critical dilettantism, and of sinking into a mere non-ethic or anti-ethic is one that must not be minimized. If Zen feels a mission as a true 'world religion,' then an open-minded confrontation with the standpoint of the 'principle' of moral

> 'principles' realized by Kant and a confrontation with various problems contained therein—such as free will, the autonomy of reason, realization of transcendental moral laws, radical evil, etc.—must be said to be inescapable.[4]

My reasons for choosing the lectures of the late Zen master, Shunryu Suzuki, as the focus of this Kantian interpretation of Zen practice are set forth briefly in the introductory chapter below. However, some additional words of explanation may help answer the questions of readers troubled by my use of the lectures of a popular contemporary Zen teacher as the focus of a philosophical analysis of Zen practice. Although Shunryu Suzuki's book, *Zen Mind, Beginner's Mind,* has been called by one American philosopher comparable in importance to the works of pioneer Buddhist scholar D.T. Suzuki (see *ZM*, 9), Suzuki's role in introducing Zen practice to Americans was that of a monastic leader and teacher, not that of a philosopher or scholar of Zen. Nevertheless, I found Suzuki's introductory lectures on Zen practice to be particularly suited to the purposes of this study for the following reasons.

First, I chose to work with Suzuki's texts because they were originally delivered in contemporary English. This choice of English-language source materials was dictated in part by necessity, as my ignorance of East Asian languages left me ill-equipped to undertake a detailed philosophical analysis of the writings of any of the well-known Asian Zen masters. But even if I had the necessary linguistic background, I still might have preferred Suzuki's texts to my own English translations of Chinese or Japanese texts, as a subject of analysis. The authenticity of any explanatory text on Zen meditation practice obviously depends a great deal upon *who* the author is: she or he must be someone well qualified to speak or write about Zen practice or the text will be of little value as a source of information on Zen. And given there is always an element of indeterminacy present in any translation of an author's text which can make it hard to tell who—the author, the translator, or some amalgam of both—is speaking or writing, I feel the use of contemporary English source materials has enabled me to present and analyze the teaching of Zen in a clearer and more straightforward way than if I had been using, say, source materials from medieval Japan.

A second reason for using Suzuki's lectures on Zen practice as the source materials for this study is that the lectures were addressed to an audience unfamiliar with the language and history of the Buddhist philosophical tradition. Because his American listeners sat, as it were, behind a veil of ignorance in respect to Buddhist philosophy and its twenty-five centuries of development, Suzuki was forced either to explain Buddhist philosophical concepts from scratch—providing fresh, new definitions in an American idiom—or else to avoid using Buddhist philosophical terms altogether. The advantage of using Suzuki's "beginner's mind" explanations of Zen practice—as opposed to more academically oriented explanations—in a comparative study of this type can be appreciated when one considers that a formidable part of the task of interpreting a text on Zen practice from the perspective of a different philosophical tradition is that of unpacking the meaning of key Buddhist terms, such as 'emptiness' or 'Buddha nature.' This work of unpacking would ordinarily require a careful, lengthy inspection of the weighty philosophical baggage these terms have accumulated, piece by piece, in their travels from culture to culture, and from language to language, over the past two thousand years. Suzuki, however, makes every effort *not* to encumber the minds of his listeners with philosophical baggage. As the following two quotations show, he advances the claim that Zen practice can—and, in a sense, must—be explained and understood in the purely practical context of one's daily life, without reference to Buddhist philosophy or history:

> The Zen school developed in many ways after it was established in China, but at the same time, it became more and more impure. But I do not want to talk about Chinese Zen or the history of Zen. I am interested in helping you keep your practice from becoming impure. [*ZM*, 21]

> The most important things in our practice are our physical posture and our way of breathing. We are not so concerned about a deep understanding of Buddhism. As a philosophy, Buddhism is a very deep, wide, and firm system of thought,

> but Zen is not concerned about philosophical understanding. We emphasize practice. We should understand why our physical posture and breathing exercise are so important. [*ZM*, 99]

Suzuki's statements that Zen is not concerned about philosophical understanding and "I do not want to talk about Chinese Zen or the history of Zen" belie the fact that many of his lectures—especially those delivered to his advanced students—are specifically devoted to explaining and analyzing Buddhist philosophical concepts, often by means of showing how these concepts developed in a particular historical context.[5] However, Suzuki's point in the above quotations would seem to be that no matter how helpful philosophical and historical understanding may be as an aid in the course of Zen study, such understanding should not be confused with the main purpose of Zen study, which is, as he says repeatedly, "practice" itself:

> Although there are people in this country who are interested in Buddhism, few of them are interested in its pure form. Most of them are interested in studying the teaching or the philosophy of Buddhism. . . . But whether Buddhism is philosophically deep or good or perfect is not the point. To keep our practice in its pure form is our purpose. [*ZM*, 123]

Thus Suzuki suggests that there is a "pure form" of Zen practice, the fundamental principles of which can best be explained and understood in the practical context of "our physical posture and breathing exercise" as we conduct our daily lives, rather than in reference to the Buddhist philosophical tradition. And therefore, as Suzuki's chief disciple, Richard Baker, points out in his introduction to *Zen Mind, Beginner's Mind*, the pedagogical approach adopted by Suzuki in his lectures is to use "the simplest language and the situations of everyday life" (*ZM*, 14) to explain and illustrate the fundamental principles of Zen practice to his beginning American students. The transcribed texts of Suzuki's lectures thus provide the comparative philosopher with fresh, "beginner's mind" explanations of the principles of Zen practice—explanations that need not be situated in any special scholarly context in order to be analyzed and understood.

A third reason for using Shunryu Suzuki's lectures on Zen practice as the focus of the present study is Suzuki's stature as a leading figure in the transmission of Zen Buddhism to America.[6] Since an underlying purpose informing this attempt to interpret Zen practice from a Kantian standpoint is that of developing a sound philosophical basis for the criticism of "wild" Zen Buddhism in America, it seems fitting to examine and interpret the fundamental principles of Zen as they have been transmitted in one of the most widely influential accounts of the practice.[7] Of course, a disadvantage of basing this Kantian interpretation of Zen practice on the writings of one contemporary Zen master is that even if the interpretation should appear plausible in respect to Suzuki's texts, questions will remain regarding its relevance to other contemporary, as well as to classical, Zen writings. Therefore, in an effort to suggest answers to some of these remaining questions, I have included an appendix that attempts to show the compatibility of the interpretation of Zen practice developed in this study with the writings of the seminal Japanese Zen teacher and philosopher, Eihei Dōgen.

A final, personal reason for using the lectures of Shunryu Suzuki as the source materials for this study is that from 1969 through 1971 I was fortunate to be one of many students who studied Zen Buddhism with Suzuki and his co-teachers, Dainin Katagiri and Kobun Chino, at San Francisco Zen Center and at Tassajara Zen Mountain Center. After Suzuki's death in December 1971, I continued my study of Buddhism with Kobun Chino, receiving monk's ordination from him in 1975. Thus, although this study approaches Suzuki's writings from a philosophical perspective, it also reflects the concerns of a member of the Zen Buddhist community. The writing of this book was, I found, a valuable opportunity to review and reevaluate Suzuki's teachings, and to reflect upon their correct transmission.

Many people in many ways helped make this study possible. In a reversal of the normal order of acknowledgments, I must start by thanking my wife, Andrea Jacobson, for financially supporting our household during the many months I spent writing this book. Without her generous assistance the book could not have been written. Similarly, I am grateful for the financial support of my parents, Phillip and Mary Ellen Olson, who helped make it possible for me to return to school at the advanced age of thirty-seven to study Buddhism and Kant. The combined years of study and writing that produced the present study also represent sacrifices on the part of my children, Marea and Eric, for which I am both grateful and apologetic: their father was often unavailable to them during that time and could not except in remote ways claim to be working for their benefit.

One of my great pleasures in returning to university life as an adult student was that of meeting many good teachers. In different ways, virtually all of my teachers in philosophy and religious studies have made a contribution to this study, and I am grateful to each one of them. In particular, my studies with Kenneth Inada of the State University of New York at Buffalo, and Carl Bielefeldt and Diana Paul of Stanford University were an invaluable and indispensable preparation for researching and writing a book on Buddhism. And studying logic with John Corcoran at SUNY Buffalo, and ethics with Michael Bratman at Stanford gave me the chance to encounter clear philosophical thinking and writing at its best. The original manuscript of the book was written as an undergraduate honors thesis at Stanford University, under the supervision of Professors Lee Yearley and Carl Bielefeldt of religious studies, and Professor Eckhart Förster of philosophy. Although they, of course, are not responsible for the contents of the study, I thank them for their advice, critical comments, and support throughout the long process of composition. Of all my teachers, I owe the greatest debt to Lee Yearley: this book was written in the wake, as it were, of his work in comparative philosophy.

The ultimate encouragement a professor can give a student is to treat the latter's academic work as worthy of respect on its own merits. Thus I want to thank Kenneth Inada, professor of philosophy and editor of the SUNY Series in Buddhist Studies, for taking an interest in my work and encouraging me to seek publication. Without his active interest and encouragement—which remained unflagging, even while the manuscript lay dormant during three years of law school—the present book would not exist. I am likewise grateful to Lois Patton, editor in chief of SUNY Press, as well as to other members of the SUNY Press staff, for their patience and support throughout the long revision and publication process. And I must add a special note of thanks to Mary Ellen Olson, who proofread first the galley sheets and then the page proofs of the book, making many valuable suggestions.

Finally, without having had the opportunity to practice Zen Buddhism in the company of sincere teachers and other Zen student friends, I would never have thought of, let alone written, this study. Thus many teachers and friends in the Buddhist community have contributed to the writing of this book, although they, like my academic teachers, are not responsible for its precise contents. More than anything else, it has been my experience of life in the midst of the Buddhist *sangha* that has convinced me of the truth of Kant's thesis (affirmed independently by Gandhi on many occasions) that true religious practice has its basis in common morality.

1

Introduction

i: Moral Law As the Basis for Zen Meditation Practice

It is a thesis of Kant's *Critique of Practical Reason* that "the moral law leads to religion" (*KP*, 130). I understand Kant to mean by this that the practice of religion is the necessary, culminating stage of a person's effort to live life in accordance with the requirements of morality. Thus the effort that human beings make to realize the requirements of morality is, when viewed from a Kantian perspective, the true foundation and raison d'être of religion, and it is only in relationship to this effort that religious principles and beliefs can be called valid (see, e.g., *KP*, 144, n.6).[1] It is another thesis of Kant's second *Critique* that without conscious and willing obedience to the requirements of moral law there can be no "consciousness of freedom"—this latter phrase referring to my awareness that I have, or at least seem to have, the capacity to be self-determining, to be the first cause of my own thoughts and actions (see *KP*, 30). This study is an attempt to organize an interpretation of the practice of Zen meditation around these two theses.

The purpose of the study is limited to sketching out one possible interpretive approach to the practice of Zen. Not wanting to lose sight of a possible forest by focusing too closely on individual trees, I felt that the risk of confusion would be too great were I to attempt both to present a coherent overview of a possible Kantian interpretation of Zen practice *and* to present rigorous arguments in support of all the various Kantian, Buddhist, and comparative philosophical theses upon which this interpretation is based. So, in the interest of providing the overview, I have chosen to leave open the question whether this interpretation can be defended against many specific criticisms that might be raised against it. Thus this book is intended only as a preparatory sketch, or outline, of a Kantian interpretation of Zen practice.

Since the terms 'freedom' and 'moral law' can be used in a variety of ways, the reader should know that I will be trying to use these terms in a manner consistent with the way Kant uses them in the *Critique of Practical Reason*—keeping in mind that Kant did not see himself in that work as using language in a manner that differed significantly from its popular use:

> I have no fear, with respect to this treatise, of the reproach that I wish to introduce a new language, since the kind of thinking it deals with is very close to the popular way of thinking. . . . To make up new words for accepted concepts when the language does not lack expressions for them is a childish effort to distinguish one's self not by new and true thoughts but by new patches on old clothes. [*KP*, 10]

Like the terms 'freedom' and 'moral law,' the term 'Zen meditation'—or *zazen* as it is called in Japanese—has been used and interpreted in a variety of ways. There are, of course, many traditions and accounts of Zen meditation practice—each of which must be understood in its particular historical, cultural, and linguistic context. Thus I have tried to make my use of the terms 'Zen meditation' and *zazen* as unambiguous as possible by limiting the focus of this study to the texts of a single Zen teacher. Also, in order to avoid problems caused by my own ignorance of Asian languages—as well as those ambiguities that inevitably arise when texts are translated from one language and culture to that of another—I have chosen to use an account of Zen practice that was given in contemporary American English. These two considerations, plus others referred to above in the preface, have led me to select as the account of Zen meditation practice to be used in this study the lectures of Zen master Shunryu Suzuki.

A Japanese Sōtō Zen teacher who lived and taught in the United States from 1959 until his death in 1971, Shunryu Suzuki's missionary efforts attracted many followers and resulted in the establishment of the first Sōtō Zen monastery in the West, the Zen Mountain Center at Tassajara, California (*ZM*, 10). Suzuki lectured to his American disciples and students in their own English language, using a minimum of Buddhist philosophical language in his talks. A series of Suzuki's lectures, addressed to beginning lay students of Zen Buddhism, has been transcribed and published in the widely disseminated book (currently in its twenty-eighth paperback printing), *Zen Mind, Beginner's Mind.* To supplement the account of Zen meditation given in these lectures, I will refer to other lectures delivered by Suzuki to his advanced students and ordained disciples at Tassajara Zen Mountain Center. Many of these Tassajara lectures have been published in the San Francisco Zen Center journal, *Wind Bell,* while others are available in unedited transcript form at the Zen Mountain Center library.

In applying Kant's theses concerning freedom and the moral basis of religious practice to the account of Zen practice given by Suzuki, I will be arguing that Buddhism, as Suzuki explains its practice, is rightly understood as a religious practice based upon respect for and obedience to moral law. I hope to demonstrate that respectful obedience to moral precepts is not, as one prominent Buddhist scholar suggests, merely "ancillary" to the full realization of the Buddhist teaching,[2] but rather ought to be considered the very essence of such teaching. Indeed, according to the interpretation of Zen practice advanced in the following chapters—an interpretation suggested by the Zen teaching story that is this book's epigraph—the practice of Zen meditation itself is ancillary (albiet essential) to a Buddhist's effort to live life according to the requirements of moral law.

This Kantian interpretation of the role of moral precepts in Zen practice is being offered in the hope it might contribute to the discussion of a question that has arisen simultaneously with the introduction of Zen meditation practice in America: What—if any—relationship is there between sitting cross-legged in meditation and respecting and obeying moral rules? Precisely because it is natural from a non-Buddhist viewpoint to ask such a question, acknowledgment that any relationship exists between practicing Zen meditation and obeying moral rules has not come spontaneously from American students of Zen. Indeed, Alan Watts—one of the first and most influential Americans to become seriously interested in the practice of Zen—suggested in his little book *Beat Zen, Square Zen, and Zen,* that the practice of Zen reveals a "comparatively limitless" sphere of existence that is "entirely beyond the categories of good and evil."[3] To dwell within this sphere, Watts said, is to view the different patterns of human conduct with the same sense of wonder and acceptance as we view different constellations of stars in the night sky:

> Looking out . . . at night, we make no comparisons between right and wrong stars, nor between well and badly arranged constellations. Stars are by nature big and little, bright and dim. Yet the whole thing is a splendor and a marvel. . . . There is a standpoint from which human affairs are as much beyond right and wrong as the stars, and from which our deeds, experiences and feelings can no more be judged than the ups and downs of a range of mountains. [ibid., 5]

In his narrative history of Buddhism in America, *How the Swans Came to the Lake,* Rick Fields cites an incident that suggests that what might be called the American temptation to sever the connection between practicing *zazen* and respecting precepts of common morality has not been confined to Americans studying the unfamiliar ways of Eastern Buddhism, but has affected some Asian teachers of Buddhism in America as well. In his discussion of Zen Buddhist practice in the United States, Fields refers to a young Japanese Zen monk of the 1960s who, "fresh from the monastery and used to the conventional morality of Japan, had been swept off his feet by the freedom of American women, and had slept with one or more of his students."[4]

Certainly, if the practice of Zen Buddhist meditation, or *zazen*, is viewed neither in the context of the Buddhist monastic tradition nor in the context of common morality, it is far from obvious why mastery of a particular cross-legged posture and way of breathing should be related to any particular kind of moral behavior. Thus it is understandable why even advanced students of Buddhist meditation in America, whether they be Asian or Caucasian, might adopt the view that the practice of *zazen*—like the practice, say, of swimming or archery—can be undertaken and developed independently of the practice of observing moral rules. If, however, *zazen* practice *is* viewed in the context of Buddhist tradition, it is clear that in addition to the study and practice of certain physical and psychological techniques such as sitting upright, following one's breath, and maintaining mental alertness, the process of becoming fully initiated into the practice of Buddhist meditation has traditionally involved an important moral dimension as well. For when one becomes an ordained member of a Zen Buddhist community, the traditional ordination ceremony culminates in the initiate's formal acceptance of a body of moral guidelines referred to as the "Bodhisattva precepts."[5] In reference to these precepts, Eihei Dōgen, the thirteenth-century Zen master whom Suzuki, in the preface to *Zen Mind, Beginner's Mind*, calls "the founder of our school" (*ZM*, 22), states categorically:

> It may be said that it is because monks strictly observe the precepts that they are the paragons of the three worlds. Therefore if you wish to do zazen and pursue Buddhism, you should first observe the precepts. How can you expect to become a Buddha or patriarch if you do not guard against faults and prevent yourself from doing wrong? . . . The words "receive the precepts first of all" already truly express the highest supreme Law.[6]

And of the *Jukai* ceremony, in which Zen Buddhist initiates formally vow to faithfully observe the Bodhisattva precepts for the entire course of their life, the contemporary British-American Zen Master, Jiyu Kennett, has written:

> This is the most important set of ceremonies in the life of a [Zen Buddhist] layman, and no person may become a [monastic] trainee unless he has undergone the week of training that these ceremonies occupy, either before his ordination or within a year of entering a training temple.[7]

The *Jukai* ceremony, as described by Kennett, includes both the taking of general vows to refrain from evil and to do good for others, and the formal acceptance of ten more specific precepts, each offering guidance in a different area of conduct.[8] Thus the practice of *zazen*, when viewed in the context of Buddhist tradition, is a practice based virtually from the beginning on vows to conscientiously observe both general and specific precepts of morality. And, given that the third of the ten specific precepts teaches restraint or detachment in respect to the promptings of sexual desire,[9] any Zen teacher "swept off his feet" by sexual desire for one or more of his students can hardly be said—from the viewpoint of such traditional accounts of Zen practice—to have mastered or even rightly understood a meditation discipline whose guiding precepts specifically entail the practice of detachment from such desire.

For Americans who question whether the practice of Zen meditation is meaningfully related to the observance of moral precepts, Kant's *Critique of Practical Reason* provides strong support for the traditional Buddhist view. For Kant's thesis that the requirements of moral law both "lead to" and provide the true foundation for religious practice seems close in spirit to Dōgen's statement, quoted above, that "the words 'receive the precepts first of all' already truly express the highest supreme [religious] Law." As Dōgen, in this same passage, goes on to say:

> People who have become Buddhas and patriarchs have done so through having never failed to receive and observe this highest supreme Law. The Buddhas and patriarchs who correctly transmitted the highest supreme Law have unfailingly received and observed the precepts, for otherwise, it would have been impossible for them to become Buddhas or patriarchs. They received the precepts either directly from the

> Buddha himself or from one of his disciples. In either case they have all inherited the essence of the Way.[10]

For Dōgen, who founded the school of Zen Buddhism to which Shunryu Suzuki belongs, to receive and observe moral precepts is to inherit and practice "the essence of the Way" of Zen. Thus it may not seem too far out of the line of Buddhist tradition to propose in this essay the following outline of a Kantian interpretation of Zen practice:

(KO) *A true religious practice in the Kantian sense is one based upon the requirements of moral law, as Kant understands these requirements.*
[proposed definition]

(K1) *A religious practice based upon the requirements of moral law is one completely subordinated to those requirements.*
[suggested interpretation of K0]

(K2) *A religious practice completely subordinated to the requirements of moral law is one performed solely as a means to the end of realizing those requirements.*
[suggested interpretation of K1]

(K3) *A religious practice performed solely as a means to the end of realizing the requirements of moral law is "a true religious practice in the Kantian sense."*
[K0-K2]

(K4) *The practice of* zazen, *when correctly performed in accordance with Shunryu Suzuki's account of this practice, is performed solely as a means to the end of realizing the requirements of moral law, as Kant understands these requirements.*
[thesis, the truth of which this study attempts to demonstrate]

(K5) *The practice of* zazen, *when performed in accordance with Shunryu Suzuki's account of this practice, is a true religious practice in the Kantian sense.*
[K0-K4]

It is my intent in this study to demonstrate the truth of thesis K4 by presenting and defending an interpretation of Shunryu Suzuki's account of *zazen* in which its practice is understood exclusively as a means to the end of fulfilling the requirements of moral law, and thus as "a true religious practice in the Kantian sense."

ii: Structure of the Study

In his prologue to *Zen Mind, Beginner's Mind,* Suzuki makes a statement that partially supports thesis K4, above:

> If we lose our original self-sufficient mind, we will lose all precepts. When your mind becomes demanding, when you long for something, you will end up violating your own precepts: not to tell lies, not to steal, not to kill, not to be immoral, and so forth. If you keep your original mind, the precepts will keep themselves. [*ZM,* 22]

The purpose of Zen practice, Suzuki says, is always to keep our "original mind"—our "beginner's mind" (*ZM,* 21). This mind is "the secret of Zen practice" (*ZM,* 22). And because he believes that "if we lose our original self-sufficient mind, we will lose all precepts," Suzuki clearly views the practice of *zazen*—the practice, that is, of keeping our "original mind"—as a necessary means for realizing the requirements of moral precepts. However, it would not be a sufficient demonstration of the truth of thesis K4 simply to present evidence that Suzuki views the practice of *zazen* as a necessary means to the end of realizing the requirements of moral law. For such a view is by no means identical to the view that *zazen,* as "a true religious practice in the Kantian sense," is practiced correctly only when it is performed *solely* as a means to the end of realizing the requirements of moral law. In refutation of this latter view, it is conceivable that Suzuki might say: "Yes, it is true that *zazen* practice is necessary for realization of the requirements of our moral precepts, but it is not *solely* in order to realize these requirements that we practice *zazen.*"

Thus it will be necessary to construct two main arguments in order to fully support the interpretation of Suzuki's account of Zen practice expressed by thesis K4. Certainly, support must be found in Suzuki for the claim that my practice of *zazen* is a necessary means for keeping those moral precepts that govern my life as a Buddhist, and thus truly is "a means to the end of realizing the requirements of moral law." But in addition, evidence must be found in Suzuki's texts to support the claim that in order to practice *zazen* correctly, I should make realization of the requirements of moral precepts my sole incentive in performing that practice.

In summation then, the Kantian interpretation of Suzuki's account of *zazen* practice that is advanced in this study is expressed by thesis K4:

K4 *The practice of* zazen, *when correctly performed in accordance with Shunryu Suzuki's account of this practice, is performed solely as a means to the end of realizing the requirements of moral law, as Kant understands these requirements.*

And the two theses that, if shown to be true, will support K4 are expressed as follows:

Z1 *The practice of* zazen, *according to Suzuki, is a necessary means to the end of realizing the requirements of moral law, as Kant understands these requirements.*

Z2 *In order to practice zazen correctly, according to Suzuki, my sole intention in performing that practice should be that of realizing the requirements of moral law, as Kant understands these requirements.*

Chapters 3 and 4 attempt to show that theses Z1 and Z2 are plausible interpretations of Suzuki's account of *zazen* practice. But first, in preparation for the arguments in these later chapters, an attempt is made in chapter 2 to develop a Kantian interpretation of the central term of theses Z1 and Z2—the term *zazen* itself.

2

Interpreting the Term *Zazen* in Kantian Language

i: Why a Kantian Interpretation of Zazen?

In order to demonstrate support in *Zen Mind, Beginner's Mind* and other Suzuki texts for theses Z1 and Z2, why should it be necessary to develop a Kantian interpretation of the term *zazen*? Why not simply use Suzuki's own explanation of the term, insert this explanation into the language of theses Z1 and Z2, and go on to demonstrate how the two theses are supported by Suzuki's account of Zen practice?

I have two related answers to these questions. The first is that in order to understand Suzuki's explanations of the term *zazen*, one must understand his frequent use of the term 'freedom' in such explanations. And in order to make sense of Suzuki's use of the term 'freedom,' I will argue, one has little choice but to interpret this term in a Kantian way—a way that then leads on to a Kantian interpretation of the term *zazen* itself. The second answer is that theses Z1 and Z2, as I shall now go on to show, are *not* conclusively supported by Suzuki's account of *zazen* unless the term 'freedom' in that account be given a Kantian interpretation. Thus, at least in respect to Suzuki's writings, the possibility of interpreting *zazen* as a religious practice based upon the requirements of moral law depends upon the possibility of developing plausible Kantian interpretations of the related terms *zazen* and 'freedom.'

While there are many statements in Suzuki that directly or indirectly support Z1 and Z2, there are also many statements that seem to rebut the claims advanced in these theses. For example, in seeming rebuttal to Z2—which advances the claim that, as a Zen student, my purpose in sitting *zazen* must be solely that of realizing the requirements of moral law—Suzuki says:

> In our practice we have no particular purpose or goal, nor any special object of worship. In this respect our practice is somewhat different from the usual religious practices. [*ZM*, 75]

The true purpose of *zazen* practice, Suzuki says elsewhere, is not that of concentrating one's mind in order to attain some purpose or goal, such as fulfilling the requirements of moral law:

> To concentrate your mind on something is not the true purpose of Zen. The true purpose is to see things as they are, to observe things as they are, and to let everything go as it goes. . . . Only in this way can you experience the vital freedom of Zen. [*ZM*, 35]

"To let everything go as it goes" would, as a maxim of conduct for one's life, seem to be the polar opposite of the maxim "to live my life in strict accordance with the requirements of moral precepts"—just as adoption of this latter maxim would seemingly stifle the spirit of anyone desiring to live life according to a principle of "vital freedom." However, Suzuki's position on the relationship between freedom and morality resists any quick understanding of the two terms as opposites. Certainly, Suzuki extolls the attainment of what might seem to be an utterly amoral kind of freedom in passages like the following:

> A Zen master once said, "To go eastward one mile is to go westward one mile." This is vital freedom. We should acquire this kind of perfect freedom. [*ZM*, 34]

Yet in the sentences immediately following this statement, Suzuki relates the attainment of "perfect freedom" to an awareness of rules:

> But perfect freedom is not found without some rules. People, especially young people, think that freedom is to do just what they want, that in Zen there is no need for rules. But it is absolutely necessary for us to have some rules. But this does not mean always to be under control. As long as you have rules, you have a chance for freedom. To try to obtain freedom without being aware of the rules means nothing. It is to acquire this perfect freedom that we practice zazen. [*ZM*, 34]

The above quotations from Suzuki show how easily differences of opinion might arise among American students of Zen regarding the relationship between *zazen* practice and obedience to moral rules. If it is "to acquire . . . perfect freedom" that I practice *zazen*, it is certainly not obvious why my attainment of such freedom should involve respect for and obedience to rules of conduct, such as those set out in the Buddhist precepts. Yet, on the other hand, Suzuki insists that "perfect freedom is not found without some rules. . . . As long as you have rules, you have a chance for freedom." Indeed, he goes on to say that it "means nothing" for me to speak of freedom apart from an awareness of rules. The term 'freedom,' according to Suzuki, loses its meaning if I use it in ignorance of the idea of acting in accordance with rules.

A Kantian reading of Suzuki's account of the relationship between perfect freedom and the observance of rules resolves the seeming ambiguity in this account. Much of Kant's second *Critique*, the *Critique of Practical Reason*, is specifically devoted to clarifying the relationship between freedom, or autonomy, and respectful obedience to moral rules. In language that seems close in spirit to the thought of Suzuki, Kant affirms a close relationship—perhaps one of identity—between the idea of freedom and the idea of unconditional practical rules, or laws:

> Thus freedom and unconditional practical law reciprocally imply each other. I do not ask here whether they are actually different, instead of an unconditional law being merely the self-consciousness of a pure practical reason, and thus identical with the positive concept of freedom. [*KP*, 29]

For Kant, like Suzuki, my consciousness of freedom can come only in association with my awareness of rules or laws. According to Kant, such laws must be *unconditional* if they are to "reciprocally imply" my freedom: that is to say, they must be rules or laws that I feel obligated to obey categorically, regardless of the situation in which I find myself. And the only type of rule or law that can command such unconditional respect and obedience, Kant says, is a *moral* law (*KP*, 30). It is meaningless, Kant claims, to talk about knowing freedom directly, separately from knowing and observing the self-imposed restraints of moral rules. This is because my knowledge of freedom:

> cannot start from freedom, for this [freedom] we can neither know immediately . . . nor infer from experience, since experience reveals us only the law of appearances and consequently the mechanism of nature, the direct opposite of freedom. [*KP*, 29]

If, as Kant says, I try to "infer from experience," it is difficult for me to conceive of the possibility of absolute freedom. I tend to think of myself as part of the world I observe—as part of that great "mechanism of nature," the physical universe, whose movements, at once vast and minute beyond my comprehension, proceed strictly according to universal laws of cause and effect. Therefore, so long as I understand my actions as taking place in the observable world, and, hence, as determined by "the law of appearances"—that is, as determined by the physical laws that govern events in that world observable by me through my senses—then I cannot infer the possibility of any action of mine being free from determination by previously existing conditions. Yet, Kant says, as soon as I develop an awareness of *moral* laws—laws whose practical necessity I acknowledge and accept as binding on my own conduct—I become aware of a way of determining my actions "which is completely independent of and not to be outweighed by any sensuous condition" (*KP*, 33).

As Suzuki points out, many people use the term 'freedom' to mean "to do just what they want." Such people equate freedom with the ability to follow and fulfill their desires—with their ability to satisfy what Kant calls the "sensuous conditions" of their lives. But this is not the way either Kant or Suzuki want to use the word 'freedom.' To make an object of desire the determining grounds for my actions, Kant says, should not be called the condition of freedom, or *autonomy* (independence[1]), but rather the condition of *heteronomy* ("subject to another's laws or rules"[2]) (*KP*, 33–34). An autonomous being is one who can be said to be independent and self-determining. By simply following my desires or drives, however, I do not, as Kant would say, *give myself* the law that governs my actions, but rather merely give myself over to "a reasonable obedience to pathological laws" (*KP*, 33).

In his second *Critique* Kant gives an example intended to illustrate both why my freedom to follow my desire is not true freedom, and why the experience of true freedom can come to me only through my encounter with moral law:

> Suppose that someone says his lust is irresistible when the desired object and opportunity are present. Ask him whether he would not control his passion if, in front of the house where he has this opportunity, a gallows were erected on which he would be hanged immediately after gratifying his lust. We do not have to guess very long what his answer would be. [*KP*, 30]

I may want to use the term 'freedom' to mean "freedom to do what I want," but in a case where doing what I want involves fearful consequences—involves perhaps the consequence of my death—I realize suddenly that I am not truly "free" to choose one course of action over another. In such a situation, it is simply not the case for me that "to go eastward one mile is to go westward one mile." If I go eastward, away from the house wherein I might fulfill my desire, I go away not with a sense of freedom but with the knowledge that I am traveling in this direction against my will, forced away from what I desire by the fear of losing my neck! And if I go westward, into the house, again I travel with no sure sense of freedom, but rather with a sense of doomed compulsion, knowing that my desire is leading me helplessly toward my death. In either case, it is what Kant calls "sensuous conditions"—those physical and psychological laws of cause and effect that we use to describe and define the "mechanism of nature"—which determine my action. There is thus no way I can experience freedom from the sensuous conditions of my life simply by following my desires and aversions.

Then Kant develops his illustration further:

> But ask him whether he thinks it would be possible for him to overcome his love of life, however great it may be, if his sovereign threatened him with the same sudden death unless he made a false deposition against an honorable man whom the ruler wished to destroy under a plausible pretext. Whether he would or not he perhaps will not venture to say; but that it would be possible for him he would certainly admit without hesitation. He judges, therefore, that he can do something because he knows that he ought, and he recognizes that he is free—a fact which, without the moral law, would have remained unknown to him. [*KP*, 30]

My desire for life is such an integral part of what I think of as "me" that it rarely, if ever, occurs to me to wonder what it might mean to attain freedom from such a desire. But should a powerful person threaten me with death in an attempt to force me, through my desire for life, to participate in the murder of an innocent person, I immediately become aware of something—Kant calls it a moral law—which tells me I *ought* not to commit murder, regardless of the sensuous conditions impelling me toward such a deed. At this moment, Kant says, I become aware of my freedom to act according to the idea of *practically necessary* laws, rather than according to "a reasonable obedience to pathological laws." And it is in reference to this ability to act according to my idea of practically necessary (that is, moral) laws or rules that, according to Kant, the term 'freedom' is rightly used.

If Suzuki's use of the term 'freedom' is given the Kantian interpretation just illustrated—an interpretation in which 'freedom' refers to my ability to determine my actions independently of the "sensuous conditions" of my life, by means of my respect for and obedience to the commands of moral laws, or rules—then there is no confusing the sense of Suzuki's statement:

> It is absolutely necessary for us to have some rules. . . . As long as you have rules, you have a chance for freedom. To try to obtain freedom without being aware of the rules means nothing. It is to acquire this perfect freedom that we practice zazen.

Viewed from a Kantian perspective, Suzuki's statement can be interpreted as follows: because (a) the experience of freedom is the experience of determining one's actions independently of the physical and psychological conditions affecting one's body and mind, and because (b) this experience of determining one's actions independently of physical and psychological conditions is realizable only as the experience of acting according to moral rules, then (c) *zazen* practice, as a way of acquiring perfect freedom, is a practice that necessarily involves respect for and obedience to such rules.

Because a Kantian interpretation of the term 'freedom' seems to fit well with Suzuki's use of this term in his account of *zazen* practice, I want now, in the next section of this chapter, to expand my Kantian interpretation of Suzuki to include the term *zazen* itself—the discipline without which, Suzuki says, "it is impossible to attain absolute freedom" (*ZM*, 31).

ii: Zazen *Interpreted As a "Discipline of Freedom"*

Quotations from Kant's *Critique of Practical Reason* that have been presented so far indicate that Kant recognizes but one practice, or discipline, as being necessary for the attainment of freedom: that of respecting and obeying moral rules. Kant's example of the house and gallows suggests that I can realize freedom, or autonomy, simply by keeping in mind and acting in accordance with the rules of morality. But if this is the only discipline needed to acquire "perfect freedom," then what *Kantian* justification is there for Suzuki's claim that *zazen* practice is necessary for the attainment of such freedom? For Suzuki explicitly says:

> If you want to discover the true meaning of Zen in your everyday life, you have to understand the meaning of keeping your mind on your breathing and your body in the right posture in zazen. You should follow the rules of practice and your study should become more subtle and careful. Only in this way can you experience the vital freedom of Zen. [*ZM*, 126]

Of course, it would be foolish to try to find support in Kant for the claim that one must sit cross-legged in meditation in order to attain "perfect freedom"—foolish not only from the viewpoint of Kant's writings, but from the viewpoint of Suzuki's as well. For Suzuki takes pains to point out that the actual practice of *zazen* has nothing to do with taking a particular posture, such as the sitting position:

> Zazen practice is the practice which includes the various activities of life. So actually, we do not emphasize the sitting posture alone. How to sit is how to act. We study how to act by sitting, and this is the most basic activity for us. That is why we practice zazen in this way. . . . Buddha taught us how to act through our practice; that is why we sit. [*ZM*, 126]

According to Suzuki, *zazen* is a practically oriented discipline whereby "we study how to act." To put emphasis on a particular posture, such as the sitting posture, is to forget that through sitting—through the practice of the Buddha's teaching of meditation—I am studying how to act in this moment right now, regardless of whether I am sitting, standing, walking, or lying down. What is important is not the particular posture I take, or even the particular activity I am involved in, but rather *how* I act. "Taking our example from Buddha," Suzuki says, we should act—should be—like Buddha in every activity (*ZM*, 126). Thus Suzuki criticizes people who put too great an emphasis upon one particular posture or activity, such as sitting cross-legged, and forget that the purpose of Zen practice is to learn how to be like Buddha in *every* activity:

> Without knowing this, people put emphasis on some activity. When they put emphasis on zazen, it is not true zazen. It looks as if they were sitting in the same way as Buddha, but there is a big difference in their understanding of our practice. They understand this sitting posture as just one of the four basic postures of man, and they think: "I now take this posture." But zazen is all the postures, and each posture is Buddha's posture. This understanding is the right understanding of the zazen posture. If you practice in this way, it is Buddhism. This is a very, very important point. [*ZM*, 126]

Zazen, then, is presented by Suzuki as a discipline through which "we study how to act." And as our actions involve all postures, so "zazen is all the postures"—"zazen practice is the practice which includes the various activities of life." Thus it will not be necessary, in order to develop a Kantian interpretation of the term *zazen*, to find passages in Kant which advocate the practice of sitting cross-legged in meditation as a necessary condition for observing the requirements of moral law! Such an interpretation will require, however, the discovery of Kantian language in which to express Suzuki's claim *linking* the practice of keeping moral precepts with the practice of a discipline whereby "we study how to act." For Suzuki, in the quote from the prologue to *Zen Mind, Beginner's Mind* given earlier, clearly connects the practice of keeping moral precepts with such a practice (here referred to as the practice of keeping one's "original self-sufficient" mind):

> If we lose our original self-sufficient mind, we will lose all precepts. When your mind becomes demanding, when you long for something, you will end up violating your own precepts: not to tell lies, not to steal, not to kill, not to be immoral, and so forth. If you keep your original mind, the precepts will keep themselves. [*ZM*, 22]

Therefore, if I am to develop a Kantian interpretation of the term *zazen*, I must show how the discipline of *zazen* practice is similar to a discipline that *Kant* thinks is necessary for keeping moral precepts. Now one obvious place to look in the *Critique of Practical Reason* for mention of a mental discipline related to keeping the requirements of moral law is in Part II of that work, the "Methodology of Pure Practical Reason." In explaining the title of this, the concluding part of his second *Critique*, Kant says, "we understand by methodology the way in which we can secure to the laws of pure practical reason [i.e., moral laws] access to the human mind and an influence on its maxims. That is to say, it is the way we can make the objectively practical reason [which gives us moral laws] also subjectively practical" (*KP*, 152).

In his "Methodology" Kant outlines a method of moral cultivation that involves two successive stages. In the first stage—which might be termed the legal stage of moral cultivation—practicers should, Kant says, focus attention upon the act of moral *judgment.* They should attempt to ensure that every action contemplated or performed, by oneself or by others, is judged in regard to its conformance to the letter of the moral law—either as this law is known in the form of precepts specifying certain actions as obligatory, permissible, or prohibited (for example, "Do not lie"), or as it is known in the form of more general moral principles functioning as guiding rules for a variety of actions (for example, "Devote your life to helping all beings attain perfect happiness and virtue").

In the initial, legal stage of moral cultivation, Kant says, the practicer's interest "is not yet interest in actions and their morality itself," for:

> It only enables one to entertain himself with such judging and gives virtue, or a turn of mind based on moral laws, a form of beauty which is admired but not yet sought ("Honesty is praised and starves"). [*KP*, 160]

According to Kant, it is only when practicers move to the second stage of moral cultivation, in which they focus attention not so much on the correctness of their deed as on the purity of the *motive* for which they do the deed, that they begin to cultivate a genuinely moral interest in the performance of an action. For, from Kant's point of view, it is the subjective disposition with which a person performs an action, and not the action or deed itself, to which moral worth is actually attributable (*KP*, 159).

Thus a politician, if judged by his many benevolent actions in the public interest, might popularly be considered a person of high moral character. Yet if his motive in performing so many benevolent actions were simply that of self-interest—for instance, an interest in convincing members of his community to vote for him in future elections—such benevolent deeds would not, for Kant, be grounds for attributing to him any real moral worth. Another politician on the other hand, if judged by her failure to perform *any* benevolent actions in the public interest while in office, might be considered a person of little moral worth. Yet if this second politician failed to accomplish anything while in office because of her repeated unwillingness to cooperate with a corrupt political machine, then her failure to act effectively in the public interest would not, for Kant, be grounds for denying her the attribution of real moral worth.

A truly moral disposition, Kant says, is one in which an agent observes the requirements of moral law *for the sake of the law itself,* not for the sake of any other incentive (*KP*, 159). Such a disposition, Kant admits, may at first be seen "only as negative perfection"—only as a negatively perfect state of mind in which no incentives or inclinations other than that of the command of morality "are the determining grounds influencing an action done as a duty" (*KP*, 160). But even though an attempt by the serious practicer of morality to cultivate a disposition of detachment and independence from the promptings of inclinations can seem purely negative in spirit—in that it involves renunciation of all objects of desire in favor of obedience to the flavorless commands of duty—nevertheless, Kant insists, there is a tremendous positive benefit that comes through such cultivation. For by cultivating independence from the requirements of his needs and inclinations, *"the pupil's attention is held to the consciousness of his freedom, and . . . by relieving him of the constraint even of his true needs it frees him from the manifold discontent in which all these needs involve him and makes his mind receptive to the feeling of contentment from other sources"* (*KP*, 160; emphasis added).[3]

Kant goes on to explain more fully what he means by "consciousness of freedom":

> The heart is freed from a burden which has secretly pressed upon it; it is lightened when in instances of pure moral resolutions there is revealed to man, who previously has not correctly known it, a faculty of inner freedom to release himself from the impetuous importunity of the inclinations, to such an extent that not even the dearest of them has an influence on a resolution for which he now makes use of his reason. [*KP*, 160]

Putting our "faculty of inner freedom" to practical use through cultivating respect for and obedience to the specific requirements of morality, Kant says, creates "respect for ourselves in the consciousness of our freedom." It is the cultivation of this sense of self-respect as a free being that is the best safeguard against moral weakness: "for the consciousness of freedom is the best, indeed the only, guard that can keep ignoble and corrupting influences from bursting in upon the mind (*KP*, 160).

This last comment of Kant's suggests that the relationship between consciousness of freedom and respectful obedience to moral laws is truly reciprocal. On the one hand, my respect for and obedience to moral laws is a necessary condition for my developing consciousness of freedom, since according to Kant it is *only* through respecting and obeying moral laws that I become aware of my ability to base my actions on something other than "a reasonable obedience to pathological laws." On the other hand, as Kant has just indicated above, consciousness of freedom is itself a necessary condition for my maintaining a capacity to respect and obey moral laws, since the sense of independence and self-respect, which such consciousness gives me, is "the only guard that can keep ignoble and corrupting influences from bursting in upon the mind."

Kant's statement that consciousness of freedom is one's only safeguard against moral weakness and corruption is clearly similar in spirit to the statement from the prologue to *Zen Mind, Beginner's Mind* already quoted:

> If we lose our original self-sufficient mind, we will lose all precepts. When your mind becomes demanding, when you long for something, you will end up violating your own pre-

> cepts: not to tell lies, not to steal, not to kill, not to be immoral, and so forth. If you keep your original mind, the precepts will keep themselves.

In this passage from the prologue to his book on Zen practice, Suzuki equates "self-sufficient mind" with "original mind" or "beginner's mind" (*ZM*, 21–22). To keep this mind, he says, is the goal of Zen practice (*ZM*, 21). And since Suzuki has also been quoted above as saying that the goal of Zen practice is the realization of "perfect" or "vital" freedom, it is reasonable to conclude that by exhorting his students not to lose their self-sufficient state of mind, Suzuki is exhorting them not to lose consciousness of their "perfect" or "vital" freedom, wherein "to go eastward one mile is to go westward one mile."

Thus it would seem that both Kant and Suzuki use the terms 'freedom' and 'awareness of rules' in ways that acknowledge a reciprocal relationship between the two. Alongside their common emphasis on the need for respectful obedience to rules as a condition for gaining consciousness of freedom, both Kant and Suzuki also emphasize the need to realize and maintain consciousness of one's freedom—the freedom to act as one thinks one ought to act, regardless of the demands and longings of one's mind and body—as a condition without which respect for and obedience to moral rules is impossible.

Suzuki uses the term *zazen* to refer to the discipline of maintaining a "self-sufficient mind," a mind in which consciousness of freedom from mental and physical demands is linked with the capacity to respect and obey moral precepts. Thus, in the title of this book I have suggested calling *zazen* a "discipline of freedom." But with what justification can it be claimed that Kant talks specifically about such a discipline? We have seen that Kant, in his "methodology of pure practical reason," describes the process of awakening to consciousness of freedom as one that involves the cultivation of a subjective disposition characterized by a "negative perfection" in which "no incentives of inclinations are the determining grounds influencing an action." Now, in chapter 3 of this study I will argue that the Kantian discipline involved in the cultivation of a disposition of "negative perfection" (and, hence, in the realization of consciousness of freedom) is none other than the practical manifestation of that *discipline of the speculative restriction of reason* that Kant describes in both the first and second *Critiques.* And, I shall go on to argue, a comparison of Kant's description of the discipline of the speculative restriction of reason with Suzuki's description of the discipline of *zazen* reveals that, in respect to their common practical aim of helping the practicer realize consciousness of freedom, these two disciplines are essentially one and the same.

3

In Defense of Thesis Z1:

Zazen practice, according to Suzuki, is a necessary means for realizing the requirements of moral law, as Kant understands these requirements

I have presented one passage from *Zen Mind, Beginner's Mind,* which suggests that Suzuki looks upon *zazen* practice as a necessary means for realizing the requirements of moral precepts. According to a possible Kantian interpretation of this passage—an interpretation loosely sketched out in chapter 2—*zazen,* as a discipline designed to develop consciousness of freedom, is a necessary means for my realizing the requirements of moral law because in order for me to observe these requirements it is necessary that I be conscious of my freedom to do so. Both Kant and Suzuki, I have claimed, assert that there is a recriprocal relationship between a person's ability to respect and observe moral laws and that person's consciousness of freedom to act independently of what Kant calls the "sensuous conditions" of life. Without the experience of respecting and observing rules, there can be no consciousness of freedom; yet without consciousness of freedom there can be no "guard that can keep ignoble and corrupting influences from bursting in upon the mind," thus rendering respect for and obedience to moral laws impossible.

Now in chapter 3 I want to develop further my Kantian interpretation of *zazen* as a "discipline of freedom," reciprocally related to the practice of respectful obedience to moral law. I will be defending the claim—expressed in thesis Z1, above—that this discipline is a necessary means for realization of the requirements of moral law. In section *i* of the chapter it is argued that the practice of a discipline of the speculative restriction of reason (as Kant describes such a discipline in both his first and second *Critiques*) is a necessary means for attaining consciousness of freedom. Section *ii* attempts to facilitate the transition from the discussion of Kant's discipline of speculative reason to the subsequent discussion of Suzuki's discipline of *zazen* by utilizing Kant's own texts to develop an interpretation of the phrase "consciousness of freedom" as "consciousness of emptiness." Then, in section *iii*, Suzuki's view that "emptiness is nothing but the practice of zazen"(*ZM*, 115) is used as the focus of a discussion that attempts to show that when Suzuki describes the practice of *zazen* as a means of awakening practicers to consciousness of their freedom, he is describing a discipline similar both in its philosophical foundations and in its practical application to Kant's critical discipline of the speculative restriction of reason.

Thus I will be advancing a Kantian interpretation of *zazen* in which the following argument is made in support of thesis Z1: because (1) the practice of a discipline of the speculative restriction of reason is a necessary means for realizing the requirements of moral law (since without this practice, consciousness of freedom is impossible), and because (2) the practice of *zazen*, as described by Suzuki, *is* a discipline of the speculative restriction of reason as Kant describes such a discipline, therefore, (3) the practice of *zazen* is indeed a necessary means for realizing the requirements of moral law, as Kant understands these requirements.

i: The Practice of a Discipline of the Speculative Restriction of Reason Is, According to Kant, a Necessary Means for Attaining Consciousness of Freedom

Kant uses the term "speculative reason" to refer our human tendency to think about objects that are totally conjectural in nature, objects that are, as Kant says, *supersensible*—seeming to exist beyond our immediate sense experience. In his first *Critique* Kant explains the need for a discipline of the speculative restriction of reason as follows:

> There is no need of a critique of reason in its empirical employment, because in this field its principles are always subject to the test of experience. . . . But where . . . reason is being considered in its transcendental employment, in accordance with mere concepts, it stands so greatly in need of a discipline, to restrain its tendency towards extension beyond the narrow limits of possible experience and to guard it against extravagance and error, that the whole philosophy of pure reason has no other than this strictly negative utility. [*KV*, B739]

When I apply my reasoning powers to the empirical world, thinking about objects observable through my senses, my experience itself will enforce discipline upon my reasoning. For example, the thought may occur to me that adding a measure of kerosene to my car's fuel tank might result in improved gas mileage. Such thinking can, as Kant says, be put to the test of experience. But when I use my reason in a purely speculative way, thinking about objects, such as immortal souls, which exist (if they exist at all) beyond the boundaries of my sense experience, here there can be no test of experience which can validate my thinking and "guard it against extravagance and error." Thus Kant considers this latter kind of thinking "greatly in need of a discipline"—so much so that the whole *Critique of Pure Reason*, Kant says, has no other utility than "this strictly negative utility" of restraining the human tendency to extend thought erroneously "beyond the narrow limits of possible experience."

Kant sees this "negative" discipline of speculative reason as intimately related to how human beings use their reason practically, in determining how to act. "Speculative restriction and practical extension of pure reason," he says, "bring pure reason into that relation of balance wherein reason as such can be suitably used" (*KP*, 141). The task of speculative reason in this "relation of balance" is not, Kant says, that of "assuming a new object beyond experience but only of approaching perfection in its employment within experience" (*KP*, 135). In this first section of chapter 3, I will try to illustrate the respective roles played by the speculative restriction and the practical extension of reason in what Kant understands to be their "relation of balance" by considering the special problem of attaining consciousness of freedom. Following Kant's thought in both first and second *Critiques*, I will be making the following argument:

(a) *In order to be conscious of my freedom I must be able to think, without contradiction, of myself as free.*

(b) *In order to think of myself without contradiction as free, I must practice a discipline of the speculative restriction of my reason, whereby I understand myself simultaneously as an object of experience (phenomenon)—of which I can have knowledge—and as a "thing in itself" (noumenon)—of which I can think, but* know *nothing.*

(c) *Therefore, in order to be consciousness of my freedom I must practice a discipline of the speculative restriction of reason.*

(a)

In order to be conscious of my freedom I must be able to think—without contradiction—of myself as free.

"Morality," Kant says in the preface to the second edition of the *Critique of Pure Reason*, "does not, indeed, require that freedom should be understood, but only that it should not contradict itself, and so should at least allow of being thought" (*KV*, Bxxix). Morality requires that freedom "should at least allow of being thought" because if I cannot conceive of the idea of freedom, then the idea of morality becomes inconceivable to me as well. My idea of morality tells me I ought to do certain things and ought not to do others: thus this idea assumes my freedom to act in accordance with my idea of what I ought and ought not to do. Were I unable to think of myself as free to choose, according to my own lights, to act in one way and not in another, then the moral thought that I ought to act in a particular way would likewise be unthinkable. "Thus," as Kant has been quoted in chapter 2 above, "freedom and unconditional practical law [moral law] reciprocally imply each other" (*KP*, 29).

Given, however, that I understand myself as part of a causally interrelated "mechanism of nature" (*KP*, 29), in which my activities as a physical being are constantly influenced by physical and psychological conditions beyond my knowledge or control, it is difficult for me to conceive how it might be possible, merely through my respectful obedience to moral law, to act independently of such conditioning influences and thereby realize true freedom. Thus a contradiction arises between my thought of myself as a being subject to the laws of the natural world and my thought of myself as a being free to follow the commands of morality, regardless of circumstances. Faced with this contradiction, I might understandably conclude that my belief in personal freedom must be false, because it is contradicted by my knowledge of nature. But, according to Kant, once I concede that freedom does not allow of being thought, then my assumption, made on behalf of morality, that I am free to choose to act in one way and not in another has to give way also:

> For since it is only on the assumption of freedom that the negation of morality contains any contradiction, freedom, and with it morality, would have to yield to the mechanism of nature. [*KV*, Bxxix]

Therefore, in order to be conscious of my freedom—and, reciprocally, in order to be conscious of moral law—I must, Kant says, be able to think of freedom without contradiction. I must be able to resolve this seeming contradiction between my knowledge of myself as part of the mechanism of nature and my thought of myself as free.

(b)
In order to think of myself without contradiction as free, I must practice a discipline of the speculative restriction of reason, whereby I understand myself simultaneously as an object of experience (phenomenon) of which I can have knowledge, and as a "thing in itself" (noumenon) of which I can think, but know *nothing.*

It is evident that I cannot think or speak of myself as free in the same way as I might think or speak of myself as an object of my sense experience. For, as Kant tries to show in both first and second *Critiques*, in the context of sense experience I must describe everything that occurs—including every action of mine—as the product of previous causes and conditions (*KV*, B560–61, B570–72; *KP*, 94–95). In thinking or speaking of myself as free, on the other hand, I must describe my actions as though they were undetermined by previous causes and conditions—as though I were a being who functioned outside the natural limitations of time and space (*KV*, B561–62). This apparent contradiction between the thought of myself as a part of the natural world and the thought of myself as free can be resolved, Kant argues, through the practice of a discipline of thought, or reason, whereby I look at an object in two ways: both as an object of sense experience (the aspect of an object that is presented to me through my sight, hearing, and all the other spatial/temporal forms of my human sensibility) and as what Kant refers to as a *thing in itself* (the aspect of an object that I think of as having an existence independent of the manner in which it appears to me through my senses).

In his first *Critique*, Kant tried to show that the concept of freedom is not self-contradictory so long as a key distinction is maintained between the thought of a person as an object of sense experience (phenomenon) and the thought of that same person as a "thing in itself" (noumenon) (*KV*, Bxx-xxi, B306–12; see also *KP*, 97–98). My spouse, thought of as an object of my sense experience, appears to me in a spatial/temporal context: I see and hear her as we chat and cook dinner together in the kitchen. I can also, however, think of my spouse as a being whose existence is utterly independent of the manner in which she appears to me through my senses. If, for example, I momentarily shut my eyes and cover my ears while we are standing together in the kitchen, I know it is not my spouse herself who disappears in blackness and silence. Thus I can distinguish between my spouse as a spatial/temporal appearance in the world of my sense experience, and my spouse as a "thing in herself" who has an existence of her own, utterly independent of my experience.

Space and time, Kant argues in his first *Critique*, are forms of our particular human sense experience, but we have no reason to assume that these forms have an existence separate from such experience. Thus, if I want to try to think of my spouse as an object existing independently of my human sense experience, I must try to think of such an object as existing independently of the *forms* of sense experience as well—that is, as existing independently of space and time (*KV*, B59, B306; *KP*, 97–98). Kant uses the term "intelligible" to describe an object thought of as existing independently of the forms of human sense experience—"intelligible" because it is thinkable but not sensible (see *KV*, B306, B566–69). However, it will be remembered that such intelligible, or "supersensible," objects are, according to Kant, only objects of "speculative" reason: the whole critical philosophy of pure reason, he has been quoted as saying, has none other than the "strictly negative utility" of guarding our thoughts about such objects against "extravagance and error."

In his first *Critique* Kant attempted to prove that those physical laws that describe and define the spatial/temporal relationships of objects in the natural world—the laws, that is to say, of natural science—are applicable only to objects as they *appear* to us through our sensory experience: such laws, that is, apply only to *phenomena.* It may seem self-evident, if not redundant, to say that the laws governing the spatial/temporal relationships of objects apply only to objects observed in space or time. But, as Kant points out repeatedly in both *Critiques,* we human beings have a natural but mistaken tendency to treat objects as they appear to us through our sense organs as "things in themselves" that have an existence, so we unthinkingly assume, independent of the spatial and temporal forms of our sense experience. Thus, for example, I unthinkingly assume that the appearance of my spouse in the kitchen is itself an object that exists on its own, independent of my sense experience. On reflection, however, I must admit that I really know nothing about my spouse as a "thing in herself."

My spouse thought of as a thing in herself, or "noumenon," might be defined as an object, X, from the thought of which I specifically subtract all phenomenal knowledge (all knowledge gained through sense experience), P. Such a noumenal object, X-P, will be knowable by me, Kant insists, only in a negative sense: that is only as something *not* extended in space, something *not* experienced in time, and so forth. Which is to say, I can abstractly think about such a hypothetical object, but I really cannot know anything about it (*KV*, B149, B306–07). My human tendency, nonetheless, is to extend erroneously my knowledge of X *as* P (my knowledge of my spouse as a spatial/temporal appearance) to my thought of X-P (my thought of my spouse as a thing in herself) thus giving X-P an altogether unwarranted *positive* interpretation. Thus I tend to "anthropomorphize" the purely negative thought of my spouse as noumenon, confusing this thought with the positive thought of her as phenomenon.

To correct this tendency of human reason to ignore the distinction between objects as they appear in sense experience and objects thought of as things in themselves, Kant proposed a critical discipline of the speculative restriction of reason. The disciplinary task to be performed by my speculative reason in its "relation of balance" with my practical reason is, as Kant says, not that "of assuming a new object beyond experience but only of approaching perfection in its employment within experience." That is to say, in my attempt to apply my reason practically, through my efforts to realize the requirements of moral law, the task of my thinking, speculating mind in this effort is "to restrain its tendency towards extension beyond the narrow limits of possible experience and to guard it[self] against extravagance and error" (*KV*, B739).

Instead of entertaining ideas about the attributes of so-called noumenal objects—objects that, by definition, are not spatial/temporal appearances—I should in my thinking, Kant says:

> Set to work . . . with these [supersensible] ideas in a negative manner, i.e., not broadening but purifying, in order to ward off anthropomorphism as the source of superstition (apparent extension of those concepts through alleged experience) and fanaticism which promises such an extension through supersensuous intuition or feelings. Both of these are obstacles to the practical use of pure reason, and the safeguard against them certainly belongs in the extension of our knowledge in a practical direction. [*KP*, 135–36]

Through the discipline of speculative reason I safeguard the practical use of my reason, according to Kant, in two ways. Taking as my example the supersensible idea of freedom—the idea of my independence from all spatial/temporal conditions—I "set to work . . . in a negative manner" with this idea in order to ward off the errors of anthropomorphism and fanaticism. The error of anthropomorphism in respect to the thought of freedom has already been illustrated in chapter 2, above. It is the error of interpreting the supersensible concept 'freedom' in terms of my own human spatial/temporal experience (as in the phrase "freedom to follow my desire"). This is an erroneous use of the concept 'freedom' because the concept is rightly used to signify a unique kind of unconditioned causality—a causality utterly independent of spatial/temporal conditions, and knowable only because it is presupposed by something we *do* know, as what Kant calls a fact of our reason (*KP*, 31): the unconditional command of moral law. The error of fanaticism, on the other hand, occurs when I use the concept 'freedom' to signify some fanciful state wherein I merely imagine myself as having an existence independent of all spatial and temporal conditions. This use of the concept is erroneous, because in my actual sense experience I do not observe myself as a being exempt from the natural laws of cause and effect. Thus, if I were to adopt what Kant calls the fanatical usage of the concept 'freedom,' the term would have absolutely no practical significance or use for me in my daily life.

It has been shown in chapter 2 that what Kant calls "anthropomorphism"—the erroneous interpretation of supersensible concepts in terms of human sense experiences—is an obstacle to the practical use of reason because it obscures my consciousness of my freedom. Anthropomorphizing the supersensible idea of freedom prevents me from being consciousness of my freedom because it extends my human sensibility and its forms of space and time to "cover," as it were, my thought of myself as a free being—my thought of myself as able to determine my actions according to unconditional moral laws, independently of all sensuous, spatial/temporal conditions. Thus, Kant says, the purely negative concept of noumena is necessary:

> to prevent sensible intuition from being extended to things in themselves, and thus to limit the objective validity of sensible knowledge. The remaining things, to which it [sensible intu-

> ition] does not apply, are entitled noumena, in order to show that this knowledge cannot extend its domain over everything which the understanding thinks. . . . The concept of a noumenon is thus a merely *limiting concept*, the function of which is to curb the pretensions of sensibility; and it is therefore only of negative employment. At the same time it is no arbitrary invention; it is bound up with the limitation of sensibility, though it cannot affirm anything positive beyond the field of sensibility. [*KV*, B311]

It is, therefore, through establishing the distinction between phenomena and noumena that Kant would curb "the pretensions of sensibility" in order to make room for the possibility of freedom. Without the limiting concept of the noumenon, my sense knowledge, including my knowledge of the laws governing the causal interactions of natural phenomena, seems to extend beyond the boundaries of my sensory experience to cover "everything which the understanding thinks"—everything, including my thought of myself as free to follow the commands of moral law. Such unlimited sense knowledge, Kant writes in his preface to the second edition of the *Critique of Pure Reason*, threatens "to make the bounds of sensibility coextensive with the real, and so to supplant reason in its pure (practical) employment" by eliminating the possibility of freedom from the realm of sensuous conditions (*KV*, Bxxv). But through positing the purely negative concept of noumenon, a concept "bound up with the limitation of sensibility," the critical discipline of the speculative restriction of reason succeeds in establishing a philosophical beachhead where there are grounds for affirming the possibility of freedom. This beachhead, however, must remain perpetually obscured in a cloud of unknowing, for "the domain that lies out beyond the sphere of appearances is for us empty" (*KV*, B310):

> What our understanding acquires through this concept of a noumenon, is a negative extension; that is to say, understanding is not limited through sensibility; on the contrary, it itself limits sensibility by applying the term noumena to things in themselves (things not regarded as appearances). But in so doing it at the same time sets limits to itself, recognizing that

> it cannot know these noumena . . . and that it must therefore think them only under the title of an unknown something. [*KV*, 312]

(c)

Therefore, in order to be conscious of my freedom I must practice Kant's critical discipline of speculative reason.

Kant's discipline of speculative reason, with its emphasis upon critically applying the purely negative concept of noumenon to our thoughts about things as they are in themselves (as opposed to our thoughts about things as they appear to us in sense perception), may seem to provide very little positive basis indeed for affirming the possibility of freedom. But this is not so, Kant says, once the discipline that restricts the speculative activity of reason is considered in its "relation of balance" with the practical, moral use of our reason:

> So far, therefore, as our Critique limits speculative reason, it is indeed *negative*; but since it thereby removes an obstacle which stands in the way of the employment of practical reason, nay threatens to destroy it, it has in reality a *positive* and very important use. At least this is so, immediately we are convinced that there is an absolutely necessary *practical* employment of pure reason—the *moral*—in which it inevitably goes beyond the limits of sensibility. Though [practical] reason, in thus proceeding, requires no assistance from speculative reason, it must yet be assured against its opposition, that reason may not be brought into conflict with itself. [*KV*, Bxxv]

In the moral employment of my reason I go "beyond the limits of sensibility" because my idea of moral law is the idea of a practical necessity that determines, or ought to determine, my actions regardless of what is going on around me in the physical world. Thus, as has been already observed, my idea of moral law includes the idea of my freedom—my freedom to act independently of the spatial/temporal conditions of life. Now let us suppose, Kant suggests, that the distinction between phenomena and noumena had not been made (*KV*, Bxxvii). In that case my reason would inevitably "be brought into conflict with itself" in thinking of freedom. For I cannot think of myself, without contradiction, both as free *and* as subject to spatial/temporal conditions. If, however, I apply the limiting concept of the noumenon to my thought of myself as free, immediately I am able to think of myself, without contradiction, in a twofold sense—both as a sensible appearance and as a thing in itself. Then, Kant says, "there is no contradiction in supposing that one and the same [being] is, in the appearance, that is, in its visible acts, necessarily subject to the law of nature, and so far *not free*, while yet, as belonging to a thing in itself, it is not subject to that law, and is therefore *free* (*KV*, Bxxvii–xxviii):

> My soul, viewed from the latter standpoint cannot indeed be known by means of speculative reason (and still less through empirical observation); and freedom as a property of a being to which I attribute effects in the sensible world, is, therefore also not knowable in any such fashion. For I should then have to know such a being as determined in its existence, and yet as not determined in time—which is impossible. But though I cannot know, I can yet *think* freedom; that is to say, the representation of it is at least not self-contradictory, provided due account be taken of our critical distinction between the two modes of representation, the sensible and the intellectual. [*KV*, Bxxviii]

The practice of a discipline of the speculative restriction of reason is, therefore, a necessary means for attaining consciousness of freedom because only by means of this practice can I think of myself as free—as the first cause of my actions—without contradiction. Of course, through such speculative thinking I cannot gain any knowledge of freedom itself; I can know freedom only indirectly, in a purely practical context, as the presupposition of my respect for, and obedience to, moral law. But, Kant says, "though I cannot *know*, I can yet *think* freedom; that is to say, the representation of it is at least not self-contradictory," given that I maintain the distinction between myself thought of as sense object (as phenomenon) and myself thought of as an unknowable (yet thinkable!) thing in itself, or noumenon. Thus, through the practice of a discipline of thought that puts severe restrictions on the way I think about things outside my immediate sense experience, I can cultivate consciousness of my noumenally based freedom and, at the same time, maintain an empirically based understanding of myself as a being whose sensible appearance is determined by spatial/temporal conditions. This allows me to think and act practically (morally) in the world without becoming ensnared in contradiction. For the purely practical (moral) exercise of my thought, Kant says, "requires no assistance from speculative reason" so long as it is "assured against its opposition" and thus "not brought into conflict with itself." And thus, through the practice of the related disciplines of the speculative restriction and the practical extension of reason, my way of thinking about myself and the world is brought "into that relation of balance wherein reason as such can be suitably used."

ii: Consciousness of Freedom Interpreted as Consciousness of Emptiness

According to Kant's view of morality, the "ought" in my life—the command of moral law that presupposes my freedom to do what I think is right—is every bit as real as the "is"—that world of nature that I know through my sense experience (*KP*, 161–62). Thus, even though I am not conscious of my freedom to follow the commands of moral law in the same way as I am conscious that I am six feet, one inch, tall, the phrase "consciousness of freedom" is not without meaning for me. The phrase loses its meaning, however, if I think of myself and my actions solely in terms of sense experience. So the question arises: What does it mean for me to say I am conscious of an aspect of myself that is not, and can never be, an object of my senses?

In section *i* above it has been argued that in order to think of myself as free without contradicting my knowledge of myself as part of the natural world, I must think of myself simultaneously both as "phenomenon" and as "noumenon"—the latter concept referring to a purely intelligible (nonsensible) being "free from all influence of sensibility and from all determination through [spatial/temporal] appearances" (*KV*, B569). But in thinking of myself as noumenon I cannot think of myself in any positive sense as an *object*, either of a sensible or of what Kant calls an "intellectual" (*KV*, B307) intuition,[1] for to do so would be to succumb to the errors of anthropomorphism or fanaticism. I can rightly think of myself as noumenon, Kant says, only in a purely negative sense, as something which is not an object of my sensible intuition:

> If by 'noumenon' we mean a thing so far as it is *not an object of our sensible intuition*, and so abstract from our mode of intuiting it, this is a noumenon in the *negative* sense of the term. But if we understand by it an *object* of a *non-sensible intuition*, we thereby presuppose a special mode of intuition, namely, the intellectual, which is not that which we possess, and of which we cannot comprehend even the possibility. This would be 'noumenon' in the *positive* sense of the term. [*KV*, B307]

My consciousness of freedom must thus be, according to Kant, a kind of *negative* consciousness in which "the domain that lies out beyond the sphere of appearances is for [me] empty" (*KV*, B310)—empty in terms of knowledge, but alive and active as the intelligible (as opposed to sensible) foundation of my freedom to do what I ought to do, regardless of what *is*. To be conscious of myself as free is to think of myself, as Kant says, "under the title of an unknown something" (*KV*, B312) utterly beyond the world in which I appear to myself, bound up by spatial/temporal conditions, as six feet, one inch, tall. And although the concept of a domain beyond the sphere of appearances must remain forever "empty," nevertheless, I can be conscious of such emptiness as the negative sign, as it were, of my freedom from the sensible conditions of life.

As was argued previously, if I am conscious of myself solely as an object in the world of nature, there is no way I can rationally think of myself as a free being who acts according to his idea of what he ought to do. For:

> The understanding can know in nature only what is, what has been, or what will be. We cannot say that anything in nature *ought to be* other than what . . . it actually is. When we

> have the course of nature alone in view, *'ought'* has no meaning whatsoever. [*KV*, B575]

However, if I am conscious of myself in a twofold sense, both as spatial/temporal phenomenon and as "empty" noumenon, then by becoming aware of the emptiness underlying and supporting my sensible appearance, I become conscious of myself as simultaneously bound by and free from sensible conditions. My empirically based knowledge of myself will not obscure my consciousness of freedom, so long as I avoid what Kant calls "the common but fallacious presupposition of the *absolute reality* of appearances" (*KV*, B564). By acknowledging that there cannot be a visual appearance—for example, the appearance of my spouse in the kitchen—without *something* being the ground of that appearance (see *KV*, Bxxvi–xxvii), then I immediately become conscious of "an unknown something"—an emptiness—beyond the limits of my sense knowledge. It is this emptiness, signified by the limiting concept of the noumenon, that curbs "the pretensions of sensibility" and makes room for the possibility of freedom.

Kant's statements in the "Methodology of Pure Practical Reason" support an interpretation of the phrase "consciousness of freedom" as "consciousness of [noumenal] emptiness." In this concluding section of the *Critique of Practical Reason*, Kant says we become conscious of our freedom through becoming conscious of a mental state of "negative perfection" wherein "no incentives of inclinations are the determining grounds influencing an action done as a duty" (*KP*, 160). In this state of negative perfection, he says, "there is a consciousness of an independence from inclinations and circumstances, and of the possibility of being sufficient to myself" (*KP*, 161). If it is correct to interpret Kant's phrase "consciousness of an independence from inclinations and circumstances" as "consciousness of an independence from sensible conditions," then it will also be correct to interpret this phrase as "consciousness of an independent, noumenal self." But I can be conscious of my noumenal self only in a negative sense as an *emptiness* that limits the pretensions of my empirical knowledge, establishing within me an awareness of the possibility of being free of all conditioning influences and, therefore, "sufficient to myself."

In interpreting the phrase "consciousness of freedom" as "consciousness of emptiness," I must be careful not to treat the concept of emptiness in a dualistic way, as though it signified some separate, metaphysical domain coexisting with the phenomenal world. For Kant uses the terms 'phenomena' and 'noumena' to make what is essentially a grammatical—not a metaphysical—distinction. Far from signifying two separate realms of existence, the phenomenal and the noumenal, these terms refer rather to two mutually inclusive ways of talking about one and the same experience. I can indeed *think* of myself in two ways, Kant affirms—both in terms of my empirical, or phenomenal, character and in terms of my intelligible, or noumenal, character (*KV*, B567). However:

> This intelligible character can never, indeed, be immediately known, for nothing can be perceived except in so far as it appears. It would have to be thought in accordance with the empirical character—just as we are constrained to think a transcendental [noumenal] object as underlying appearances, though we know nothing of what it is in itself. [*KV*, B568]

In this statement Kant asserts that his critical distinction between things as they appear in our sense experience and "things in themselves" is a sword that cuts two ways. Just as I am constrained, by the critical discipline of speculative reason, to think of an empty "transcendental object" as underlying the sensible appearance of my spouse in the kitchen, so, Kant insists, I am also constrained to think of that purely intelligible object—my spouse thought of as a thing in herself—"in accordance with [its] empirical character." Thus my empirical knowledge of my spouse as a woman of medium height with dark hair and brown eyes, should include my thought of her as empty noumenon, *and* my thought of her as empty noumenon should include my awareness of her physical appearance.

When, therefore, through the practice of Kant's discipline of speculative reason, I go beyond the thought of myself as an object of sense experience by applying the "limiting concept" of noumenon to this thought, I must be sure to go beyond the thought of myself as empty noumenon as well, by applying what Kant refers to as the "sensible sign" of empirical knowledge (*KV*, B574) to that latter thought. For since "nothing can be perceived except in so far as it appears," I have no way at all of becoming conscious of myself as free—except through consciousness of myself as an object of sense experience. Therefore, if my thought of myself as an intelligible being free of spatial/temporal conditions is to escape the error of fanaticism, it has "to be thought in accordance with [my] empirical character."

This means that I should not, in thinking of my *intelligibly* perceived self as free, commit the error of thinking of my *sensibly* perceived self as somehow *exempt* from those laws of natural necessity that common sense tells me apply to me, just like they apply to everyone else. For:

> To allow such exemption would be to set [myself as] an appearance outside all possible experience, to distinguish it from all objects of possible experience, and so to make of it a mere thought-entity, a phantom of the brain. [KV, B571]

Thus, if I am not to reduce the thought of myself as free to "a mere thought-entity, a phantom of the brain," I must pay all due respect to my empirical character—the aspect of myself that I know as an object of my senses. In regard to those acts of mine that I observe through my senses, I must:

> Take their strictly empirical character as the supreme ground of explanation, leaving entirely out of account their intelligible character (that is, the transcendental cause of their empirical character) as being completely unknown, save insofar as the empirical serves for its sensible sign. [KV, B574]

As has been pointed out above, to think of my actions both as free and as subject to empirical conditions "as the supreme ground of explanation" does not constitute a contradiction, for the thought of myself as noumenon does not negate, but rather is complementary to, the thought of myself as phenomenon. As Kant puts it:

> the same act which as belonging to the world of sense is always sensuously conditioned, i.e., mechanically necessary, can at the same time, as belonging to the causality of the acting being in so far as it belongs to the intelligible [noumenal] world, have a sensuously unconditioned causality as its foundation. That is, it can be thought of as free. [*KP*, 104]

Of course, as Kant goes on to point out, "causality through freedom must always be sought outside the world of sense . . . [and] . . . things which are not sensuous are not given to our perception and observation" (*KP*, 104–05). Thus, it is *only* through my awareness of the unconditional commands of moral law, and not through anything I can ever know directly through sense experience, that I come to be conscious of a causality of freedom within me that truly must be sought outside the world of sense. But although it is true that I cannot come to consciousness of freedom solely through sense experience, neither can I come to such consciousness apart from sense experience. My consciousness of emptiness—as that state of "negative perfection" in which I am aware of "an independence from inclinations and circumstances and of the possibility of being sufficient to myself"—serves indeed as the negative sign of my freedom from the spatial/temporal conditions of the world of nature. But because this freedom, as the intelligible cause of my actions in the world, must remain "completely unknown save insofar as the empirical serves for its sensible sign," my consciousness of freedom as emptiness can come to me only through the "sensible sign" of these same spatial/temporal conditions.

A formula for the practice of Kant's discipline of speculative reason, which expresses both the sharp distinction *and* the mutually inclusive relationship between consciousness of freedom as emptiness (consciousness of the noumenal world) and consciousness of objects of sense experience (consciousness of the phenomenal world), might be stated as follows:

(1) *Phenomena are noumena:*
By means of this insight I go beyond my "anthropomorphic" belief in the absolute reality of spatial/temporal appearances. In this way I establish an awareness of the limits of my sense knowledge and affirm my own freedom, as a noumenal being, from determination by the laws of that knowledge.

(2) *Noumena are phenomena:*
By means of this insight I go beyond the "fanatical" view that my noumenal self is an object that I can know through some special kind of intuition. In this way I restrict my speculative thinking to "the narrow limits of possible experience." At the same time, I extend my practical thinking beyond these narrow limits through my respect for and obedience to a supersensible moral law. This balanced relationship between the speculative restriction and the practical extension of my reason enables me to express my freedom through the "sensible sign" of morally inspired actions in the world of sense.

(3) *Noumena are noumena:*
By means of this insight I go beyond a dualistic view of noumena and phenomena. Once I understand that phenomena are noumena and noumena are phenomena, then there is no longer any need for me to discriminate between them. "Noumena are noumena" thus expresses the oneness—the nondualistic nature—of my actual experience, in which I remain simultaneously "in my right senses" and consciousness of myself as free.

(4) *Phenomena are phenomena:*
If phenomena and noumena are actually one, then there is no need to emphasize even this oneness. By means of this fourth insight I leave concepts behind and turn my attention to the variegated world of actual experience, in order to engage myself in "fruitful, practical employment" (see *KV*, B421). Liberated from the false views of anthropomorphism, fanaticism, and dualism, and unhindered by contradictions and conflicts in my thinking, I engage in a whole hearted effort to fulfill the commands of moral law in all my activities and interactions in the world.

iii: Zazen Interpreted as a Discipline of the Speculative Restriction of Reason

In sections *i* and *ii* it was argued that, for Kant, consciousness of freedom as emptiness is a mental state necessary for respectful obedience to moral law because only through such consciousness—in which I recognize that the self "which lies out beyond the sphere of appearances is for [me] empty" (*KV*, B310)—do I attain awareness of my "independence from inclinations and circumstances," and, hence, "of the possibility of being sufficient to myself" and therefore free to act in accordance with my idea of what I ought to do. And, it was also argued, attainment of consciousness of freedom as emptiness is the direct result of the practice of a discipline of the speculative restriction of reason, whereby I apply what Kant calls the "limiting concept" of an empty noumenon to all that which appears to me in the world of natural phenomena, and in this way "limit the objective validity of sensible knowledge . . . in order to show that this knowledge cannot extend its domain over everything which the understanding thinks" (*KV*, B311). Now, in this concluding section of chapter 3, I want to argue that Shunryu Suzuki's account of *zazen* practice can plausibly be interpreted as the account of a practice that, for practical purposes, is identical to the practice of Kant's discipline of speculative reason. By the phrase "for practical purposes," I mean "for the purpose of attaining that consciousness of freedom as emptiness, which is a necessary means for realizing the requirements of moral law."

In the following subsections I will present arguments for three theses, each of which partially supports the claim that zazen and Kant's discipline of the speculative restriction of reason are, for practical purposes, the same discipline:

> *Argument a: Both Suzuki's* zazen *and Kant's "discipline of speculative reason" involve the practice of the same critical discipline of thought, in which a key distinction is made and maintained between objects of experience understood as phenomena—as appearances in*

consciousness—and objects of experience understood as noumena—as unknowable things in themselves.

Argument b: The practice of this critical discipline of thought is described, in both Kant and Suzuki, as leading to the awakening of consciousness of freedom as emptiness in the practicer.

Argument c: Suzuki acknowledges the same practical use of this discipline as does Kant, each treating the discipline as a necessary means for realizing the requirements of morality.

(a)
Suzuki's distinction between form and emptiness parallels Kant's distinction between phenomena and noumena

It is the *Prajñāpāramitā Hridaya Sūtra*, or "Heart Sutra"—a Buddhist teaching text chanted morning, noon, and before bedtime in many Zen Buddhist training centers—to which Suzuki often refers in discussing a critical distinction in Buddhism: the distinction between one's normal, empirical consciousness and one's consciousness of something called "emptiness," which, he says, is cultivated and realized through *zazen* practice:

> In the Prajñā Pāramitā Sūtra the most important point . . . is the idea of emptiness. Before we understand the idea of emptiness, everything seems to exist substantially. But after we realize the emptiness of things, everything becomes real—not substantial [*ZM*, 113]

The Heart Sutra contains a formula expressing the relationship between the idea of emptiness and our empirical consciousness of form and color, feelings, perceptions and so forth—all of which, as Suzuki says, may erroneously seem to us to exist substantially, as substances having their own, independent being. This formula is expressed by Suzuki as follows:

> *Form is emptiness.*
> *Emptiness is form.*
> *Emptiness is emptiness*
> *Form is form.*
>
> [*WB*, VII, Summer 1968:16]

My effort in this subsection will be to show that Suzuki uses the terms 'form' and 'emptiness' in the above formula to establish the same critical distinction established by Kant in his discussion of the discipline of the speculative restriction of reason. The distinction is, of course, that between phenomena and noumena: the distinction between things as they appear to us and things as they are in themselves "beyond the sphere of appearances." Thus I will be arguing that the above formula from the Heart Sutra is equivalent to the Kantian formula developed in section *ii* above:

Phenomena are noumena.
Noumena are phenomena.
Noumena are noumena.
Phenomena are phenomena.

After arguing that Suzuki's 'form' and 'emptiness' are indeed properly translatable as 'phenomena' and 'noumena,' as this latter set of terms has been used in sections *i* and *ii* of chapter 3, I will go on to discuss a short lecture of Suzuki's in which he explains the fourfold formula from the Heart Sutra.

In describing 'emptiness,' the Heart Sutra states:

> In emptiness there is no form, nor feeling, nor perception, nor impulse, nor consciousness; no eye, ear, nose, tongue, body, mind.[2]

In this description, all the data of our human experience are categorized into five groups, or *skandhas*[3]—form, feelings, perceptions, impulses, and consciousness. In Suzuki's four-part formula ("Form is emptiness, emptiness is form . . ."), as well as in the language of the sutra itself, the term "form" is used as an abbreviation signifying all five of the *skandhas* considered together—that is, "all the data of our experience."[4]

Referring to the text of the Heart Sutra in a lecture to his advanced students and ordained disciples at Tassajara Zen Mountain Center, Suzuki uses the Japanese Buddhist technical terms *Ri* and *Ji* to help explain the difference between the data of our conscious experience ("whatever . . . can be introduced into your consciousness") and "something which is beyond our conscious world" (*SL*, III,4). *Ri*, he says, "is a more noumenal word," and *Ji* "is a more phenomenal word. . . . Phenomenal or noumenal is not right, but tentatively I have to say so." (*SL* III,3). Suzuki finds 'phenomena' and 'noumena' to be perhaps the best available English terms to translate *Ji* and *Ri*, although he says they are "not right." However, Suzuki's use of the terms *Ri* and *Ji* shows that this pair of terms is indeed closely equivalent to 'noumena' and 'phenomena' as this latter pair of terms is being used in the present study.

Suzuki says:

> *Ji* is something which you can see, which you can hear, or which you can smell or taste, and it includes objects of thinking, or ideas. Whatever . . . can be introduced into your consciousness is *Ji*. And . . . something which is beyond our conscious world is *Ri*. In the *Prajñā Pāramitā Sūtra*, "no taste, no eyes, no ears, no nose . . ."—that is actually this one, *Ri*. [*SL* III, 4]

The "usual person," Suzuki says, will "stick to *Ji*" (*SL*, IV,1). Usually I "stick" to a view that equates what *is* with "whatever . . . can be introduced into [my] consciousness"—a consciousness whose contents include not only objects of sight, hearing, smell, taste, and touch, but also thoughts and feelings that appear and disappear in time. But the "characteristic of Buddha's teaching," Suzuki says, "is to go beyond things" (*SL*, IV,1). In order to awaken from a "hasty, primitive understanding" (*SL*, III,2) of the contents of my consciousness, I should go beyond the view that treats appearances in my consciousness as "things" that exist outside and apart from that consciousness:

> You say, "outside of yourself," but it is not true. You feel in that way, but actually when you say, "There is a river," the river is already within your mind. So hasty people may say, "The river is there," but if you think more about it, you will find out the river is something which is in your mind—something which is in your mind is the river. So it is a kind of thought we have in our mind. And if you say, "There is the

> river, and here is my mind," this is a dualistic understanding. [*SL*, III,2)

Here Suzuki is implicitly pointing out the distinction between the river as an appearance in my empirical consciousness ("a kind of thought we have in our mind"), and the river thought of as something existing separately from that appearance. This latter thought of the river, Suzuki would insist, cannot lead to knowledge or be discussed directly. For to say, "*There* is the river, and *here* is my mind," as if the appearance of the river and the mind within which the river appears were separate, independent entities, is immediately to involve oneself in an ignorant, dualistic view that treats the *spatial/temporal appearance* of the river as a thing in itself— a thing existing separately and independently from the empirical consciousness in which that appearance appears.

Of course, I can talk about the river and I can talk about my mind; but I should not forget to discipline my speaking and thinking in order to avoid the mistake of talking about the *appearance* of the river as if it were a thing existing beyond and outside this mind. It is important that I understand the river in two ways: both in terms of *Ji*—that is, as something that appears in my consciousness—*and* in terms of *Ri*—as something that exists beyond consciousness. This latter way of understanding the river—wherein it is thought of as something apart from its appearance in my consciousness—must not be spoken of in a "hasty" way, in terms of *Ji* only, if the error of dualism is to be avoided.

Thus, for Suzuki, "to go beyond things"—to cease sticking to *Ji*—is indeed to go beyond what Kant calls "the absolute reality of appearances." By recognizing the sensible appearance of the river as a phenomenon of my own empirical consciousness, I establish within this consciousness both a nondualistic awareness of the identity of that consciousness with its contents (the identity of my consciousness with the appearance of the river), and an awareness of the *limits* of consciousness. The technical term *Ri* is used—precisely as Kant uses the technical term 'noumena'—as a limiting concept pointing to that which lies beyond the sphere of consciousness as something that "is absolutely independent and has its own value" (*SL*, IV, 6) but which is, at the same time, utterly unknowable:

> Stainless means no stain of thought or words. If you describe it, that is the stain, to put limitation to the Truth. So it means you stain the Truth. You put some mark on the Truth. . . . *Ri* . . . is beyond words. Something which is stainless . . . that is actually [*Ri*]. [*SL*, III, 3–4]

"So," Suzuki says, "we are always involved in this world, only without knowing *Ri*" (*SL*, III, 9). Nevertheless, even though we can never directly know *Ri*, it is also true that "to follow or to realize or to have complete understanding of *Ri* . . . to accept *Ri* is our practice" (*SL*, III, 7). Or, as Suzuki says in *Zen Mind, Beginner's Mind*: "Emptiness is nothing but the practice of *zazen*" (*ZM*, 115). Thus Suzuki describes *zazen* as a practice that both limits the applicability of "thought or words" to that which can be introduced into consciousness, and that simultaneously affirms the existence of an unknowable realm beyond our conscious world as empty, or stainless. This is a strong indication that *zazen* practice as Suzuki describes it is truly a discipline of the speculative restriction of reason, as Kant describes such a discipline in his first and second *Critiques.*

> *Form is emptiness and emptiness is form. Form is form and emptiness is emptiness. Thus we understand things in four ways.* [*WB*, VII, Summer 1968:16]

One might think that in identifying emptiness with the practice of *zazen* Suzuki is saying that *zazen* practice involves the cultivation of some special mental state in which the practicer is transported to a world beyond that of normal sense experience. But this is clearly not the case. In explaining the relationship between a person's empirical consciousness of form and feelings, and that person's nonempirical consciousness of emptiness, Suzuki warns that the relationship between form and emptiness "is easily misunderstood" (*WB*, VII, Summer 1968:16). A "hasty person," he says, might think "that emptiness should be quite unusual [but] it is really something very common" (*WB*, VII, Summer 1968:17). Thus, while it is certainly important to accept the view that "form is emptiness" in order to correct the mistaken view of reality that treats appearances in consciousness as substantial—as if "they are permanent and have self-nature" (*WB*, VII, Summer 1968:17)—it is equally important to accept the view that "emptiness is form" in order to correct the mistake of treating emptiness, or enlightenment, as a special kind of mental state that transports one utterly beyond the boundaries of ordinary human experience:

> People may think Zen is a wonderful teaching, that they will acquire perfect freedom by studying it, that whatever you do, if you are in a Buddhist robe, it is all right. This looks like the teaching that form is emptiness, but this is not what is meant by it. [*WB*, VII, Summer 1968:18]

"Reality," Suzuki says, "is experienced only when you are in some particular circumstance. That is why we say *emptiness is form.* Emptiness is very good but it can only be experienced in some form or color or under some limitation" (*WB*, VII, Summer 1968:18, emphasis added). This is what Suzuki means by "emptiness is form" and this also would seem to be what Kant means when he says that the intelligible, or noumenal character "can never, indeed, be immediately known, for nothing can be perceived except in so far as it appears. It would have to be thought in accordance with the empirical character" (*KV*, B568). Both Suzuki and Kant reject the "fanatical" view of the noumenal world as an object of experience that can in some way be directly known. As Suzuki tells his Tassajara students:

> If you make some point about *Ri*, [this] is not enlightenment. Enlightenment is not something you can experience actually. Enlightenment is beyond our experience. At the same time, if you understand that enlightenment is beyond our experience, something which you cannot experience, *that* is enlightenment. So if someone says, "I attained enlightenment," he is wrong! [*SL*, III, 5]

"Enlightenment"—or emptiness, or *Ri*—is, according to Suzuki, something that by definition is "beyond our experience." Therefore, when we use the words "enlightenment" and "experience" we should pay attention to our grammar! And the grammatical key to the correct usage of these words is to be found, Suzuki suggests, in the latter half of the four-part Heart Sutra formula: emptiness is emptiness and form is form. Suzuki explains this latter half of the Heart Sutra formula by referring to the words of Dogen: "When the moon is in the water, the moon does not get wet, nor is the water broken" (*WB*, VII, Summer 1968:17). Emptiness and form, like noumena and phenomena, are related terms that refer to the same reality from different viewpoints. So my understanding of reality as form (the world as it appears in my conscious experience) is not shattered or broken by my understanding of reality as emptiness (my acknowledgment of the limits of consciousness). Nor is my understanding of reality as emptiness disturbed—or dampened!—by my conscious experience of events in the world of form. "Moon is moon," Suzuki says, "and water is water" (*WB*, VII, Summer 1968:17). Or, as Kant unpoetically puts it, in regard to events in the phenomenal world I must always:

> take their strictly empirical character as the supreme ground of explanation, leaving entirely out of account their intelligible character (that is, the transcendental cause of their empirical character) as being completely unknown, save insofar as the empirical serves for its sensible sign. [*KV*, B574]

Because the moon's reflection in the bright water of consciousness is the sensible sign of the moon itself, I must be careful not to treat the distinction between the moon and its reflection (the distinction between emptiness and its sensible sign) dualistically, as though there were two different moons: one in the water and one in the sky. Emptiness is emptiness and form is form—"moon is moon and water is water"—means that there is one truth, or reality, which can be talked about in two ways, each way implicitly including the other. Thus, Suzuki says, "*Ji* and *Ri* are the same thing":

> Things you have in your mind, things you think about are *Ji*. *Ri* is something beyond your understanding or perception. And again, *Ji* and *Ri* are the same thing. [For] when we think about something [even when we are thinking about *Ri*] what we think about is this, *Ji*. So actually it is same thing, but we

> must understand in two ways. Our understanding should not be limited to this area of *Ji*. [*SL*, XI,8]

Precisely because "our understanding should not be limited to this area of *Ji*," it is important that my understanding of "emptiness is emptiness and form is form" include an understanding of the first half of the Heart Sutra formula, in which a dynamic tension between the two terms—the dynamic tension of Zen practice itself—is stressed. Form must be understood and experienced as emptiness; emptiness must be understood and experienced as form. Otherwise, Suzuki says, "there may be a misunderstanding, because if form is form and emptiness is emptiness, you may think there is no need to practice Zen" (*WB*, VII, Summer 1968:17). Because our thoughts and words are ultimately incapable of signifying that which is beyond consciousness ("for when we think about something, what we think about is this, *Ji*") our tendency, as Suzuki has said, is to stick completely to thoughts and words, and to ignore the practice of *zazen*, which is "to follow or to realize or to have complete understanding of *Ri*." Thus it is important, Suzuki says, that each part of the Heart Sutra formula be understood as implicitly embracing all the others:

> An understanding of each view should include the other three. Actually they are all the same. So instead of saying "form is form and emptiness is emptiness, form is emptiness and emptiness is form," it is really enough to say just one. This is the true understanding of the *prajñā pāramitā*. [*WB*, VII, Summer 1968:17]

Suzuki's explanations of 'form' and 'emptiness' as *Ji* and *Ri* indicate that the philosophical distinction expressed in the four-part Heart Sutra formula is closely equivalent to that expressed in Kant's distinction between phenomena and noumena. Thus the Buddhist terms 'form' and 'emptiness' can be substituted in the Kantian formula given at the end of section *ii*, above, without significantly altering its meaning.

(b)
Like Kant, Suzuki treats insight into the critical distinction between form and emptiness, or

phenomena and noumena, as a necessary means for realizing consciousness of freedom.

As emptiness, *Ri* must remain untainted, without "stain of thought or words." For to identify *Ri* with a particular experience in space or time is to identify the absolute, unconditioned truth of emptiness with the conditioned truth of sensible appearances—which is to destroy the enlightened consciousness of emptiness completely. In using the phrase, "the absolute, unconditioned truth of emptiness," I mean to point out that for Suzuki, just as for Kant, to practice insight into the noumenal world of emptiness is to practice insight into one's absolute freedom from spatial/temporal conditions. As Suzuki tells his Tassajara students, "You should not be involved in time or space. Our practice shouldn't be disturbed by some framework of time or space" (*SL*, III,17). And at the conclusion of his lecture on the four-part formula from the Heart Sutra, he says:

> When you have enlightenment you are independent from everything and have your own past and future, just as Buddha had his own past and future. And his position is as independent as your position is independent. If so, this realization is beyond time and space. [*WB*, VII, Summer 1968:19]

In his explanation of how the practice of *zazen*, as the practice of insight into emptiness, establishes consciousness of freedom in the practicer, Suzuki adopts an explanatory approach quite different from Kant's. Nonetheless, Suzuki's different explanatory approach leads to a view of consciousness of freedom as emptiness, which is remarkably similar to the Kantian view developed in sections *i* and *ii* above. In his lectures to his Tassajara students, Suzuki emphasizes the point that through *Ji*—that is, through awareness of that which appears in my consciousness—I become aware of my interrelatedness, my causal interconnectedness, with the entire phenomenal world. However, if I "stick to *Ji*"—stick to a belief in the absolute reality of appearances—my knowledge of my causal interrelatedness with everything else may produce in me the helpless feeling of being totally determined by the conditions of this world. Thus it becomes crucially important, if I am to escape the trap of a passive determinism, to understand all things as appearances within a consciousness that can itself be understood—in terms of *Ri*, or emptiness—as transcendentally grounded and therefore free. Through such an understanding I come to see myself, as Suzuki puts it, as the "boss" of my own surroundings (*SL*, IV, 4).

If the chattering of a bird outside my window causes me to lose concentration while I am trying to write these sentences, I may become annoyed and frustrated, feeling harassed by the circumstances of my life. However, through establishing an awareness of the critical distinction between (a) myself and the bird as appearances in my consciousness and (b) myself and the bird each as an unknown "something which is beyond [the] conscious world" and therefore free of its causal laws, I become aware of my own, and every other thing's, absolute independence from the phenomenal world—while remaining aware as well of the simultaneous interrelatedness of all phenomena. Through making the distinction between *Ji* and *Ri*, I recognize that phenomena do not exist independently or separately from me. They are not alien "things" that have power over my thoughts and actions, but, rather, are integral parts of an independent consciousness that I call "myself." Thus, using noise as a metaphor for the entire phenomenal world, Suzuki says:

> A Buddhist understands everything, every noise, as a sound which we ourselves make. You may say "the bird is singing over there." But . . . when I hear the bird, bird is me already. Actually, I am not listening to bird. Bird is here, in my mind already, and I am singing with bird: "Peep-peep-peep." If you think when you are reading something that a bird is *there*—"Blue Jay is over my room, Blue Jay is singing but his voice is not so good"—if you think in that way, that is noise. When you are not disturbed by the Blue Jay, the Blue Jay will come right into your heart, and you will be a Blue Jay and Blue Jay will be reading something, and then the Blue Jay will not disturb your reading. When you think the Blue Jay is *there*—"Blue Jay should not be over my room"—when you think in that way, that is more primitive understanding of being. Why we understand things in that way is because of

> our want of practice. When you practice zazen more you can accept things as your own, whatever it is. [*SL*, IV, 3]

To practice *zazen*, then, means to "accept things as your own, whatever it is." Suzuki uses the expression "big mind" to refer to the mind of *zazen* practice, the mind that understands all phenomena as a part of itself:

> No one exists . . . nothing exists outside of yourself. This understanding is understanding which includes everything—understanding of Big Mind, which includes everything. So things happen only within yourself . . . it is activity of life within yourself, like your stomach digesting things. [*SL*, V,10]

An appearance in my consciousness is not something that exists separately from me, Suzuki says, any more than my stomach is something that exists separately from my heart: "things are as closely related [to us] as our tummy and our heart are closely related. So there is no need to say tummy or heart anymore" (*SL*, V,10).

Although Suzuki's language may not sound at all Kantian, Kant also emphasizes the oneness of mind and its contents in a way that, like Suzuki, affirms my so-called outer experience of the blue jay singing as an integral part of what Kant calls the "empirically determined consciousness of my own existence" (*KV*, B275). In attempting to refute the view he calls "material idealism"—"the theory which declares the existence of objects in space outside us to be merely doubtful and indemonstrable or to be false and impossible" (*KV*, B274)—Kant acknowledges that such a refutation cannot be achieved "save by proof that even our inner experience, which for Descartes is indubitable, is possible only on the assumption of outer experience" (*KV*, B275). In order to prove that the blue jay I hear chattering is not a fabrication of my imagination, Kant is saying, I must prove that it is the blue jay's chatter itself that makes possible the experience in which I am aware of myself hearing this chatter. In other words, Kant says, I must prove that "the consciousness of my existence is at the same time an immediate consciousness of the existence of other things outside me" (*KV*, B276).

In his "Refutation of Idealism," Kant *does* attempt to prove "that outer experience is really immediate and that only by means of it is inner experience [in which I come to think of myself as something separate from other appearances in my consciousness] . . . possible" (*KV*, B276–77). Thus his words would seem to support Suzuki's view of the self as a "big mind" in which the activity of phenomena is the "activity of your life within yourself like your stomach digesting things." Admittedly, it is not clear from Suzuki's statement, "No one exists . . . nothing exists outside of yourself," that the Zen master himself is not professing precisely the kind of idealism that Kant is attempting to refute! But I think it is clear from the way Suzuki talks about the blue jay that he is *not* talking about the bird either as an imaginary entity or as something whose existence is doubtful. Thus Kant's descriptions of dogmatic and problematic idealism (see *KV*, B274) do not describe Suzuki's view of a "big mind" that includes everything. And thus it would seem that Suzuki, like Kant, views consciousness of one's own existence in a nonidealistic way, as "empirically determined."

Therefore, just as it is a mistaken view to think dualistically, "the bird is *there*,' so it is equally mistaken to think dualistically, "I am *here*." For the bird and I are so closely interrelated, Suzuki says:

> It is difficult to say "this is bird and this is me." Because it is interrelated very closely it is difficult to separate Blue Jay from me. [*SL*, IV,4]

Through accepting things, whatever they are, as integral parts of one's own consciousness, Suzuki says, "every being, each being can be a boss . . . each one of us can be a boss because we are so closely related" (*SL*, IV, 4). It is meaningless for me to talk about being independent—being the "boss"—of something to which I am utterly unrelated. It is because that which I call "I" is interrelated so closely with the blue jay's chatter that I can "be the boss" of that chatter, accepting and enjoying it as my own—and, at the same time, not allowing it to disturb my work. Suzuki uses the example of his own relationship to the students of Zen Mountain Center to illustrate how independence is associated with interrelatedness:

> If you say, "Suzuki," then I am very closely related to you, so I can be president of Zen Center. So if I say, "Mel," Mel already is not just Mel. He is already one of [my] Zen Center students, and to see Mel is to see Zen Center. If you see Mel, you understand what Zen Center is. But if you think, "Oh, he is just Mel," then your understanding is not good enough. You don't know who Mel is. [*SL*, IV,4]

"So," Suzuki says, "if you have good understanding of things, by things you will understand the whole world" (*SL*, IV,4). Just as a "good understanding" of Mel, the Zen Center student, must include an understanding of Mel's interrelatedness with his teacher and all of Zen Center, so a good understanding of each thing must include an understanding of that thing's interrelatedness with all the world. And it is through this interrelatedness with everything else, as Suzuki says, that "each one of us is the boss of the whole world" (*SL*, IV,4):

> So, if you understand this way, [each thing] is not interrelated. It is independent. We are independent. Each one of us is completely independent, absolutely independent. There is nothing to compare with you. You are you, just you. We have to understand things from both ways. One is inter-relatedness—to understand things as interrelated beings. The other way of understanding is to understand ourselves as quite independent from everything. When we include everything we are completely independent because [there is] nothing to compare to you. Do you understand? If there is only one thing, how can you compare things to you, because there is nothing [else] to compare to you. This is absolute independence. [*SL*, IV,4–5]

"If there is only one thing," Suzuki says— if there is only one consciousness, within which all phenomena appear—then there is "nothing to compare to you." This "you" does not refer to what I can know about myself as *Ji*, as an appearance conditioned by other appearances in consciousness. It can only refer to what lies "beyond the sphere of appearances"—that transcendental ground of all appearances in consciousness, the noumenal subject, which I can think of only in terms of emptiness, or *Ri*. So to understand myself as this "one thing" is to understand myself as existing beyond the conditioned world of appearances and, hence, as absolutely independent. "So," Suzuki says, "various beings which we see, which we hear, are things which are interrelated, but at the same time each being is absolutely independent and has its own value. . . . That value means *Ri*" (*SL*, IV,6). *Ri*, or emptiness, is thus used by Suzuki to refer to the transcendental ground of absolute independence, or freedom, just as the expression "noumenal world" is used to refer to the transcendental ground of absolute freedom in Kant.

And just as the noumenal world can be described in Kant's philosophy only as an "unknown something," so Suzuki finds it impossible to explain *Ri*:

> *Ri* is something which makes something meaningful. Which is not theory or anything. This is rather difficult to understand, *Ri*. It may take time before you understand *Ri*. Even though you don't attain enlightenment, you [already] have enlightenment, we say. That enlightenment means *Ri*. That something exists here means something had already some reason why it exists here. And because of that reason it makes some sense. I don't know what sense. No one knows, but there must be some reason, and everything must have some virtue for itself, and it is very strange that everything, that no things are the same. One is different from other. So there's nothing to compare with you, so you have your own value. And that value is not comparative value or exchange value. That value is something more than that. So when you are just on the cushion [sitting *zazen*] you have your own value. And because that value is related to everything, so that value is also absolute value. Maybe better not to say too much. [*SL*, IV, 6]

"That something exists here" as an appearance in my "big mind" "means something had already some reason why it exists here." Thus Suzuki uses the term *Ri* to refer to the unknown reason, the transcendental cause, of *Ji*—whatever can be introduced into my consciousness—just as Kant uses the term 'noumena' to refer to the transcendental, or "intelligible," cause of phenomena.

It is significant that Kant, like Suzuki, argues that a transcendental or intelligible cause can only be a cause of things in the world if it is, as Suzuki says, "related to everything." Thus Kant, in describing how the intelligible, or noumenal, character of human beings manifests itself through the free utilization of practical reason, points out that:

> This freedom ought not . . . to be conceived only negatively as independence of empirical conditions. The faculty of reason, so regarded, would cease to be a cause of appearances. It must also be described in positive terms, as the power of originating a series of events. [*KV*, B581–82]

And similarly, in the second *Critique*, Kant insists that the existence of a relationship between an intelligible, noumenal causality—that is to say, the causality of a will determined by moral law—and events in the world of sense must be assumed by people "in a definite way" when they act for moral reasons. For if I were ignorant of any such relationship, I would be unable to translate my ideas of morality into practical actions in the world of sense: "Causality with respect to the actions of the will in the world of sense must, of course, be known by reason in a definite way, for otherwise practical reason could produce no act" (*KP*, 49).

Because "appearances are not things in themselves and therefore not causes in themselves" (*KV*, B584), the ground of every independent action of mine in the world is to be found in what Kant calls "the relation to which the action stands to reason" (*KV*, B584). Thus, in the course of arguing that there must be an independent, unconditioned source of "the causality of free actions" (*KV*, B585), both Kant and Suzuki postulate the existence of an intelligible cause of things. "That something exists here," Suzuki says, "means something had . . . some reason why it exists here; and because of that reason it makes some sense" (*SL*, IV,6). And Kant and Suzuki also both admit in effect that "I don't know what sense. No one knows, but there must be some reason" (*SL*, IV, 6):

> Thus in our judgments in regard to the casuality of free actions we can get as far as the intelligible cause, but not beyond it. We can know that it is free, that is, that it is deter-

> mined independently of sensibility, and that in this way it may be the sensibly unconditioned condition of appearances. But to explain why in the given circumstances the intelligible character should give just these appearances and this empirical character transcends all the powers of our reason, indeed all its rights of questioning. [*KV*, B585]

Even though Suzuki and Kant approach the problem of attaining consciousness of freedom from different philosophical perspectives, the quotations and commentary in this subsection show that the key philosophical distinction informing both approaches is the distinction between form and emptiness, or phenomena and noumena. Without relying on this distinction, neither Kant nor Suzuki could possibly explain the existence of consciousness of freedom as emptiness, which, as I will now demonstrate, they both consider a necessary condition for respecting and observing moral laws.

(c)
Zazen *practice, as a method of cultivating consciousness of freedom as emptiness, is a necessary means for the realization of the requirements of moral law.*

At the beginning of chapter 2, a quotation from *Zen Mind, Beginner's Mind* was presented as evidence in support of the claim that Suzuki considers the mental state cultivated in *zazen* practice to be a necessary condition for the realization of the requirements of moral law. I want now to use the interpretation of Suzuki's account of Zen practice developed so far in this chapter—the interpretation of *zazen* as a discipline of the speculative restriction of reason leading to consciousness of freedom as emptiness—to provide further arguments in support of this claim. In providing these further arguments I will need to demonstrate that Suzuki's practice of *zazen* is indeed a *method of moral cultivation* similar to the method suggested in the text of Kant's "Methodology of Pure Practical Reason." However, because Kant himself never actually presented a fully developed method of moral cultivation, either in the *Critique of Practical Reason* or in his later work on ethics, *The Metaphysic of Morals*, it will be necessary, before proceeding any further, to demonstrate the degree to which such a method is *implicit* (perhaps "latent" would be a better term) in Kant's ethical writings, when these writings are considered in the context of the critical philosophy as a whole.

That there is no fully developed method of moral cultivation presented in the "Methodology of Pure Practical Reason," Kant acknowledges in the final paragraph of that concluding section of the *Critique of Practical Reason*:

> With these remarks I have intended only to point out the most general maxims of the methodology of moral cultivation and exercise. Since the manifold variety of duties requires specific definitions of each kind, and these would constitute a prolix affair, the reader will excuse me if in a work like this, which is only preliminary, I go no further than these outlines. [*KP*, 161]

As indicated by these concluding remarks to the second *Critique*, Kant saw the task of defining "the manifold variety of duties" as the focus of his future efforts to develop a methodology of moral cultivation. This task he indeed went on to accomplish in *The Metaphysic of Morals*. However, at the close of that work, just as at the close of the *Critique of Practical Reason*, Kant again appended a few suggestions concerning a possible *method* of moral cultivation, acknowledging that "one does not, merely by the theory of how one should behave in keeping with the concept of virtue, acquire the strength to put the rule into practice" (*MM*, 477). Thus Kant has acknowledged that there must be more to a methodology of moral cultivation than merely providing specific definitions of the various moral duties.

Unfortunately, the few suggestions that Kant gives us in his extremely short "Ethical Doctrine of Method" at the close of the *Metaphysic of Morals* are even less helpful than the text of the "Methodology of Pure Practical Reason" in pointing out how one might actually cultivate "the strength to put the [moral] rule into practice." In the "Ethical Didactic" (*MM*, 477–83), Kant outlines the beginning of a "moral catechism," by which "the subjective autonomy of each [person's] practical reason" can be "encouraged and developed" through a question and answer exchange. Then, in an extremely brief section entitled "Ethical Ascetic," Kant brings "The Ethical Doctrine of Method" to a quick close by exorting his readers to "aim at a frame of mind that is *brave* and *cheerful* in the observance of duty" (*MM*, 483).

That Kant devoted the concluding sections of two major works on morality to the topic of a methodology of moral cultivation indicates that he considered the development of a way to acquire "the strength to put the rule into practice" both a relevant and an important part of his moral philosophy. On the other hand, the fact that Kant failed to present, in either work, anything more than an extremely sketchy outline of what such a method might be is a good indication that Kant himself never developed such a method beyond the point of articulating what he calls "the most general maxims of moral cultivation and exercise." As was noted in chapter 2, however, Kant does suggest in the "Methodology of Pure Practical Reason" that there are two definite stages of moral cultivation: a legalistic stage that "teaches how to distinguish between the different duties which come together in an action," and a second, truly moral stage focusing on whether or not an action "not only is morally correct as a deed, but also has moral worth as a disposition" (*KP*, 159). So, if we assume that Kant, in the *Metaphysic of Morals*, did succeed in showing us the way to distinguish (legalistically, as it were) among "the different duties which come together in an action," then we can conclude that it is the second stage of moral cultivation—the stage involving what Kant refers to as the "negative perfection" of the moral disposition (see *KP*, 160)—which remains insufficiently articulated in Kant. More specifically, in the context of the structure of the "Ethical Doctrine of Method" outlined by Kant in the *Metaphysic of Morals*, it is the realm of what Kant calls the "ethical ascetic"—which "teaches not merely the concept of virtue but also how to put into practice and cultivate the *capacity for* and the *will to* virtue" (*MM*, 411) — that is left largely unexplored in Kant's moral philosophy. And it is precisely as an "ethical ascetic", I believe, that *zazen* as a true religious practice in the Kantian sense should be understood.

In sections *i* and *ii* of this chapter, the text of Kant's "Methodology of Pure Practical Reason" has been interpreted rather freely in an effort to demonstrate a relationship between the nonlegalistic, "ascetic" stage of moral cultivation and the practice of the critical discipline of the speculative restriction of reason. Where Kant states that "consciousness of freedom is the best, indeed the only, guard that can keep ignoble and corrupting influences from bursting in upon the mind" (*KP*, 161), I have understood him to mean that consciousness of freedom is a *necessary characteristic* of a truly moral disposition. And where Kant associates consciousness of freedom with an ideal moral disposition characterized by a "negative perfection . . . indicating that no incentives of inclinations are the determining grounds influencing an action done as a duty" (*KP*, 160), I have understood him to mean that consciousness of freedom does not involve awareness of freedom in any positive sense (a form of awareness that must, in the context of the critical philosophy, be considered illusory), but rather is accurately described by the phrase "consciousness of emptiness"—that is, it is a mental state best described negatively, by reference to its "independence from inclinations and circumstances" (*KP*, 161).[5]

These admittedly problematic interpretations of Kant's "Methodology" are incorporated into the following argument, which sums up my case for treating the practice of Kant's critical discipline of speculative reason as a method of moral cultivation:

(a) One cannot truly fulfill the requirements of morality so long as "incentives of inclinations are the determining grounds influencing an action" (*KP*, 21–27; 159–60).
(b) One cannot eliminate incentives of inclinations as the determining grounds of one's actions so long as one's mind is susceptible to "ignoble and corrupting influences" (*KP*, 161).
(c) "Consciousness of freedom is the . . . only guard that can keep ignoble and corrupting influences from bursting in upon the mind" (*KP*, 161).
(d) Consciousness of freedom is "consciousness of an independence from inclinations and circumstances and of the possibility of being sufficient to myself" (*KP*, 161).

(e) To be conscious "of an independence from inclinations and circumstances and of the possibility of being sufficient to myself" is to be conscious of my noumenal self (as argued in chapter 3, section *i*, above).
(f) To be conscious of my noumenal self in a nonanthropomorphic, nonfanatical way is to be conscious of this noumenal self as *empty*—that is, to be conscious of freedom as emptiness (as argued in chapter 3, section *ii*, above).
(g) Thus, in order to truly fulfill the requirements of morality, I must realize and maintain consciousness of freedom as emptiness (as argued in *a* through *f* above).
(h) To realize and maintain consciousness of freedom as emptiness is to constantly practice Kant's critical discipline of the speculative restriction of reason (as argued in chapter 3, sections *i* and *ii*, above).
(i) Thus, in order to truly fulfill the requirements of morality I must constantly practice Kant's critical discipline of the speculative restriction of reason (as argued in *a* through *h* above).

I acknowledge both that the plausibility of my Kantian interpretation of Zen practice hangs upon the thread of this argument, and that this thread is, from the point of view of Kantian scholarship, a tenuous one. Nevertheless, since this essay is intended merely to outline—not to exhaustively defend—a possible interpretive approach to the practice of Zen, I will not try to make the argument in any more detail (it may well be that Kant's texts will not support a more detailed argument), but will move on now, and attempt to demonstrate how the discipline of *zazen*, when understood in the practical context of the argument just given, plays essentially the same role as Kant's discipline of the speculative restriction of reason in helping the practicer observe the requirements of morality.

In support of my claim that *zazen* and Kant's critical discipline of speculative reason are, for *practical* purposes, essentially the same, I shall now argue that the two disciplines are put to the same practical use as a method of cultivating a mental condition considered by both Suzuki and Kant as necessary for the fulfillment of the requirements of moral law. This mental condition is referred to by Suzuki as "our original self-sufficient mind" (*ZM*, 22) and by Kant as "consciousness of an independence from inclinations and circumstances and of the possibility of being sufficient to myself" (*KP*, 161). Kant has asserted that consciousness of one's freedom from inclinations and circumstances is "the only guard that can keep ignoble and corrupting influences from bursting in upon the mind." Now I will attempt to show how Suzuki, like Kant, asserts that consciousness of freedom as emptiness—a form of consciousness realized through the practice of *zazen*—is a necessary condition for the attainment of freedom from greed, anger, and various other "ignoble and corrupting influences" that can destroy the moral purity of our intentions, if not the "legalistic" correctness of our deeds themselves.

Like Kant in the "Methodology," Suzuki holds that it is the purity of intention with which a person performs an action, and not the correctness of the deed actually performed, that is the supreme determinant of moral praiseworthiness or blameworthiness. Thus, for Suzuki, to cultivate a state of mind free from the influencing conditions of greed, anger, and other selfish incentives is to cultivate morality itself. In a lecture addressed to his Tassajara students, Suzuki uses a popular Zen teaching story to illustrate how the practice of *zazen* is a necessary means for realizing the requirements of moral law, because through this practice the mind is freed from all inclinations and incentives. The subject of the story is an ancient Buddhist monastic rule prohibiting monks from associating with—or even looking at—women.

> There is a Zen story. Once there were two monks traveling together. And they came to a big river where there was no bridge to cross. So they were waiting on one side of the bank. While they were waiting a beautiful woman came. So they were very much encouraged to cross the river with her. And at last one of them carried her on his back and crossed the river.
>
> After crossing the river, and on the way to somewhere, the other monk became furious: "You are a monk. You violated the precept not to look at a woman. As a monk it is not so good. Why did you do that?" The monk who helped the lady

> said, "You are still carrying a woman. I forgot about her a long time ago. You are still carrying her—you are still violating the precepts," he said. [*SL*, VIII, 8]

Referring to the words of an ancient scripture discussing the Buddhist precepts, Suzuki explains what he feels is the true sense of the prohibition against looking at women: "To see," he says, "is not to see, and not to see is to see" (*SL*, VIII, 7). So long as the other monk remains obsessed with *not seeing*, so long as he continues to struggle with his desire to look at the beautiful woman, he is, in fact, seeing: morally, he is looking at the woman even though legalistically he is obeying the letter of the precept by averting his eyes. Thus, the monk's literal obedience to the precepts is, morally, a violation of them. His behavior brings to mind Jesus's refusal, in the Sermon on the Mount, to accept a legalistic interpretation of adultery that would tolerate a man's committing adultery "in his heart." On the other hand, it is the monk carrying the woman on his back who, in violating the letter of the precepts, actually fulfills their true spirit. Because his intention in acting is that of helping all human beings as a friend, he is able to free himself and his actions from the taint of selfish incentives and inclinations:

> As a monk it may not be perfectly right [to help the woman]. Even so, as a man—as all human beings are our friend we should help them. Even if we violate the precepts we should help her. But if you think about it uselessly when there's no need to think about it, to think about it is actually violating the precepts. So to see a woman is not to see the woman. To help her, actually, he is not helping her. If he crosses with her on his back, actually he is not helping her. Do you understand? Actually he is not helping her. So not to help her is to help her in its true sense. [*SL*, VIII, 8]

Because the mind of one monk is not free of inclinations and incentives, he is unable to see reality as it is: he turns his eyes away from it in shame. Involved in dualistic thoughts about the appearance of the woman as an object of desire, separate from himself, he treats her appearance as a separate object that can be pursued or avoided. He forgets that, just like the river he is crossing, the attractive woman is also intimately a part of his own "big mind":

> Usually, why [people] become attached to the objective world, or to something they see, is because they understand things in only one way: "Here is something very good, very sweet—I have to eat." And we think that something exists here without us—whether we try to eat it or not, we think the cake exists. That is the normal way of understanding. But cake becomes cake because we want to eat it. So *we make cake.* There's no cake, actually, without us. When we understand in that way we are seeing cake, but we are not seeing cake. That is how we keep our precepts. [*SL*, VIII, 3]

When I understand that a sexual object becomes a sexual object only because I want to possess it sexually, then I understand that there is no object of desire without me, the subject of desire. And when I understand in that way, Suzuki says, then when I see a sexual object I do not see a sexual object: I recognize the appearance of the attractive woman as the appearance of my own sexual desire. This is truly to see things as they are:

> Because of our discrimination, or because of our desires, we are not observing things as it is. So Buddhist way is trying very hard to eliminate this kind of emotional discrimination, or prejudice, of good or bad: to see things as it is. After doing so it is possible to see things as it is. So when we say "things as it is," we mean to practice hard to get rid of our desires. Not to get rid of our desires, but to *count* our desires—to calculate or make allowance for them. If there is a computer, you must put in the data [and] one of the data will be our desire: this much desire, and this much nourishment, and this kind of color and how heavy it is. So we should count our desires in it. Then you will see the thing as it is. [*SL*, I, 5]

"How you observe the precepts," Suzuki tells his Tassajara students, "is to have complete understanding of reality" (*SL*, VIII, 4). How to observe the precepts—how to avoid treating a woman as a sexual object—is to see the woman as she is in her own right, as a thing in herself, apart from how she appears as a phenomenon of my subjective consciousness. And to "see" her in this way means actually *not to see* her: it is to go beyond the sphere of subjective appearances by realizing consciousness of form as emptiness, or *Ri*, which, Suzuki has said, is "nothing but the practice of zazen" (*ZM*, 115):

> When we go beyond subjective and objective world, which is *Ji*, we come to the understanding, oneness of everything, oneness of subjectivity and objectivity, oneness of inside and outside. For instance, if you sit zazen you are not thinking anything, you are not watching anything. Your focus is four feet, four or five feet ahead, but actually we are not watching anything. Focus is there but we don't watch anything. Even though many ideas come, we don't think. They come in and go out, that's all. We do not entertain various ideas. We do not serve food or anything. If they come in O.K. and if they go out, O.K. That's all. That is zazen. [*SL*, IV,1]

Here Suzuki describes *zazen* as a practice in which the conscious division of reality into subject and object is rejected in favor of the cultivation of consciousness of emptiness, or *Ri*: "oneness of everything, oneness of subjectivity and objectivity, oneness of inside and outside." The actual practice of *zazen*, he says, is "not thinking . . . not watching. . . . Focus is there but we don't watch anything." If I come upon a person in distress, I help her because I ought to help her—but without thinking about her as an object, without watching her as an object. Even if the idea of her beauty enters my mind, I do not "entertain" this idea: I do not "serve food or anything" to it. If it comes in, O.K.—I do not encourage the idea by struggling to repress it, or by getting "involved in dualistic sense of [observing or] violating precepts, or man or woman." If it goes out, O.K.—I do not "think about it uselessly when there's no need to think about it." So, "even though many ideas come," *I* do not think: I do not make the mistake of identifying my unconditioned noumenal self with the conditioned phenomena of consciousness. Through practicing consciousness of freedom as emptiness, I maintain awareness of what Suzuki calls "our original self-sufficient mind"—which would seem indeed to be close in spirit, if not identical, to what Kant refers to as awareness of an "independence from inclinations and circumstances and of the possibility of being sufficient to myself."

It is, therefore, as a method of going "beyond [the] subjective and objective world, which is *Ji*," by cultivating consciousness of freedom as emptiness, or *Ri*, that *zazen* practice makes it possible for the Buddhist practicer to observe the requirements of morality. Cultivating consciousness of freedom as emptiness is necessary for fulfilling the requirements of moral precepts, because it is only by acting with complete purity of intention—by acting with what Kant, in his "Methodology of Pure Practical Reason," calls "purity of will" (*KP*, 160)—that these requirements can be fulfilled. And such purity is attainable only by going beyond the dualistic world of inclination and its objects through the practice of a discipline that radically restricts the speculative activity of reason:

> When you are involved in dualistic sense of [observing or] violating precepts, or man or woman, or monk and layman, that is violating the precepts and poor understanding of Buddha's teaching. That is [the idea behind] how we sit. We just sit without any idea of attainment. Without any idea of doing anything, just to sit is our way. To be involved, completely involved in sitting meditation is our zazen. Without any idea of attainment, any idea of waste of time or meaningful practice, just to sit is our way. And this is how you keep our precepts. [*SL*, VIII,8]

4

In Defense of Thesis Z2:

In order to practice zazen *correctly, according to Suzuki, my sole intention in performing that practice must be that of realizing the requirements of moral law, as Kant understands these requirements.*

In chapter 3, arguments were advanced in support of the claim that Suzuki, like Kant, affirms there is a necessary relationship between a person's practice of a discipline of the speculative restriction of reason, leading to consciousness of freedom as emptiness, and that person's ability to realize the requirements of moral law. But Kant, in the *Critique of Practical Reason*, goes on to describe this relationship as a reciprocal one in which the negative discipline of speculative restriction works in tandem with the positive discipline of the practical, moral extension of reason in a "relation of balance, wherein reason as such can be suitably used" (*KP*, 142). In the writings of Suzuki, on the other hand, the reciprocal relationship between the cultivation of consciousness of freedom as emptiness and the practice of observing the requirements of moral laws would seem to be in danger of collapsing into one of identity. For Suzuki speaks of *zazen* practice as being *itself* the fulfillment of the requirements of morality: "Just to sit is our way. And this is how you keep our precepts" (*SL*, VIII,8).

Kant strictly limits the task of speculative reason in its working relationship with practical reason to that of "approaching perfection in its employment within experience" (*KP*, 135). Practical reason, he has stated in the preface to the second edition of the *Critique of Pure Reason*, "requires no assistance from speculative reason," so long as the former is assured against the latter's opposition, "that reason may not be brought into conflict with itself" (*KV*, Bxxv). But when Suzuki states, "How you observe the precepts is to have complete understanding of reality," he would seem to be advancing the clearly un-Kantian view that the practice of a discipline of the speculative restriction of reason—through which we see "things as they are," and thus "have complete understanding of reality"—is not only necessary but also *sufficient* for the fulfillment of moral requirements. Thus, even if it is agreed that *zazen* and Kant's discipline of the speculative restriction of reason are, for the practical purpose of moral cultivation, one and the same discipline, such agreement does not preclude disagreement over whether *zazen* is indeed "a true religious practice in the Kantian sense."

Does Suzuki mean to say that whatever one does, if one does it while practicing *zazen*, then—almost by definition—it fulfills the requirements of morality? Obviously, if this is Suzuki's view, it is not only un-Kantian but counter-intuitive as well. For such a view would justify committing patently immoral actions in the name of morality. And Suzuki's own words to his Tassajara students hardly discourage such an interpretation of *zazen* as a practice in the course of which any activity is morally permissible, so long as one is "completely involved in sitting meditation":

> Without any idea of doing anything, just to sit is our way. To be involved, completely involved in sitting meditation is our zazen. Without any idea of attainment, any idea of waste of time or meaningful practice, just to sit is our way. And this is how you keep our precepts. Sometimes we will be angry and sometimes we will smile; sometime we will murder people—your friend—sometime you will give a kind word to them. But, actually, what we are doing is just to observe our way. O.K.? I cannot explain it to well, but I think you must have understood what I mean. [*SL*, VIII,8–9]

Unfortunately, what Suzuki means by "just to sit is our way—and this is how you keep our precepts" has, in all likelihood, *not* been clearly understood by many students and teachers of Buddhism in America. For it is clearly possible to derive from the above statement what I have just referred to as a counter-intuitive view of morality. A Zen student might infer from Suzuki's words that there is no contradiction between observing moral precepts and murdering one's friend—just so long as one is, somehow, "involved, completely involved" in *zazen* practice. And it is likewise clearly possible for a Zen teacher, such as the monk "fresh out of the monastery" referred to in the introduction of this study, to interpret such a statement to mean that there is no contradiction between observing moral precepts as a Zen teacher and engaging in casual sexual relations with one's students—again, just so long as one is "completely involved" in *zazen* practice. Therefore, because certain statements of Suzuki's can be interpreted in ways that contradict the views most people have about morality—for example, it is usually considered morally blameworthy for someone to murder a friend, or for a religious leader to allow sexuality to insert itself into the relationship with followers—I believe it is important to discover an interpretation of Suzuki's account of *zazen* practice that connects the seemingly unrelated ideas of freedom, or autonomy, and respectful obedience to moral rules.

The Kantian interpretation of Suzuki that I am arguing for in this study affirms a truly reciprocal relationship between the attainment of consciousness of freedom as emptiness and the practice of respectful obedience to moral law. In presenting this interpretation I have, in chapter 3, followed Kant in arguing that a discipline that restricts speculative thinking (for example, *zazen*) is a necessary means for fulfilling the requirements of moral laws. And now in chapter 4 I will continue to follow Kant in arguing that the commands of morality must have *primacy* over the practice of a discipline of speculative reason (see *KP*, 119–21), if perfect freedom, or autonomy, is to be attained.

Although certain statements of Suzuki extolling *zazen* practice as a means of realizing the requirements of morality do seem to ignore Kant's thesis of the reciprocity of the relationship between consciousness of freedom and consciousness of moral law, other statements strongly affirm a relationship between freedom and respect for rules (see, e.g., *ZM*, 34). Thus in chapter 2 it was suggested that Suzuki, like Kant, can plausibly be interpreted as holding that it is my respectful obedience to unconditional moral rules that first makes possible my consciousness of freedom.

Because freedom is unknowable in itself, being neither a sensible experience nor a concept deducible from sensible experience (*KP*, 29), it is, Kant says in his "Methodology of Pure Practical Reason," only:

> Instances of pure moral resolutions . . . [which reveal] to man, who previously has not correctly known it, a faculty of inner freedom to release himself from the impetuous importunity of the inclinations, to such an extent that not even the dearest of them has an influence on a resolution for which he now makes use of his reason. [*KP*, 161]

And similarly, near the beginning of the second *Critique*, Kant argues that "no one would dare introduce freedom into science had not the moral law and, with it, practical reason come and forced this concept upon us" (*KP*, 30). Therefore, to complete my outline of a Kantian interpretation of Suzuki's account of *zazen*, I must present evidence from Suzuki's writings clearly demonstrating his belief that the mental state of consciousness of freedom as emptiness cultivated in *zazen* practice is necessarily subordinate to—and not above, beyond, or free from—the respectful observance of the commands of morality. That is to say, I must argue in support of thesis Z2, which expresses the view that *zazen*, when practiced correctly according to Suzuki, is practiced solely with the intention of fulfilling the requirements of moral law, as Kant understands these requirements.

My arguments in support of thesis Z2 are presented in the three sections of this chapter. First, in section *i*, evidence is presented from Suzuki's texts showing that Suzuki indeed shares Kant's view that the relationship between consciousness of freedom and dutiful obedience to moral laws is truly reciprocal. Just as both Suzuki and Kant view *consciousness of freedom* as a necessary means for realizing the requirements of moral laws, it is argued, so both Suzuki and Kant view *consciousness of duty*—my awareness of what is unconditionally required of me—as a necessary means for attaining consciousness of freedom. Secondly, in section *ii*, the compatibility of the ideas of duty in Suzuki and Kant is discussed. From the fact that the terms "morality" or "moral law" hardly ever appear in Suzuki's lectures, it is possible to conclude that Suzuki's idea of duty, unlike Kant's, does not contain a truly moral dimension—and if this were indeed the case, of course, the claim advanced in thesis Z2 could not be substantiated. Finally, in section *iii*, it is argued that it is the "Bodhisattva vow" to save all beings from suffering that Suzuki sees as the motivating intention behind *zazen* practice, and that the object of this vow is not different from that which Kant calls "the object and final end of pure practical reason" (*KP*, 129, 108–10). Thus, if I can successfully demonstrate that, according to Suzuki, one must practice *zazen* with the sole intention of realizing an end that Kant considers to be the summation of all the requirements of morality, I will have demonstrated the truth of thesis Z2.

i: Consciousness of Duty is Necessary, According to Both Suzuki and Kant, for Attainment of Consciousness of Freedom

In the *Critique of Practical Reason* Kant specifically asserts that the notion of duty is derived from the obligations imposed by morality (*KP*, 32), and that it is knowledge of these obligations that "leads directly to the concept of freedom" (*KP*, 32). The moral law, Kant says, "is an imperative, commanding categorically because it is unconditioned" (*KP*, 32). And the relation of my human will to this law is always "one of dependence under the name of 'obligation' . . . [which] implies a constraint to an action . . . called *duty*" (*KP*, 32). In Kant's house and gallows illustration, referred to in chapter 2, it is the man's awareness that he has a duty—an unconditional obligation to abstain from the murder of an innocent person—that causes him to recognize that he is free to act as he thinks he ought to act, regardless of his inclinations or circumstances.

Therefore, according to Kant, it is always in the form of an objective duty—never in the form, say, of a subjective *desire* to do good—that I am conscious of the requirements of morality:

> It is a very beautiful thing to do good to men because of love and a sympathetic good will, or to do justice because of a love of order. But this is not the genuine moral maxim of our conduct . . . when we presume, like volunteers, to flout with proud conceit the thought of duty and, as independent of command, merely to will of our own good pleasure to do something to which we think we need no command. We stand under a *discipline* of reason, and in all our maxims we must not forget our subjection to it, or withdraw anything from it, or by an egotistical illusion detract from the authority of the law. . . . Duty and obligation are the only names which we must give to our relation to the moral law. We are indeed legislative members of a moral realm which is possible through freedom . . . yet we are at the same time subjects in it, not sovereigns. [*KP*, 82]

It is this strict notion of duty as an unconditional obligation, coupled with the notion that there is a necessary, means-to-end relationship between my consciousness of duty and my consciousness of freedom, which Suzuki shares with Kant. In the epilogue to *Zen Mind, Beginner's Mind*, for example, Suzuki tells his students:

> Physical practice and rules are not so easy to understand, maybe especially for Americans. You have an idea of freedom which concentrates on physical freedom, on freedom of activity. This idea causes you some mental suffering and loss of freedom. You think you want to limit your thinking, you think some of your thinking is unnecessary or painful or entangling; but you do not think you want to limit your physical activity. For this reason Hyakujo established the rules and way of Zen life in China. He was interested in expressing and transmitting the freedom of true mind. Zen mind is transmitted in our Zen way of life based on Hyakujo's rules. [*ZM*, 135–36]

In this passage Suzuki contrasts what he calls "the freedom of true mind" with "an idea of freedom which concentrates on physical freedom, on freedom of activity." The latter idea of freedom, he says, "causes you some mental suffering and loss of freedom." Following the Kantian interpretation of Suzuki developed so far in this essay leads me to identify what Suzuki calls "an idea of freedom, which concentrates on physical freedom, on freedom of activity" as the idea that one can sometimes act in this world independently of the limitations imposed by spatial/temporal conditions. In chapter 3 it was pointed out that such an idea is self-contradictory so long as I think of myself *solely* in spatial/temporal terms—so long, that is, as I fail to understand myself simultaneously as form, or phenomenon, and as emptiness, or noumenon. From this perspective, the "mental suffering and loss of freedom" of which Suzuki speaks can be understood as stemming from the contradiction inherent in an idea of freedom that concentrates on physical—that is, spatial/temporal, or "sensuous"—freedom. Without a transcendental understanding of my phenomenal self as empty noumenon—without consciousness of freedom as emptiness—my idea of physical freedom is a fantasy that impedes rather than empowers me in my effort to express true freedom in the activities of daily life. It is for this reason—in order both to dispell my illusory ideas of freedom, and to express and transmit "the freedom of true mind"—that Suzuki says the rules and way of Zen life have been established.

But why must the freedom of true mind—the freedom of a mind conscious of form as emptiness and emptiness as form—be expressed and transmitted through rules? Suzuki's answer to this question is that the enlightened consciousness of freedom as emptiness requires special means for its transmission. Just like Kant, Suzuki rejects the view that true freedom, which is based on noumenal emptiness, can be known either directly through experience, or "antecedently" (see *KP*, 31) through some special intuition:

> We talk about enlightenment experience, but it is not some experience we will have in terms of good or bad, time or space, past or future. It is experience or consciousness beyond those distinctions or feelings. So we should not ask, "What is enlightenment experience?" That kind of question means you do not know what Zen experience is. Enlightenment experience cannot be asked for in your ordinary way of thinking.

> When you are not involved in this way of thinking, you have some chance of understanding what Zen experience is. [*ZM*, 133–34]

To be attached to "an idea of freedom which concentrates on physical freedom" is to envision the liberating enlightenment experience in terms of my ordinary way of thinking—in terms of "good or bad, time or space, past or future." But so long as I am involved in this ordinary way of thinking, I have no chance to experience the reality of freedom based upon consciousness of emptiness. "Reality," Suzuki says, "cannot be caught by thinking or feeling mind" (*ZM*, 135). And in another passage he states, "If you seek for freedom, you cannot find it" (*ZM*, 112). So, because thinking about freedom in terms of my ordinary "thinking or feeling mind" results in nothing but "mental suffering and loss of freedom," the rules and way of Zen life have been established to help me go beyond the limitations of my ordinary mind and actually realize what Suzuki has called "freedom of true mind." Because, as Suzuki says, "absolute freedom itself is necessary before you can acquire absolute freedom" (*ZM*, 112), the observance of the rules of Zen life constitutes a kind of training whereby the freedom of true mind, which "at first . . . may be a kind of belief" becomes, through the practice of observing rules, or precepts, "something the student feels or already has" (*ZM*, 135).

Freedom, Kant insists, is "an inscrutable faculty which no experience can prove"—the very possibility of freedom being "incomprehensible to speculative reason" (*KP*, 47–48). Thus, in the context of a Kantian interpretation of *zazen*, it makes sense for Suzuki to say "not by reading or contemplation of philosophy, but only through practice, actual practice, can we understand what Buddhism is" (*ZM*, 102). To understand the significance of "physical practice and rules" in relationship to the attainment of freedom is to understand that thinking speculatively about freedom—or having faith in the reality of such speculations—can never produce consciousness of freedom as emptiness. However, by my "actual practice" of following the rules of Zen life—by which "we train our mind, our emotions, our body"—I learn to *express* my freedom in the context of the necessary limitations under which it can actually be acquired:

> When you are in your position, are limited, the realization of truth will be there, will happen to you. But if you do not work anywhere, wandering from this place to that place, without knowing where you are, without knowing the place where you work, there will be no chance for you to realize your true nature. . . . Reality is experienced only when you are in some particular circumstance. That is why we say emptiness is form. Emptiness is very good but it can only be experienced in some form or color or under some limitation. . . . You should appreciate what you are doing right now, moment after moment, and to do that you must know what condition you are actually under. If you are a teacher you should behave like a teacher. If you are a student you should behave like a student. So first of all you should know what your position is, or else the realization of the truth will not happen to you. To realize our position and find ourselves is our Way. [*WB*, VII, Summer 1968:18]

Suzuki's words recall Kant's warning that I should never, in thinking of my noumenal self as free, commit the error of thinking of my phenomenal self as exempt from those laws of natural necessity, which, as I know, apply to the person standing next to me. For, to repeat Kant's words from the first *Critique:* "To allow such exemption would be to set [myself as] an appearance outside all possible experience, to distinguish it from all objects of possible experience, and so to make of it a mere thought-entity, a phantom of the brain" (*KV*, B570–71). Because the freedom of true mind based upon noumenal emptiness "can only be experienced in some form or color or under some limitation," it is necessary, according to both Kant and Suzuki, to understand noumena, or emptiness, in terms of phenomena, or form. If freedom is to be more than "a mere thought-entity, a phantom of the brain" to me, then, as Suzuki says, I "must know what condition . . . [I] am actually under." I must, in Kant's words, take the "strictly empirical character" of my actions "as the supreme ground of explanation, leaving entirely out of account their intelligible character (that is, the transcendental cause of their empirical character) as being completely unknown, save insofar as the empirical serves for its sensible sign" (*KV*, B574). And thus, because *zazen* practice necessarily involves consciousness of "what condition you are actually under"—

because it involves the experience of emptiness "in some form or color or under some limitation"—the rules and way of Zen life have been developed:

> The only way to study pure mind is through practice. Our inmost nature wants some medium, some way to express and realize itself. We answer this inmost request through our rules, and Patriarch after Patriarch shows us his true mind. [*ZM*, 136]

In order for the rules of Zen practice to actually work as a means to the end of attaining consciousness of freedom, my attitude toward them must, according to Suzuki, be one of unconditional respect and obedience (*ZM*, 136). Thus he cautions his American students that, if new rules are to be fashioned for "an American way of Zen life," we should be very careful to make such rules worthy of our respect and obedience:

> Little by little with patience and endurance we must find the way for ourselves, find out how to live with ourselves and with each other. In this way we will find out our precepts. [*ZM*, 136]

However, once such rules, or precepts, have been decided upon, Suzuki says, "we should obey them completely until they are changed":

> It is not a matter of good or bad, convenient or inconvenient. You just do it without question. That way your mind is free. The important thing is to obey your rules without discrimination. This way you will know the pure Zen mind. [*ZM*, 136]

According to Suzuki, then, it will be only through my dutiful obedience to a set of precepts, which I treat as unconditionally binding upon my behavior, that I come to "know the pure Zen mind"—the mind conscious of a supersensible reality which "cannot be caught by thinking or feeling." And, as has already been shown, the same means-to-end relationship between humble obedience to duty and the sublime consciousness of freedom is affirmed—"apotheosized" might be a better word!—by Kant:

> Duty! Thou sublime and mighty name that dost embrace nothing charming or insinuating but requires submission. . . . What origin is there worthy of thee, and where is to be found the root of thy noble descent which proudly rejects all kinship with the inclinations and from which to be descended is the indispensable condition of the only worth which men can give themselves? It cannot be less than something which elevates man above himself as a part of the world of sense, something which connects him with an order of things which only the understanding can think and which has under it the entire world of sense, including the empirically determinable existence of man in time. . . . It is nothing else than personality, i.e., the freedom and independence from the mechanism of nature regarded as a capacity of a being which is subject to special laws (pure practical laws given by its own reason), so that the person as belonging to the world of sense is subject to his own personality so far as he belongs to the intelligible world. For it is then not to be wondered at that man, as belonging to two worlds, must regard his own being in relation to his second and higher vocation with reverence and the laws of this vocation [i.e., the laws of duty] with the deepest respect. [*KP*, 87]

The following quotations provide additional evidence of Suzuki's belief in the view that consciousness of duty is a fundamental aspect of Zen Buddhist practice:

"We are doing what we should do. That is Buddhism."

> When I was at Eiheiji monastery in Japan everyone was just doing what he should do. That is all. It is the same as waking up in the morning; we have to get up. At Eiheiji monastery, when we had to sit, we sat; when we had to bow to Buddha, we bowed to Buddha. That is all. And when we were practicing, we did not feel anything special. . . . So to feel something about Buddhism is not the main point. Whether that feeling is good or bad is out of the question. We do not mind, whatever it is. Buddhism is not good or bad. We are doing what we should do. That is Buddhism. [*ZM*, 78]

Getting up in the morning is "a very good chance to practice our way."

The following dialogue took place at Tassajara Zen Monastery, where students are awakened very early in the morning for group *zazen* practice:

Student: When I am fully awake I have, maybe, a little control over my desires, but in the *morning* . . .

Suzuki: That is what I am saying. In the morning you have trouble, I know that. So that is why I say, "Get up!"

Student: How do you do that?

Suzuki: Just do it. Or else someone will go and hit you!

Student: I *just* got up a couple of times—jumped out of bed. But it was such a big thing!

Suzuki: Yes. Big thing. So if you can get up pretty well I think your practice is almost O.K. That is a very good chance to practice our way. Just get up. O.K.? That is a most important thing. [*WB*, XVI, Winter 1978–79: 31]

On strict practice

Student: Would you explain what you mean by strict practice?

Suzuki: Things are going on in a very strict way. There is no exception. Wherever there is something, there is some rule, some truth behind it, which is going on strictly, controlling things without any exception. We think we care for freedom, but the other side of freedom is strict rules. Within the strict rules there is complete freedom; freedom and strict rules are not two separate things. . . . Originally we are supported by strict rules or truths. That is the other side of freedom.

Student: Can you give us some more examples of strict practice?

Suzuki: When you get up you should get up. When everyone sleeps you should sleep. That is an example. [*WB*, XII, 1973:50]

More rules—not fewer rules—are needed for American Zen

In the following passage Rick Fields describes the beginning years of Suzuki's teaching in San Francisco of the mid–1960s:

> [Suzuki] even went so far as to suggest—much to everyone's amazement—that American Zen ought to have more rules than Japanese Zen. "You think two-hundred and fifty precepts for men and five hundred for women is awful and that it should be made simpler," he said. "But I think you will have more difficulty in practicing zazen in America than we do in Japan. This kind of difficulty should be continued forever or we will not have peace in the world."
>
> He declined to say what additional precepts he might have had in mind . . . but he did increase the number of bows after zazen from three to nine. When it was suggested that this might discourage some people, he answered, "It is true, very true. I know people will be discouraged. I know we are causing a lot of discouragement for American people when we bow nine times, when they bow only three times in Japan. I know that very well. So I bow nine times here in America.". . .
>
> So there were rules—etiquette, decorum. These did not change for anyone. If you wanted to sit in the morning, you were there, on your zafu, by five-thirty. There was freedom, but within form. As Suzuki-roshi explained it, in an astute analysis of that generational conflict that obsessed the decade: older people might understand what the *Heart Sutra* meant when it said, "emptiness is form," and younger people might understand what it meant when it said, "form is emptiness," but both were necessary.[1]

As the above quotations indicate, Suzuki, like Kant, views the relationship between my consciousness of a duty to obey certain unconditional rules, or precepts, and my consciousness of freedom as truly reciprocal. Suzuki clearly does not equate zazen practice with total freedom from the commands and restrictions imposed by societal rules. Instead, he emphasizes that it is precisely the rules of everyday behavior—rules as humble as the time we must get up in the morning—that, by revealing to us the way of "doing what we should do," constitute the form of freedom itself:

> We think we care for freedom, but the other side of freedom is strict rules. Within the strict rules there is complete freedom; freedom and strict rules are not two separate things. . . . Originally we are supported by strict rules or truths. That is the other side of freedom. [*WB*, XII, 1973: 50]

However, what is not evident from the quotations from Suzuki presented so far is that it is respect for and obedience to *moral* rules that Suzuki considers necessary in order to acquire consciousness of freedom. Suzuki's examples of the rules of strict practice—such as getting up at the right time in the morning, or bowing nine times after sitting in meditation—seem singularly lacking in any moral component. In fact, Suzuki seems to derive his concept of "strict practice" more from the concept of necessary natural laws, than from the concept of a necessary moral law:

> Things are going on in a very strict way. There is no exception. Wherever there is something, there is some rule, some truth behind it, which is going on strictly, controlling things without any exception. [*WB*, XII, 1973: 50]

Therefore, in the next section of this chapter, I will try to show that Suzuki's idea of duty, despite its seemingly amoral—and ritualistic—components, is nonetheless compatible with Kant's idea of duty as an obligation based upon moral law.

ii: Compatibility of the Idea of Duty in Suzuki and Kant

In this section three arguments are presented in defense of the claim that Suzuki and Kant share a similar understanding of the nature of duty and its role in religious practice. Subsection *a*, below, is a response to the criticism that Suzuki's idea of duty is incompatible with Kant's moral theory, because Suzuki rarely uses the term "morality" in his lectures and actually seems to reject the idea that there is any moral purpose in following the rules and way of Zen life. For example:

> In our practice we have no particular purpose or goal, nor any special object of worship. In this respect our practice is somewhat different from the usual religious practices. [*ZM*, 75]

In this first subsection I shall argue that Kant's notion of moral law as a fact, or original characteristic, of human reason renders unnecessary any attempt to prove that Suzuki's idea of duty involves an idea of obedience to specific moral rules or precepts. By showing that Suzuki urges his students to cultivate awareness of what he calls their "original nature"—such awareness being, he believes, both a necessary and a sufficient condition for being able to act in a morally praiseworthy way—I will be showing that it is at least possible that Suzuki, like Kant, believes that the purpose of religious practice is that of cultivating awareness of a fundamental moral principle inherent in the human mind—that is, cultivating awareness of a sense of moral duty that is a fact of my "original nature" as a rational being.

Subsection *b*, below, is a response to the potential criticism that Suzuki is guilty of a type of naturalistic fallacy when he explains the need for strict rules and precepts in terms of the existence of strict laws of nature—for instance, "Wherever there is something, there is some rule, some truth behind it, which is going on strictly, controlling things without any exception" (*WB*, XII, 1973: 50). I will argue that the analogy that Suzuki draws between the strictness of laws of nature and the strictness of rules of Zen life is not at all inconsistent with Kant's moral philosophy. The fundamental law of pure practical reason—as Kant points out repeatedly in the second *Critique*—is itself void of any specific moral content, or material, being only a *formula* to which, according to Kant, all maxims of conduct that are truly moral must conform (see Kant's note at *KP*, 8). Moreover, in explaining how to apply this fundamental moral principle as a general formula for all moral rules, Kant—in a manner very similar to Suzuki—repeatedly draws an analogy between the form of moral rules and the form of laws of nature. For example:

> If the maxim of action is not so constituted as to stand the test of being made the form of a natural law in general, it is morally impossible. Even common sense judges in this way, for its most ordinary judgments, even those of experience, are always based on natural law. Thus . . . natural law serves . . . as the *type* of a law of freedom, for if common sense did not have something to use in actual experience as an example, it could make no use of the law of pure practical reason in applying it to that experience. [*KP*, 69–70]

Finally, subsection *c* responds to the potential criticism that the duties and rules of Zen life, such as getting up early in the morning or bowing nine times after *zazen*, cannot properly be called *moral* duties or rules. In this subsection I will try to show how the purpose of all the rules, or precepts, which form the foundation of the Zen way of life, is, according to Suzuki, that of eliminating selfishness. This would indicate that Suzuki understands the *function* of duties and rules in a manner similar to the way in which Kant understands the function of moral law:

> The moral law, which alone is truly, i.e., in every respect, objective, completely excludes the influence of self love . . . and forever checks self-conceit, which decrees the subjective conditions of self-love as laws. [*KP*, 74]

(a)
Interpreting what Suzuki refers to as awareness of "true nature" (or "original" or "Buddha" nature) as awareness of a fundamental principle of morality, which is a fact of human reason

There is, Kant says, a "fundamental law of pure practical reason," which functions rather like the voice of conscience within me. "The consciousness of this fundamental law," Kant has said, "may be called a fact of reason" (*KP*, 31):

> In order to regard this law without any misinterpretation as given, one must note that it is not an empirical fact but the sole fact of pure reason, which by it proclaims itself as originating law. [*KP*, 31]

Thus Kant claims that my consciousness of moral law originates in my very nature as a rational being. It is a "fact" of my reason, and when I allow my awareness of this fact to determine my idea of what I should and should not do, then I can rightfully proclaim myself (my reasoning self) "as originating law."

Because Kant states that my knowledge of the fundamental law of pure practical reason is originally present within me, as it is within all rational beings, and because he also states that through my knowledge of and application of this fundamental principle, I myself am the "legislative" source of all the specific moral laws upon which I base my actions, it will not be necessary—in order to prove that Suzuki's idea of dutiful obedience to rules is, like Kant's, based upon the idea of moral obligation—to prove that Suzuki advocates respectful obedience to any *specific* set of moral obligations. For, according to Kant's view of moral law as a fundamental fact of reason, it is conceivable that someone might be innocent of a sense of obligation to obey a specific set of moral rules, and yet still naturally act in a morally praiseworthy way, solely due to her or his attention to that original, inborn moral principle, which, as Kant claims, is the source and inspiration for all truly moral maxims of conduct.

In the *Groundwork of the Metaphysic of Morals*, Kant acknowledges the capacity of each person to know what he or she is obliged to do, solely by maintaining consciousness of the fundamental principle of morality and by using it alone "as a norm of judgment." After deriving this principle from an analysis of ordinary moral judgments, he writes:

> In studying the moral knowledge of ordinary human reason we have now arrived at its first principle. This principle it admittedly does not conceive thus abstractly in its universal form, but it does always have it actually before its eyes and does use it as a norm of judgment. It would be easy to show here how human reason, with this compass in hand, is well able to distinguish in all cases that present themselves, what is good or evil, right or wrong—provided that, without the least attempt to teach it anything new, we merely make reason attend, as Socrates did, to its own principle; and how in consequence there is no need of science or philosophy for

> knowing what man has to do in order to be honest and good, and indeed to be wise and virtuous. It might even be surmised in advance that acquaintance with what every man is obliged to do, and so also to know, will be the affair of every man, even the most ordinary. [*GW*, 403–4]

Referring no doubt to the example of Socrates teaching mathematics to an uneducated slave boy in the *Meno*, Kant says that all that is necessary for teaching knowledge of what is morally right and wrong is to "make reason attend, as Socrates did, to its own principle." My consciousness of this fundamental principle is a "compass in hand" enabling me "to distinguish in all cases that present themselves, what is good or evil, right or wrong." I need not be able to understand or to formulate this principle philosophically "in its universal form" in order to use it—for, as a fundamental fact of my reason, it is always "actually before [my] eyes . . . as a norm of judgment." And thus, if it can be shown that Suzuki, "without the least attempt to teach [his students] anything new . . . merely [tries to make each of their minds] attend, as Socrates did, to its own principle," then I will have established the possibility at least that Suzuki, like Kant, views attention to a fundamental moral principle as the very basis of religious practice.

In order to establish grounds for such a possibility it will not, of course, be necessary to show that Suzuki and Kant use the same language to describe this fundamental principle. For, as Kant points out, "even the most ordinary" person—even, one must assume, a Japanese Zen teacher!—can know and make use of this principle without having made any attempt to describe it or analyze it philosophically. Thus it is possible that Suzuki in his writings might be referring to the same fundamental moral principle as Kant, yet be talking about it in quite a different way. My purpose in this subsection, however, is not even to argue that Kant and Suzuki advocate respectful obedience to the same moral principle. I merely want to show that Suzuki in his lectures, like Kant in his writings, points to *something*—whether it be a "fundamental principle," or our "original nature"—that is a "fact" of our human consciousness, respectful attention to which is both necessary and sufficient for acquiring knowledge of what we should and should not do.

Suzuki's statement in the prologue to *Zen Mind, Beginner's Mind*—a statement already quoted several times in this study—lends itself to the Kantian interpretation I am suggesting in this subsection:

> If we lose our original self-sufficient mind, we will lose all precepts. . . . If you keep your original mind, the precepts will keep themselves. [*ZM*, 22]

It is at least possible that Suzuki in this statement is trying to make his students attend to some original, fundamental principle of their own minds—attention to which, as he indicates, is both necessary (if we lose it, "we will lose all precepts") and sufficient (if we keep it, "the precepts will keep themselves") for fulfilling the requirements of morality.

If this statement is given the Kantian interpretation I am suggesting, then what I have called, at the beginning of chapter 2 of this book, Suzuki's "seeming rebuttal" to thesis Z2 would no longer contradict the claim advanced in that thesis. Thesis Z2 advances the claim that, as a Zen student, my purpose in sitting *zazen* must be solely that of realizing the requirements of moral law. Suzuki, in seeming rebuttal to that claim, has been quoted as saying that "in our practice we have no particular purpose or goal" (*ZM*, 75) and "to concentrate your mind on something is not the true purpose of Zen" (*ZM*, 33). But under a Kantian interpretation of Suzuki's statement from the prologue of *Zen Mind, Beginner's Mind*, a religious practice that has no particular goal, nor any special object of worship can still, without contradiction, be called a practice whose *general* purpose is that of realizing the requirements of morality. If one describes the general purpose of a religious practice as that of attending to an original principle of the mind, the observance of which is both a necessary and sufficient means of fulfilling moral requirements, it is not contradictory to go on to describe such a practice as having no particular goal—that is, no goal of realizing any particular moral requirements—apart from that general purpose.

Moreover, Kant himself quite evidently does not view the fundamental principle of pure practical reason as an object of experience that one might concentrate one's mind on. Kant specifically states that this principle "is not an empirical fact" (*KP*, 31). We come to know pure practical laws, he says, by simply "attending to the necessity with which reason prescribes them to us and to the elimination from them of all empirical conditions, which reason directs" (*KP*, 30). Thus, according to Kant, I come to know moral laws not by concentrating my mind upon any specific principle of morality, but rather by first *eliminating* the influence of "empirical conditions" upon my thinking and then by simply "attending" to what I must do in the course of my daily life. Because moral law is a fact of my original nature as a rational being, I naturally and continually experience its prescriptive effect on my thoughts and conduct, without trying to force myself to concentrate on any specific precept of morality. "We become immediately conscious" of the moral law, Kant says, "as soon as we construct maxims [of conduct] for the will" (*KP*, 29). So, if the purpose of my religious practice is that of attending carefully to what I do in the light of my original nature as a rational human being, such a purpose not only does not conflict, but accords well with Kant's view of religious practice.

I want now to present a few quotations in which Suzuki speaks of attending to and accepting the "true nature" of the mind. These quotations are presented as grounds for the claim that Suzuki, like Kant, advocates both attention and submission to the guidance of an inner, fundamental principle of the mind.

True nature as sincerity

> Our way is not to sit to acquire something; it is to express our true nature. That is our practice. . . . Whatever you do, it should be an expression of the same deep activity. . . . The Bodhisattva's way is called "the single-minded way," or "one railway track thousands of miles long." The railway track is always the same. If it were to become wider or narrower, it

would be disastrous. Wherever you go, the railway track is always the same. That is the Bodhisattva's way. So even if the sun were to rise from the west, the Bodhisattva has only one way. His way is in each moment to express his nature and his sincerity.

We say railway track, but actually there is no such thing. Sincerity itself is the railway track. . . . There is no starting point, no goal, nothing to attain. Just to run on the track is our way. This is the nature of our Zen practice. [*ZM*, 54]

Danger of naive speculation about true nature

But when you become curious about the railway track, danger is there. You should not see the railway track. If you look at the track you will become dizzy. . . . But sometimes we try to explain the railway track because we become curious if something is always the same. We wonder, "How is it possible for the Bodhisattva always to be the same? What is his secret?" But there is no secret. Everyone has the same nature as the railway track. [*ZM*, 54]

True nature as an "inmost desire"

To think, "Because it is possible we will do it," is not Buddhism. Even though it is impossible, we have to do it because our true nature wants us to. But actually, whether or not it is possible is not the point. If it is our inmost desire to get rid of our self-centered ideas, we have to do it. When we make this effort, our inmost desire is appeased and Nirvana is there. Before you determine to do it, you have difficulty, but once you start to do it, you have none. Your effort appeases your inmost desire. [*ZM*, 45–46]

Buddha nature is human nature

By Buddha-nature, we mean human nature. To be faithful to our nature will be the only way to live in this world as a human being. So we call our nature buddha-nature and accept it. . . Accept does not mean to understand it psychologically or biologically. It means actual practice. [*WB*, XIII, 1974:4]

To find your true nature is not to observe yourself as an object, but to stand on your own legs and realize "I am here."

Buddha attained this enlightenment when he found his true nature and knew exactly who he was . . . [and] he saw that everything had the same nature as himself . . .

"So everything is Buddha," we say; but when we say so, in its true sense it means "I am Buddha." Only when we have this view, when we stand on our own legs, can we help others. Before this, when you observe yourself with ideas like "Who am I?" "Have I attained enlightenment or not?" "Am I able to help others?" you cannot help others. When you become just you yourself, without comparing yourself to others, just "I am I," "I am here," and when you have difficulty, just "I can manage myself pretty well," that is Buddha. . . .

When we understand ourselves in this way we will live in this world to continuously try to express Buddha nature, moment after moment. That is the effort we should make, instead of being caught by some certain color or form. We should make our best effort at each moment. [*WB*, VIII, Spring 1969:10–11,16]

(b) *How Kant and Suzuki both model their ideas of duty after the way things happen in nature, according to natural laws*

In the preceding subsection, mention was made of Kant"s "fundamental principle of pure practical reason," but no attempt was made to articulate the principle itself. This was because the purpose of that subsection was solely to argue that Suzuki, like Kant, refers to an original fact, or feature, of the human mind, attention to which is both necessary and sufficient for realizing how we ought to act in our daily lives. Now, however, I want to try to articulate Kant's fundamental principle in a way that suggests its affinity both with Suzuki's idea of "true nature" or "Buddha nature" and with what I have called Suzuki's naturalistic way of explaining the need for strict rules in Zen life.

If Suzuki's idea of Buddha nature is indeed compatible with Kant's idea of a moral principle fundamental to human reason, then there must be some good Kantian explanation for why Suzuki typically refers to the world of nature ("things are going on in a strict way"; "by Buddha nature we mean human nature") rather than to traditional moral concepts of good and evil, or right and wrong, when he offers analogies for Buddha nature. For in the absence of any such explanation, it would seem that Suzuki, by equating Buddha nature with nature or human nature, is vulnerable to criticism from a Kantian viewpoint, not only because he seemingly ignores the moral dimension of this fundamental principle, but also because he incorrectly "anthropomorphizes" it by analogizing it to events in the world of human sense experience. In regard to the latter criticism, however, it has already been shown in chapter 3 and in section *i* of chapter 4, above, how Suzuki and Kant share both the view that the concepts of phenomena and noumena are interrelated, and the view that my intelligible character must remain completely unknown to me, save insofar as my empirical character serves as its sensible sign. So, a fundamental principle of mind, which is a "fact" of my nature as a rational being, must, from both Kant and Suzuki's point of view, be understood and described in terms of my empirical human nature—this empirical nature being itself understood, in reciprocal fashion, as the sensible sign of a purely intelligible (noumenal) nature.

It will be my purpose in this subsection to show first how Kant recommends that we use the empirically based descriptions of the natural world given by *laws of nature* as the sensible signs of fundamental laws of the intelligible world (fundamental moral laws) and then to show how Suzuki makes use of similar analogies taken from the natural world in his own descriptions of Buddha nature.

1
Kant's "law of nature" formula for the fundamental moral principle

There is, it would seem, a problem with Kant's thesis that the empirical character of my actions can serve as the sensible sign of that fundamental moral principle, which, allegedly, is the intelligible source of such actions. For how can my knowledge of the empirical, "sensuous" conditions of my life—the same knowledge that, as Kant has said, threatens "to make the bounds of sensibility coextensive with the real, and so to supplant reason in its pure (practical) employment"—possibly serve as a sign of that purely intelligible principle of practical reason that is the source of my freedom from such conditions? For, as Kant points out:

> Since all instances of possible actions are only empirical and can belong only to experience and nature, it seems absurd to wish to find a case in the world of sense, and thus standing under the law of nature, which admits the application of a law of freedom to it, and to which we could apply the supersensuous ideal of the morally good, so that the latter could be exhibited *in concreto.* [*KP*, 68]

Throughout the vast "is" of the "world of sense" that is nature, I can find no sign of an "ought." How, then, can this empirical "is" possibly serve as the sensible sign of a supersensuous principle—that is, of the moral law that is the intelligible source of my freedom? Kant's answer to this question can be given in the form of two arguments: *A,* that the causality of freedom can be understood only in terms of my sensible experience (and thus there can be no sign of freedom other than a sensible one), and *B,* that those natural laws that I use to describe and define my sensible experience, due to the characteristics of necessity and universality that they share with moral laws, can serve as *types* of my idea of the moral law.

Argument A: The causality of freedom can be understood only in empirical terms

The concept of freedom, Kant notes, is a special example of the concept of causality (*KP*, 103) in which I understand myself as the first, *unconditioned* cause of my actions, and thus as perfectly free to act in accordance with what I think I ought to do. Yet, Kant points out, when I apply the general concept of causality—according to which one condition, B, is always thought of as the product of a previous condition, A—directly to the notion of a free, noumenal self existing independently of spatial/temporal conditions, I immediately become ensnarled in contradiction (*KP*, 94–95). Therefore, the only way the concept of freedom becomes understandable to me in practice is, according to Kant, by *analogy*, through which, as Kant says in the *Critique of Pure Reason*, "we employ the concepts of experience in order to form some sort of concept of intelligible things—things of which as they are in themselves we have yet not the least knowledge" (see *KV*, B594). In the *Critique of Practical Reason*, Kant justifies the need for an "analogical" understanding of freedom by pointing out that "if common sense did not have something to use in actual experience as an example, it could make no use of the law of pure practical reason in applying it to that experience" (*KP*, 70).

Because, as Kant has been quoted above, "nothing can be perceived except insofar as it appears"—and because freedom can never be known from spatial/temporal appearances—it is never freedom itself that appears as the cause of an action of mine in actual experience, but always some condition in the sensible world. If my respectful obedience to the command of the moral law within me should lead me to return a wallet stuffed with cash that I find lying on the sidewalk, then this moral law—and my freedom, which is presupposed by it—can indeed be thought of as the cause of an effect in the sensible world. But this thought of myself as a free being causing an event in the spatial/temporal world can be thought only in reference to the actual experience of observing myself—as an object of my senses—bending over and picking up the wallet, finding the owner's identification, telephoning her, and thus, in various sensibly observable ways, causing the wallet to be returned. Thus my actions in the world, as Kant points out, have a dual character:

> On the one side the actions are under a law which is a law of freedom instead of a natural law and thus belong to the conduct of intelligible beings, and on the other side as events in the world of sense they belong to appearances; *so that the rules of a practical reason are possible only with respect to the latter.* [*KP*, 65: emphasis added]

"The rules of a practical reason"—those moral rules that presuppose my existence as a free, noumenal being—are possible *only with respect to my existence as a phenomenal being.* For my attempts to apply my reason practically (for example, in acting to return a lost wallet) take place in the real world of my sense experience, not in some abstract, supersensuous setting! And since it is only as "events in the world of sense" that I both perceive and judge my actions, the moral rules of my practical reason are incomprehensible in isolation from the actual sensuous conditions of my life. It is, therefore, only in reference to what is presented to me in my sensible experience—the experience that I describe, define, and understand in terms of natural causal laws—that I can actually apply the practical "law of freedom" in my efforts to act morally in the world.

Argument B: My actual experience of how things happen according to natural laws can serve as the sensible sign of a practical law of freedom

Although I must, according to Kant, be able to refer to something in my actual sense experience as an example before I can make use of the concept of freedom in applying it to that experience, it is not the *sensible* aspect of empirically observable events that makes them fit to serve as examples for the application of my practical reason. Rather, Kant argues, it is through the *lawful* character of these events that they become "sensible signs" of the causality of a moral law of freedom.

Despite various problems of inconsistency and incompleteness in the theoretical structures of the physical sciences, it continues to make sense for me to speak of the accelerating speed of a hammer dropped from the top of my household ladder, or the evaporation of water from my boiling teapot—or even the travel of electrons inside the cathode–ray tube of my television set—as events that can be described and understood through reference to laws of nature. What distinguishes a law—whether it be a natural or a moral law—is, according to Kant, its aspects of necessity and universality; a true law, as Kant wants to use the term 'law,' must be "a necessary and universal rule" (*KP*, 34). And thus, just as the behavior of electrons inside my television set can be said to occur in accordance with certain universal and necessary rules of nature, so, Kant wants to say, *moral* behavior can likewise be said to occur in accordance with a universal and necessary "law of freedom" (*KP*, 70). In regard to their shared characteristics of necessity and universality, Kant argues, "laws as such are all equivalent, regardless of whence they derive their determining grounds" (*KP*, 70). And so it follows that my idea of a moral law—"I must always cause B"—is equivalent to my idea of a natural law—"A must always cause B"—in that I think of both types of laws as necessary and universal rules.

Because a moral law, due to what Kant understands to be the unconditional nature of its command, is always a necessary and universal rule, then it follows—so Kant goes on to argue—that any rule of behavior adopted by me, which cannot possibly be willed by me as a universal and necessary rule, cannot qualify as a law of morality (*KP*, 69–70). And in this way Kant arrives at the conclusion that universal and necessary laws of nature can serve as the type, or standard, for moral laws. For, "if the maxim of action is not so constituted as to stand the test of being made the form of a natural law in general, it is morally impossible" (*KP*, 69–70)—impossible because such a rule of conduct would not satisfy the formal criteria of necessity and universality that, according to Kant's view, makes a moral law a moral law.

Therefore, although I cannot apply any test of experience directly to determine the reality of that which is signified by my supersensuous idea of freedom, I *can* apply such a test of experience to the rules, or maxims, by which I live my life in order to determine whether or not they could quality as universal and necessary laws of nature—and hence, as universal and necessary *practical* laws of action within the world of nature (*KP*, 69–70). And because, as Kant has argued, the capacity to live one's life according to universal and necessary moral laws is freedom itself (see *KP*, 93–94), such a test of experience truly provides me with a "sensible sign" of my intelligible character as a free being.

The test, Kant says, is to "ask yourself whether, if the action which you propose should take place by a law of nature of which you yourself were a part, you could regard it as possible through your will" (*KP*, 69):

> Everyone does, in fact, decide by this rule whether actions are morally good or bad. Thus people ask: If one belonged to such an order of things that anyone would allow himself to deceive when he thought it to his advantage, or felt justified in shortening his life as soon as he was thoroughly weary of it, or looked with complete indifference on the need of others, would he assent of this own will to being a member of such an order of things? Now everyone knows very well that if he secretly permits himself to deceive, it does not follow that everyone else will do so, or that if, unnoticed by others, he is lacking in compassion, it does not mean that everyone else will immediately take the same attitude toward him. This comparison of the maxims of his actions with a universal natural law, therefore, is not the determining ground of his will. But such a law is still a type for the estimation of maxims according to moral principles. If the maxim of action is not so constituted as to stand the test of being made the form of a natural law in general, it is morally impossible [though it still may be possible in nature. [*KP*, 69–70]

However, despite Kant's claim that "everyone does, in fact, decide by this rule whether actions are morally good or bad," many philosophers have found Kant's "law of nature" test, as it has just been given, grossly inadequate as a means of determining the morality of an action. Thus John Stuart Mill wrote that Kant "fails, almost grotesquely, to show that there would be any contradiction, any logical (not to say physical) impossibility in the adoption by all rational beings of the most outrageously immoral rules of conduct."[2] Nonetheless, since it is precisely this seemingly amoral, or naturalistic, aspect of Kant's fundamental moral principle that I wish to emphasize as I try to show the similarity between Kant's and Suzuki's idea of duty, I will not try to defend Kant against Mill's criticism. I want at this point merely to try to show how the "law of nature" test—a test that Kant thinks everyone intuitively applies in deciding "whether actions are morally good or bad"—is applied in practice as a working principle of practical reason.

The egocentric maxim "seek my own happiness in all situations" can be used as an example to show how applying the test of universal natural law to a personal rule of conduct can, at least in theory, take me beyond thoughts of personal satisfaction and help me establish a truly empty state of mind, in which the form of universal law alone becomes the determining ground of what I do. Applying Kant's "law of nature" test to the personal rule of furthering my own happiness means that, from a moral standpoint, I may act on this rule only if I can, at the same time, will it into existence as a universal law of nature. However, when I envision the universalization of this rule—that is to say, when I envision it as universally adopted by all human beings—I discover that my original maxim to seek my own happiness "can become an objective practical law only if I include within it the happiness of others" (*KP*, 34). I cannot rationally will the universal adoption of the original, egocentric form of the rule, since I cannot rationally will that other human beings seek their own happiness in all situations *at my expense.* The only possible rational universalization of the rule is "to seek the happiness of all beings—myself included—in all situations." Thus, universalizing my egocentric maxim by making it applicable to all human beings eliminates its component of selfishness. And thus, if I succeed in basing my actions on this new, universalizable rule, I thereby succeed in making the *form of universal law itself,* rather than the physical or psychological circumstances of my life, determine what I choose to do:

> Therefore, the law that we should further the happiness of others arises . . . from the fact that the *form of universality,* which reason requires as condition for giving to the maxim of self-love the objective validity of law, is itself the determining

> ground of the will. Therefore not the object [that is, the happiness of myself and of others] . . . was the determining ground of the pure will but rather it was the lawful form alone. Through it I restricted my maxim, founded on inclination, by giving it the universality of a law, thus making it conformable to the pure practical reason. From this limitation alone, and not from the addition of any external incentive, the concept of obligation arises to extend the maxim of self-love also to the happiness of others. [*KP*, 34]

In this manner, by first developing an enlightened awareness of the world of sense experience as the *sign* of necessary and universal laws, and then by successfully making such laws my constant example in forming my own personal rules of behavior, I can establish consciousness of an intelligible causality of freedom within me—a causality originating from my idea of practically necessary, universal laws, rather than from my inclination to move toward, or away from, objects of sense experience (see *KV*, 567–86; *KP*, 94–104).

2
Compatibility of Suzuki's idea of Buddha nature with Kant's idea of a fundamental moral principle modeled upon natural laws

"Natural law," Kant says, "can, for the purposes of [moral] judgment, be used only in its formal aspect, and it may, therefore, be called the *type* of the moral law. . . . We are therefore allowed to use the nature of the sensuous world as the type of an intelligible nature, so long as we do not carry over to the latter intuitions and what depends on them but only apply to it the form of lawfulness in general." (*KP*, 69–70). Based on this passage, a Kantian interpretation of Suzuki's "naturalistic" account of Zen practice might be stated as follows: because natural law can serve as the type of the moral law, Suzuki is "allowed to use the nature of the sensuous world as the type of an intelligible nature"—that is, as the type of a "Buddha nature" understood as the noumenal ground of personal freedom—so long as he does not make the mistake of attributing sensuous characteristics to this Buddha nature, but rather is content to "only apply to it the form of lawfulness in general." In this subsection, quotations from Suzuki are presented that indicate that Suzuki does indeed follow the above Kantian guidelines in his description of Buddha nature. Thus I will be arguing that Suzuki's naturalistic descriptions of Buddha nature do not rule out a possible Kantian interpretation of this Buddha nature as the intelligible, noumenally based principle of practical reason, which is the source of my ability to act as a free being in this world.

In a lecture on the "Trikāya"—or "three bodies" of Buddha—Suzuki distinguishes between nature as form, or "what we see," and nature as truth itself: "There is, you know, Nature. When we say Nature, Nature is, of course, Truth; but Nature includes what we see, and Truth is not, in its strict sense, something which we can see" (*WB*, VIII, Spring 1969:12). In order to distinguish between the aspect of truth that we can see (what we have been referring to in this study as the "phenomenal" aspect of reality) and what he calls the "strict sense" of truth, Suzuki suggests using the terms "Dharma nature" to signify truth as nature (the world of phenomena) and "Dharma body" to signify truth in this latter, strict sense:

> There is some Truth, yet Truth is something which you cannot see; you can see the apple; you cannot see the theory of gravitation. But nothing happens just by accident. When something happens there must be some reason. . . . We can understand it in some way, we can figure out some rules. We call Dharma *Body* the source of all Truth, of all rules, of all Nature.
>
> Dharmakāya Buddha, or the Dharma Body of Buddha, is called the fundamental, undeveloped Buddha Body. When we say undeveloped body, or fundamental body, we mean that it is the Original Source itself. . . . We understand this reality in two ways, as activity and as non-activity; we have two understandings for one reality. In one case we call it Dharma *Nature*, meaning something in action, or Sambhogakāya, and in the other, Dharma *Body*, or Dharmakāya, meaning something which is not active, which is not developed. Rather, all Dharma Nature exists in the Dharma Body as potentiality. [*WB*, VIII, Spring 1969:12–13]

Suzuki's description of the relationship between Dharma body (Dharmakāya) and Dharma nature (Sambhogakāya) is similar in several ways to Kant's description—discussed in both chapter 3 and in section *i* of the present chapter—of the relationship between the intelligible and the empirical character of a subject belonging to the sensible world.

As we have seen, Kant, like Suzuki, advocates "two understandings for one reality":

> We should . . . in a subject belonging to the sensible world have, first, an *empirical character*, whereby its actions, as appearances, stand in thoroughgoing connection with other appearances in accordance with unvarying laws of nature. . . . Secondly, we should also have to allow the subject an *intelligible character*, by which it is indeed the cause of those same actions as appearances, but which does not itself stand under any conditions of sensibility, and is not itself appearance. We can entitle the former the character of the thing in the field of appearance, and the latter its character as thing in itself. [*KV*, B567]

Also like Suzuki, Kant contrasts the "activity" of a thing understood according to its empirical character with the "inactivity" of a thing understood according to its intelligible character:

> Now this acting subject would not, in its intelligible character, stand under any conditions of time; time is only a condition of appearances, not of things in themselves. In this subject no *action* would *begin* or *cease*, and it would not, therefore, have to conform to the law of the determination of all that is alterable in time, namely, that everything *which happens* must have its cause in the *appearances* which precede it.
>
> In its empirical character . . . [however], this subject, as appearance, would have to conform to all the laws of causal determination. To this extent it could be nothing more than a part of the world of sense, and its effects, like all other appearances, must be the inevitable outcome of nature. [*KV*, B567–68]

And finally, Kant's description of intelligible character parallels Suzuki's account of Dharma body as "fundamental"—as the "original source itself"—of activity in the empirical world:

> In its intelligible character (though we can only have a general concept of that character) this . . . subject must be considered to be free from all influence of sensibility and from all determination through appearances. Inasmuch as it is *noumenon*, nothing *happens* in it. . . . No action begins *in* this active being itself; but we may yet quite correctly say that the active being *of itself* begins its effects in the sensible world. . . . In this way freedom and nature, in the full sense of these terms, can exist together, without any conflict, in the same actions, according as the actions are referred to their intelligible or to their sensible cause. [*KV*, B569]

Thus when Suzuki says that the strict rules and precepts of Zen life are analogous to laws of nature, and when he speaks of Buddha nature alternately in naturalistic and in supersensuous terms—both as "human nature" and as "original source itself"—it should be remembered that, just like Kant, Suzuki acknowledges "two understandings for one reality." Like Kant, Suzuki understands the natural world as the sensible sign of universal, noumenal reality that is "the source of all truth, of all rules, of all nature." And also like Kant, Suzuki claims that it is our realization of the true, noumenal foundation of our empirical human nature that empowers us to live our lives in morally exemplary ways:

> When we realize Dharma Nature in its true sense, we are the Sambhogakāya Buddha. [At that time] when we observe . . . the objective world, and when we want to help people who are involved in the objective, or materialistic, world, then we are the . . . [historical] Buddha. How can we help others as . . . [the historical] Buddha? We must take various forms and give them some handy help, that is how to help others as [the historical] Buddha. But as Sambhogakāya Buddha [as Dharma nature itself] we should know our own nature. . . . When we realize this universal nature, we can help others without trying to help others because whatever we do, that is our helping activity. [*WB*, VIII, Spring 1969:13]

(c)
In defense of the claim that the rules of Zen life, as Suzuki explains them, do have a truly moral component when viewed from a Kantian perspective, because the stated function of these rules is the elimination of selfishness

I have argued in section *i* above that both Kant and Suzuki emphasize strict obedience to the unconditional commands of duty as the way to attain true freedom. Kant clearly understands such unconditional commands to be grounded in respect for and obedience to the fundamental law of pure practical reason—that is, grounded in respectful obedience to moral law: "Pure practical reason . . . forbids us to place the subjective determining ground of dutiful actions, i.e., their moral incentive, anywhere else than in the [moral] law itself" (*KP*, 85–86). For Suzuki, however, the "dutiful actions" that he prescribes as rules of Zen life—actions such as waking up early in the morning, or bowing nine times after *zazen*—seem singularly devoid of any moral content. Suzuki even made "no jaywalking" a precept for his students, many of them erstwhile hippies practicing *zazen* together in San Francisco of the late 1960s:

> There was no traffic to speak of at five twenty-five in the morning when the students crossed Bush Street to sit at Sokoji, but they waited at the corner before the deserted street until the light clicked into green, and then, and only then, did they walk across within the white crosswalks. It was something their contemporaries only a few blocks away in the Haight-Ashbury would never have thought of doing.[3]

Given the seemingly arbitrary and ritualistic nature of Suzuki's rules of Zen life, the claim that there is what Kant calls a "moral incentive" behind such activities seems implausible. However, when one looks more closely at the concept of a moral incentive, as Kant presents this concept in Book I, chapter 3 of the *Critique of Practical Reason*, it becomes clear that Suzuki's view of the general function of Zen rules is quite compatible with Kant's view of the general function of rules of duty In this final subsection of section *ii* of this chapter I will first introduce Kant's notion of a moral incentive and show how this notion is related to his view of duty and its central importance for living the moral life. Then I will demonstrate how Suzuki's explanations of why one should observe the rules of Zen life lend themselves to a Kantian interpretation.

1

Kant insists that the moral incentive behind all dutiful actions must be the moral law itself. However, as he acknowledges, the question "how a law in itself can be the direct determining ground [the incentive] of the will . . . is an insoluble problem for the human reason. It is identical with the problem of how a free will is possible" (*KP*, 72). Therefore, Kant says, rather than try to talk about *how* the moral law can possibly be an incentive for an action, it is better to try to understand what kind of *effect* such a law would have to have "in the mind, so far as it is an incentive" (*KP*, 72).

In regard to what kind of effect the moral law would have to have on me, assuming that it indeed functions as an incentive determining my will, Kant says the "essential point" is that my will must not be determined by anything but the law itself: "As a free will, and thus not only without cooperating with sensuous impulses but even rejecting all of them and checking all inclinations so far as they could be antagonistic to the law, it is determined merely by the law" (*KP*, 72). The effect of the moral law on the mind is thus, according to Kant, the "negative" effect of purging the will of all sensuous impulses "and checking all inclinations so far as they could be antagonistic to the law" (*KP*, 72). An example of this effect was provided in subsection *b*, above, where it was shown how, by imposing the form of universality upon my egocentric maxim "to seek my own happiness in all situations," I do indeed check my selfish inclinations insofar as they find expression in such a selfish rule of conduct. Through my respectful obedience to moral law, Kant says, I restrict my selfish maxim, "founded on inclination, by giving it the universality of a law, thus making it conformable to pure practical reason" (*KP*, 34–35). Thus, the concept of obligation, or duty, arises "not from the addition of any external incentive" (*KP*, 35), but solely from the limitations, or constraints, imposed upon my inclinations by the moral law.

"When one's own happiness is made the determining ground of the will," Kant says, "the result is the direct opposite of the principle of morality; and I have previously shown [see *KP*, 25] that, whenever the determining ground which is to serve as a law is located elsewhere than in the legislative form of the maxim, we have to reckon with this result" (*KP*, 35). Thus, according to Kant, whenever the "legislative form" of my personal maxims, or rules of conduct, fails to determine what I do, I must reckon with the result that happiness, or what Kant calls the principle of self-love (*KP*, 22), will be the incentive for my action. Of course, in the example from subsection *b* referred to above, the principle of self-love—that is, my desire for happiness—*is* in a sense viewed by Kant as an incentive for my action of helping others. For it is this maxim of self-love which is, as it were, *shaped* by the influence of the moral law into the universalized rule of conduct: "seek the happiness of all beings (myself included)." Kant's point is, however, that the truly moral aspect of the maxim of seeking the happiness of all beings arises not from my desire for personal happiness, but rather from the restriction, or limitation, put upon my selfish maxim founded on this desire by the universal form of moral law. Thus it is this "form of universality" and not my *inclination* toward something—even toward the happiness of others— that Kant sees as the true incentive for working to further the happiness of others:

> Therefore, the law that we should further the happiness of others arises . . . from the fact that the form of universality, which reason requires as condition for giving to the maxim of self-love the objective validity of law, is itself the determining ground of the will. Therefore not the object, i.e., the happiness of others, was the determining ground of the pure will but rather it was the lawful form alone. [*KP*, 34]

And thus Kant would divide the class of all possible incentives for an action into two mutually exclusive categories: incentives of self-love and incentives of morality. All material or sensuous incentives for action—all "inclinations," as Kant calls them—"without exception . . . revolve about the principle of one's own happiness" (*KP*, 34), while any action that is *not* motivated primarily by inclination must, necessarily, be motivated primarily by moral law: "for no other law precludes all inclinations from having a direct influence on the will" (*KP*, 80). And from this perceived division between material and moral incentives arises what Kant calls "a practical conflict" between self-love and moral law—a conflict that, "were the voice of reason with respect to the will not so distinct, so irrepressible, and so clearly audible to even the commonest man . . . would drive morality to ruin" (*KP*, 35).

Any action that "excludes inclination from its determining ground is called duty," Kant says "and, because of this exclusion, in the concept of duty there is that of practical constraint, i.e., determination to actions, however reluctantly they may be done" (*KP*, 80). So, simply through willingly doing what I perceive to be my duty—simply through willingly accepting, despite any attendant feelings of reluctance, the practical constraint of unconditionally having to perform an action—I exclude inclination, or self-love, as an incentive for my action. And by excluding self-love as an incentive I—by default as it were—make the legislative form of moral law my incentive. For again, according to Kant, it can be nothing else but the moral law that "precludes all inclinations from having a direct influence on the will."

Kant's view of duty as respectful, voluntary submission to the commands of law, plus his view that "laws as such are all equivalent" (*KP*, 70), leads him to identify the thought of duty itself with the moral principle:

> [Pure practical reason] . . . commands that we make the thought of duty, which strikes down all arrogance as well as vain self-love, the supreme life principle of all human morality. [*KP*, 86]

Thus in Kant's view, respectful obedience to moral law and respectful obedience to duty are one and the same thing. By striking down "all arrogance as well as vain self-love," my willing observance of duty for its own sake is itself the realization of the basic requirement of moral law: the requirement, that is, the form of law itself (all true laws being universal and necessary rules) be the sole determining ground of my action.

Thus, in response to the criticism that Suzuki's rules of Zen life are not truly *moral* rules, one can argue that by the mere fact that Zen practice is organized around a set of *duties*—for example, the duty to get up when it is time to get up, or the duty to cross the street only at the crosswalks—it follows that Zen is a practice organized around what Kant understands to be the essential principle of moral law: that the legislative form of law itself be the sole incentive for one's actions. For by performing an action with the sole incentive of doing one's duty for its own sake, Zen practicers necessarily exclude self-love as an incentive for their actions. And in this way, simply by precluding "all inclinations from having a direct influence on [their] will" through the thought of duty, they make the idea of moral law—the idea of a universal, practically necessary law—the sole incentive of their actions.

Does Kant claim, then, that mere devotion to duty is sufficient to ensure that one acts in morally praiseworthy ways? In the spirit of Mill's criticism of Kant's notion of moral law, as noted in subsection *b* above, it might be pointed out that many of the Nazi officials and soldiers who participated in the killing of Jews in extermination camps probably did so under the rationale that they were doing their duty. In response to this criticism, I would point in turn to Kant's thesis that all rational beings have built into the structure of their reasoning faculty the means of determining what they morally should and should not do. Thus if "the subjective determining ground of dutiful actions," as Kant says, is placed not in a person's fear of authority but truly "in the law itself"—that is, in the person's inner knowledge, as a rational being, of what he or she should and should not do—then, even as an official or soldier under orders, a person should be able to distinguish between the true duty (to obey the inner sense of right and wrong) and one's official duty.

The human problem, of course, is that the subjective determining ground of the actions of soldiers and common citizens alike is usually not an inner sense of right and wrong, but rather what Kant would call incentives of self-love, or inclinations. Thus Kant emphasizes the distinction between acting *according to duty*—according to the commands of a higher authority—and acting *from duty*—that is, from my respect for and my obedience to my idea of what I ought and ought not to do:

> The former, legality, is possible even if inclinations alone are the determining grounds of the will, but the latter, morality or moral worth, can be conceded only where the action occurs from duty, i.e., merely for the sake of the law. [*KP*, 81]

Whenever inclinations are made the determining ground of the will, Kant has said, "the result is the direct opposite of the principle of morality." Therefore, merely acting "according to duty"—for example, acting out of my human inclination to please my superiors—does not mean I am acting from the "thought of duty" that Kant calls "the supreme life principle of all human morality." It is only when I set aside my human inclinations or fears and manage to perform a duty completely for its own sake—for no incentive other than that of doing what I think ought to be done, according to my idea of moral law—that I truly act "from duty." And it is then, that the thought of duty, striking down "all arrogance as well as vain self-love," performs its function as the life principle of morality.

2

The following quotations and commentary are presented as evidence that Suzuki does indeed view the function of dutiful obedience to Zen rules and precepts as being that of excluding self-love as an incentive for one's actions.

> I have been reading much lately on the subject of rules for monasteries, thinking that it is important for our practice here that we have certain rules to follow which will help us avoid egoistic practice. All of us here may want to do away with the idea of self, but in fact it is impossible to do away with this idea without the help of certain rules. [*PO*, 1/18/70][4]

It is clear that by "rules" Suzuki does not mean only written rules, such as the Buddhist precepts, or a similar code of monastic conduct. He is also intensely concerned with matters of etiquette or manners—with the often unwritten rules of everyday societal behavior.[5] Suzuki wants to help his students become aware of egotism as it manifests itself—and effects others—in their daily lives. Thus he comments on the students' daily practice of hitting the *mokugyo*—a wooden drum whose beat helps Zen students maintain the same rhythm and pace as they chant Buddhist sutras during morning, noon, and evening services:

> For instance, each person who hits the *mokugyo* does so at a different speed. If there is no standard here then unconsciously we are helplessly engaged in a type of egoistic practice when we drum the *mokugyo*—some hitting very fast, others very slow. This type of egoism has its effect on those who chant the sutra—it cannot help but have an effect. Without unspoken rules, such as the right pace to drum the *mokugyo*, we will have a difficult time indeed escaping from self-centered practice. [*PO*, 1/18/70]

In *Zen Mind, Beginner's Mind,* Suzuki says that the rule of bowing nine times after *zazen* also has the function of eliminating egotism:

> After zazen we bow to the floor nine times. By bowing we are giving up ourselves. To give up ourselves means to give up our dualistic ideas. So there is no difference between zazen and bowing. . . . Bowing helps to eliminate our self-centered ideas. This is not so easy. It is difficult to get rid of these ideas, and bowing is a very valuable practice. [*ZM*, 43–45]

And in regard to its function of eliminating "dualistic" or "self-centered" ideas, bowing, of course is not different from *zazen* itself. In fact, Suzuki understands *all* rules and practices of Zen life to have this same function:

> So why do we bow? Of course, the idea behind all our practice—not just rituals, but when we practice zazen—is to be free of selfish thoughts and emotions. This is why we practice zazen, just to sit without being caught up in changing ideas of self. We cultivate the feeling of our being right here and now practicing on our black cushion—and so we find our true nature by just being ourselves. [*PO*, 7/28/70]

Because "the idea behind *all* our practice . . . is to be free of selfish thoughts and emotions," it is wrong, according to Suzuki, to discriminate between the respectful observance of rituals and the respectful observance of moral rules, such as the Buddhist precepts. For the rules of Zen life include both kinds of rules, plus rules for *zazen* practice as well, and in fact, these three kinds of rules are not different:

> We observe the precepts in the same way we practice our rituals—just as we practice our rituals in the same way we practice zazen. These three are really not different practices. So following our schedule here means to observe the precepts, just as it means to practice zazen and perform rituals. . . .
>
> Each part of our practice—zazen, rituals, precepts—actually should include all other parts: in reality we only have one practice, of realizing our true self-nature right here and now. So while you are here with us at Zen Center you should follow our schedule and be a Zen Center student each step of the way. . . . If you do this you can become aware of your own self-nature or Buddha nature; without developing any ideas of self or Buddha you will naturally express this true nature for the benefit of your own life and the lives of all sentient beings. [*PO*, 7/28/70]

Like Kant, Suzuki seems to hold an either/or view concerning incentives for an action: *either* an action is motivated by "selfish thoughts and emotions" *or* it is the expression of one's "true," "original," or "Buddha" nature:

> According to the traditional Buddhist understanding, our human nature is without ego. When we have no idea of ego, we have Buddha's view of life. Our egoistic ideas are delusions, covering our Buddha nature. We are always creating and following them, and in repeating this process over and over again, our life becomes completely occupied by ego-centered ideas. This is called karmic life, or karma. The Buddhist life should not be karmic life. The purpose of our practice is to cut off the karmic spinning mind. [*ZM*, 100]

Thus, it would seem to be Suzuki's view that simply by allowing the written and unwritten laws of societal behavior to replace "egoistic ideas" as the determining grounds of one's actions, one naturally cuts off "the karmic spinning mind," and naturally cultivates and expresses "human nature . . . without ego," or Buddha nature itself. And—as has previously been argued in subsection *a* above—cultivation of Buddha nature is, for Suzuki, both a necessary and a sufficient means for realizing all the requirements of moral precepts (*ZM*, 22). Therefore, simply by being a Zen Center student "each step of the way," one naturally—without needing to develop "any ideas of self or Buddha"—comes to express one's true nature "for the benefit of your own life and the lives of all sentient beings." Realization of a morally praiseworthy way of life is the intended end achieved through the means of dutifully following the rules and way of Zen life.

"We are doing what we should do," Suzuki has said in *Zen Mind, Beginner's Mind*, "that is Buddhism" (*ZM*, 78). Simply by doing one's duty—simply by getting up in the morning when it is time to get up, by crossing the street when it is time to cross the street, by bowing when it is time to bow—"we give our body and mind up completely to our practice in the here and now" (*PO*, 7/28/70). Following the maxim of duty—to do what one should do—obviously means giving up self-centered thoughts like, "shall I or shall I not obey the rule about crossing the street only at the crosswalk?" Or, "If I go to a Zen monastery, will I be able to follow the rule of getting up at 3:40 in the morning?" People do not act with the thought of duty when—"like volunteers,"as Kant has said—they think "I will follow this rule *if*. . . ." For both Suzuki and Kant, the command of a duty is absolute—this absoluteness being the source of its efficacy as a means of striking down what Suzuki refers to as egoism or "karmic life" and what Kant calls "arrogance as well as vain self-love." The written and unwritten rules of social behavior are thereby established in the place of selfish, individual inclinations as the incentives for personal action.

So, instead of thinking about moral precepts as particular rules that I may or may not be able to follow, it is better that I focus on their nature as absolute commands, "forgetting myself" (see

ZM, 76–79), and giving my body and mind up completely to practice in the here and now. In this way I "will observe the precepts actually without knowing anything about them," simply by saying *yes:*

> You may think that the precepts are some specific rules to be followed—*Don't Kill*—but observing precepts is not like following rules. It is true that the origin of the precepts was in Shakyamuni Buddha's commandments to his disciples: "Don't do that! Don't behave like that!" But to hold to such commandments is to have dualistic ideas—"I must obey the Buddha's commandments—*sixteen* precepts! Oh, no—not *sixteen*! How can I? Buddhism is too difficult!" With this frame of mind you will never be able to follow our way. What you should do is simply say *"Hi!* [*"Hi!"* means *"Yes!"* in Japanese]. No matter how difficult, just *"Hi!"* In this way, though Buddhism may seem very difficult indeed, all you need do is say *"Hi"* to our practice from one step to the next. The question of "difficult" or "easy" need never arise. [*PO*, 7/28/70]

Here Suzuki expresses the pure thought of duty, the thought of respectful submission to an absolute command, simply as *Hi!* or *Yes!* But what if a command of duty is impossible to follow? As in Suzuki's example of the two monks crossing the river, it may be impossible to follow every moral precept literally in every situation. And it may be impossible to follow some moral precepts literally in any situation! If, for instance, we wish to observe the Buddhist precept, "Don't Kill," it is, as Suzuki points out, already too late:

> If you say "Ah! a fly—I must not kill it," it is already too late to follow the Buddha's law. We should realize before any specific incident arises the fact that countless numbers of living beings have been sacrificed so that we might be alive this moment. [*PO*, 7/28/70]

Suzuki's approach to this dilemma reveals his close kinship with Kant in respect to the *unconditional* nature of moral duties. "To think, 'Because it is possible we will do it,' is not Buddhism," he says in *Zen Mind, Beginner's Mind.* Perhaps it is impossible, strictly speaking, to observe the Buddhist precepts. Nevertheless:

> Even though it is impossible, we have to do it because our true nature wants us to. But actually, whether or not it is possible is not the point. If it is our inmost desire to get rid of our self-centered ideas, we have to do it. [*ZM*, 46]

By "inmost desire" Suzuki is quite evidently referring to an incentive for action whose source is "our true nature" itself. The command of our true nature, Suzuki says, is categorical: whether or not an action is possible "is not the point." Similarly, Kant, at the very start of the *Critique of Practical Reason*, distinguishes between a hypothetical and a categorical imperative:

> Imperatives determine either the conditions of causality of a rational being as an efficient cause only in respect to its effect and its sufficiency to bring this effect about, or *they determine only the will, whether it be adequate to the effect or not.* In the former case, imperatives would be hypothetical and would contain only precepts of skill; in the latter, on the contrary, they would be categorical and would alone be practical [moral] laws. . . . Laws must completely determine the will as will, even before I ask whether I am capable of achieving a desired effect or what should be done to realize it. [*KP*, 20; emphasis added]

It thus seems clear that Suzuki, like Kant, speaks of the commands of duty as categorical, rather than as hypothetical, imperatives—imperatives whose function is to "determine only the will, whether it be adequate to the effect or not." "Even before I ask whether I am capable of achieving a desired effect or what should be done to realize it," Suzuki is clearly saying, "I should say *'Hi!'* ":

> No matter how difficult, just *"Hi!"* In this way, though Buddhism may seem very difficult indeed, all you need do is say *"Hi!"* to our practice from one step to the next—the question of difficult or easy need never arise.

This view of duty seems truly compatible with Kant's view that the function of duty as the "supreme life-principle of all human morality" is to help human beings free themselves from the bonds of self-love by making the idea of law itself "completely determine the will as will."

iii: The Bodhisattva Vow Interpreted As a Commitment to Realize the Highest Possible Good in this World

In section *ii* of this chapter Suzuki was quoted as saying:

> According to the traditional Buddhist understanding, our human nature is without ego. When we have no idea of ego, we have Buddha's view of life. Our egoistic ideas are delusions, covering our Buddha nature. We are always creating and following them, and in repeating this process over and over again, our life becomes completely occupied by ego-centered ideas. This is called karmic life, or karma. The Buddhist life should not be karmic life. The purpose of our practice is to cut off the karmic spinning mind. [*ZM*, 100]

In this passage Suzuki is expressing the purpose of Zen practice in negative terms as "to cut off the karmic spinning mind"—to cut off, that is to say, attachment to "ego-centered ideas." Thus, as was argued above, the function of the rules and way of Zen life can be viewed in negative terms as that of eliminating selfishness, or self-love, as a determining ground for action in the world. However, Suzuki also expresses the purpose of Zen practice in positive terms. "Our egoistic ideas" are, he says, only "delusions, covering our Buddha nature." When we succeed in cutting off "the karmic spinning mind," "when we have no idea of ego," he says, then "we have Buddha's view of life." It will be the purpose of this last section of chapter 4: *(a)* to present the purpose of Zen practice in positive terms, as what Suzuki calls "Buddha's view of life," *(b)* to present Kant's view, expressed in the "Dialectic" portion of the *Critique of Practical Reason*, that "the moral law commands us to make the highest possible good in a world the final object of all our conduct" (*KP*, 129), and finally, *(c)* to demonstrate the affinity of Buddha's way of life with Kant's view of a life lived according to the requirements of moral law by constructing a complete argument in support of thesis Z2—*In order to practice* zazen *correctly, according to Suzuki, my sole intention in performing that practice must be that of realizing the requirements of moral law, as Kant understands these requirements.*

(a)
Buddha's view of life: the Bodhisattva vow

For people who do not understand Buddha's view of life, Suzuki says, "life is karmic life." However:

> For those who know this point, life is not karmic life. . . . The Nirmānakāya [the historical] Buddha comes into this world, not through karma, but with a vow to save all sentient beings. By a vow he appears in this world, and practices the Bodhisattva's way and attains enlightenment as Buddha did, to save all human beings. He changes his form in various ways—sometimes he's a Bodhisattva, sometimes a Buddha; to help people, he takes various forms. So, in a wide sense, everything is Nirmānakāya Buddha. And in the narrow sense, people who appear in this world because of a vow, instead of karma, are called Nirmānakāya Buddhas. [*WB*, VIII, Spring 1969:17]

The Nirmānakāya, or historical Buddha, Suzuki says, comes into this world "not through karma"—not through self-centered, egoistic thinking—"but with a vow to save all sentient beings." This vow is called in Buddhism the "Bodhisattva vow," a "Bodhisattva" being a person who seeks and labors for salvation for everyone—"all sentient beings"—putting aside the egoistic incentive of attaining salvation for herself or himself alone:

> A Bodhisattva (literally: Enlightenment-being) is an enlightened being . . . who has postponed his entrance into Nirvana, and his escape from this world of birth-and-death, for the purpose of helping suffering creatures.[6]
>
> The identity of *self* and *not-self* cannot be fully understood by people who in actual practice oppose their own advantage to that of others. If a man exerts himself for the purpose of obtaining salvation and liberation for himself, and if he enters the freedom of Nirvana which cuts him off from the other suffering creatures whom he leaves behind, he can be said to

make a difference between himself and others. Not so the Bodhisattva.[7]

Although, according to Suzuki, "every sentient being is a Bodhisattva, whether or not he is aware of it" (*WB*, IX, Fall-Winter 1970–71:9), the archetypal Bodhisattva in Buddhism is Avalokiteśvara Bodhisattva, whose name means "looking down compassionately on this world."[8] Avalokiteśvara, whose practice and perfection of wisdom is the subject of the *Prajñā Pāramitā Hridaya Sūtra* referred to earlier in of this study, is known for the ability to take on different human (and nonhuman) forms in order to help others in the most skillful way possible. Here is how Suzuki describes the way of life of this Bodhisattva:

> Our way is like Avalokiteśvara Bodhisattva. When he wants to save ladies he takes the form of a lady; for boys he takes the form of a boy; for fishermen he becomes a fisherman. A more sophisticated Chinese expression is to be like a white bird in the snow. When people are like snow, we should be like snow. When people become black, we should be black. And always being with them, without any idea of discrimination, we can help others in its true sense, without giving anything, any special teaching or materials. This is actually the Bodhisattva way. [*WB*, IX, Fall-Winter 1970–71:9]

Here Suzuki gives a positive description of the purpose of Zen practice as the way of being "like a white bird in the snow." In this way there is no dualistic thought of self or other—no thought, even, that I have something to give others (some "special teaching or materials") which dualistically sets me apart from them. "Just to be with people," Suzuki says, "will be enough" (*WB*, IX, Fall-winter 1970–71:10). Just "always being with them, without any idea of discrimination"—this, Suzuki says, is the point of Zen practice:

> When you practice zazen in this way, you have the point of zazen and the point of practice. . . . None of us, including various great teachers, find it easy to be like a white bird in the snow. But somehow, we should make our best effort. If you help yourself through practice, you can help others without anything. [ibid.]

Now it is possible to understand more clearly, in a positive light, the moral context of many of Suzuki's seemingly amoral descriptions of *zazen* practice and the rules and way of Zen life:

> Without any idea of doing anything, just to sit is our way. To be involved, completely involved in sitting meditation is our *zazen*. Without any idea of attainment, any idea of waste of time or meaningful practice, just to sit is our way. And this is how you keep our precepts. [*SL*, VIII, 8]

When Suzuki says this, he is evidently talking about practicing the Bodhisattva's way of dropping off all egocentric thoughts, including even the thought "*I* am obeying moral precepts," in order to be just a white bird in the snow. And similarly, what I have called the "amoral" rules of Zen training would seem to have this same purpose behind them:

> Softness of mind is the foundation of our practice to help others. You may think we are forcing you into some form, forcing some rituals on you or some special teaching; forcing you to say "Yes, I will." But these things are provided for you just to be like a white bird in the snow. [*WB*, IX, Fall-Winter 1970–71:10]

Suzuki was aware that when he asked his students simply to say "*Hi!*" to the duties required of them as Zen students, they might interpret this as a request to submit to a kind of militaristic regimen:

> Some people will say, seeing us drop to the floor [bowing] when the bell rings, that we are practicing military way. I think it may be true that the Japanese army has copied much of our way of practice. But they cannot copy our spirit. [*PO*, 7/28/70]

The spirit,which is the "foundation" of Zen practice, is, Suzuki says above, "softness of mind." And in *Zen Mind, Beginner's Mind* he links softness of mind with Avalokiteśvara's practice of seeing all phenomenal things in the context of emptiness, or "nothingness":

> We say *shin ku myo u*, "from true emptiness, the wondrous being appears"
>
> Without nothingness, there is no naturalness—no true being. True being comes out of nothingness, moment after moment. Nothingness is always there, and from it everything appears. But usually, forgetting all about nothingness, you behave as if you have something. What you do is based on some possessive idea or some concrete idea, and that is not natural. . . . When you do something, you should be completely involved in it. You should devote yourself to it completely. Then you have nothing. So if there is no true emptiness in your activity, it is not natural.
>
> Whatever you do, this attitude is necessary. Sometimes we say *nyu nan shin*, "soft or flexible mind." *Nyu* is "soft feeling"; *nan* is "something which is not hard"; *shin* is "mind" *Nyu nan shin* means a smooth, natural mind. When you have that mind, you have the joy of life. When you lose it, you lose everything. You have nothing. Although you think you have something, you have nothing. But when all you do comes out of nothingness, then you have everything. [*ZM*, 109–10]

In linking Avalokiteśvara's practice of insight into emptiness with that Bodhisattva's practice of softness or flexibility of mind as "the foundation of our practice to help others," Suzuki reveals the link between the practice of *zazen*, as a discipline of the speculative restriction of thought leading to consciousness of emptiness, and the practice of practically extending my thoughts into action by making the vow to save all sentient beings the determining ground of all my actions in the world. The practice of *zazen*, as a discipline of the speculative restriction of reason, is incorrectly performed, according to Suzuki, if I perform it for the selfish incentive of gaining enlightenment for myself:

> If you are trying to attain enlightenment, that is a part of karma, you are creating and being driven by karma, and you are wasting your time on your black cushion. According to Bodhidharma's understanding, practice based on any gaining idea is just a repetition of your karma. [*ZM*, 100]

In order to practice *zazen* correctly, according to Suzuki, my purpose in performing that practice should be solely that of helping people:

> Our practice is to help people, and how to help people is to practice our way in each moment. That is how to live in this world and how to practice zazen. [*WB*, IX, Fall-Winter 1970–71: 47]

Thus Suzuki understands *zazen* practice as a *means* of realizing the Bodhisattva's vow to save all sentient beings. This means that there is truly an underlying purpose, or intent, behind the practice of *zazen* as this practice is understood by Suzuki. Because sentient beings are numberless, and yet each one is unique, there must be numberless, unique ways of realizing a vow to help each being deal with his or her particular form of suffering. And it is *zazen*, as the practice of utter emptiness or "softness of mind," that "is the foundation of our practice to help others." By emptying the mind of its dualistic notions of self versus others—by becoming like a white bird in the snow—Suzuki says, "just to be with people will be enough."

> And always being with them, without any idea of discrimination, we can help others in its true sense, without giving anything, any special teaching or materials. This is actually the Bodhisattva way. [*WB*, IX, Fall-Winter 1970–71:9]

To live according to the vow to save all sentient beings is, as Suzuki has said, to live as the historical Buddha did. And because so-called Buddha nature is not unique to the historical Buddha but rather is an ultimate fact of our human nature, the Buddha's vow to work for the salvation of all beings is likewise a "fact" of our human nature. Thus, as Suzuki says, "Every sentient being is a Bodhisattva, whether or not he is aware of it."

The Bodhisattva's way of life is based not upon karma, which has at its root egoistic ideas, or what Kant has called "incentives of self-love," but rather upon a *vow* through which we categorically commit ourselves to realize a certain object in this world: the salvation of all beings. In the following two subsections I want to relate this object of the Bodhisattva vow to what Kant understands as the final object of pure practical reason: the realization of the highest possible good in this world.

(b)
Kant's view of life: the "vow" to realize the highest good in the world

> The achievement of the highest good in the world is the necessary object of a will determinable by the moral law. [*KP*, 122]

In this subsection I want to present Kant's reasons for making the above claim. I will first show why Kant claims that there is such a thing as a "necessary object of a will determinable by the moral law." Then I will go on to discuss the characteristics of that object, "the highest good," itself.[9]

1
The highest good as the necessary object of a will under moral laws

In chapter 3 it was noted that the empirical concept 'phenomenon' is meaningless when used independently of the intelligible, or supersensible, concept 'noumenon'—the idea of something outside my conscious experience, which is a ground, or cause, of this appearance. "Otherwise," as Kant has been quoted above, "we should be landed in the absurd conclusion [of "material idealism"] that there can be appearance without anything that appears" (*KV*, Bxxvii).

And in a similar way, Kant has argued, my concept of performing an action in the world solely according to my idea of what I ought or ought not do is meaningless when entertained independently of the intelligible, or supersensible, concept of myself as a free being—as the first cause of my actions, a cause itself unconditioned by inclinations or natural needs. This is because an action that is initiated solely on the basis of voluntary obedience to moral law, independently of any physiological or psychological incentive, yet which takes place in the world of sense where every effect is understood as necessarily proceeding from a previous cause, "would be absolutely impossible save on the assumption of freedom" (*KV*, Bxxvix).

Thus there occurs what Kant calls a "dialectic" in my reasoning as I try to understand my life and the world I live in. On the one hand, I must base all my knowledge of things in the world—as well as all my practical, action-oriented thinking—on sensible experience, for I cannot have any reliable knowledge of that which lies beyond the bounds of human sensibility. On the other hand, in order to *complete* my understanding of things in the world I live in it is absolutely necessary that I go beyond the boundaries of sensible experience and demand, as Kant says, "the absolute totality of conditions for a conditioned thing" (*KP*, 107). In the realm of empirical knowledge, this demand for the absolute totality of conditions leads me to the unknowable—but, as Kant insists, thinkable—concept of noumena as the supersensible ground of all sensible appearances. And in the realm of practical, morally based actions, my rational demand for knowledge of that absolute totality of conditions—reference to which would explain how it is possible for me, a being determined by spatial/temporal conditions, to act solely in accordance with my idea of what I should and should not do—leads me necessarily to the supersensible idea of an *unconditioned* cause of action in the world as a possible determining ground of my will (*KP*, 108). This "dialectical" search for an unconditioned determining ground of the will—i.e., freedom—is satisfied by my knowledge of "a fact wherein pure reason shows itself actually to be practical. This fact is autonomy in the principle of morality by which reason determines the will to action" (*KP*, 42).

My "factual" knowledge of moral law as an unconditioned, supersensible determining ground of my will satisfies my need to know the totality of explanatory conditions necessary for resolving that seeming contradiction between my thought of myself as a being totally determined by the causal relations of phenomena in the natural world and my thought of myself as free to act as I think I ought to act. However, a second dialectical demand arises, Kant says, in regard to "the unconditioned totality of the object of the pure practical reason, under the name of the *highest good*" (*KP*, 108). The next few paragraphs will be devoted to an explication of this phrase, in order to introduce Kant's notion of the highest good and the role it plays in his moral philosophy.

In respect to the term "object of pure practical reason," Kant understands the practical (as opposed to the speculative or theoretical) function of reason to be either that of (a) physically bringing forth into existence some object that I have in mind (for instance, making my lunch for today), or that of (b) "determining [my]self" to bring forth that object, "whether the physical power is sufficient to this or not" (*KP*, 15). By "pure" practical reason, Kant means practical thinking that is not empirically conditioned (*KP*, 15)—thinking, that is to say, which is based on purely rational grounds, uninfluenced by physical or psychological conditions. A major motivation behind Kant's efforts in both first and second *Critiques* was, of course, to defend the possibility of this kind of "pure" reasoning or thinking—both in the realm of scientific, or theoretical, thought, and in the realm of practical, or moral, thinking—against the attacks of skeptical empiricists like Hume.

My thought that it is time to "bring forth" lunch is normally an empirically conditioned thought, influenced by my experience of the sensuous condition of hunger or my desire to maintain my personal health and happiness. But if I were suffering from anorexia, and had neither any desire to eat nor even any desire to keep myself alive by eating, then my thought of bringing forth lunch would have to be based not upon empirical conditions—not even upon my basic desire to live—but rather upon some purely *rational* ground. And this idea of a purely rational will, a will totally uninfluenced by physical or psychological conditions that can initiate practical action in the world solely on the basis of the prescriptions of rational thinking, is what Kant means by "pure practical reason" (*KP*, 55).

As has been pointed out many times in this study, the only form in which I, as a human being, can exercise my "pure practical reason" is (according to Kant's view) in the form of my respect for and obedience to moral law—a law requiring that I universalize my selfish maxims of conduct, and act in the world on the basis of such universalized maxims. The "object of pure practical reason," then, is the effect in the world that the moral law requires me, as an (ideally) free agent, to cause. "By a concept of an object of practical reason," Kant says, "I understand the idea of an object as an effect possible through freedom" (*KP*, 57) Thus, an object of the pure practical reason is the state of affairs that might possibly be brought about in this world by the causal action of a free agent acting according to the commands of moral law. This object, Kant says, is rightly called the "highest good":

> For, in fact, the moral law ideally transfers us into a nature in which reason would bring forth the highest good were it accompanied by sufficient physical capacities; and it determines our will to impart to the sensuous world the form of a system of rational beings. The least attention to ourself shows that this idea really stands as a model for the determination of our will. [*KP*, 43]

Just as universal and necessary laws of nature can stand "as a model for the determination of our will" by revealing to us the form of universality and necessity that all truly moral maxims of conduct should have, so the natural world itself, as a world governed by universal and necessary laws, can likewise serve as a model for the determination of our will. This happens, Kant has said, when we "use the nature of the sensuous world as the *type* of an intelligible nature" (*KP*, 70; emphasis added). Understanding the sensible world of nature in this way—as the *type* of a world in which pure reason, exercising causality through freedom, "would bring forth the highest good were it accompanied by sufficient physical capacities"—fosters a "dialectical" tension between my sensible perception of what is and my practically oriented thought of what ought to be. "A demand therefore arises within me," Kant argues, to seek "the unconditioned totality of the object of the pure practical reason"—to realize, that is, the highest good in this world as "the necessary object of a will determinable by the moral law" (*KP*, 122).

Of course, in the actual world my will is determined largely by selfish inclinations whose combined effects "form a natural whole according to pathological (physical) laws, but not a system of nature which is possible only through our will acting according to pure practical laws" (*KP*, 44). Nevertheless, through consciousness of moral law as a fact of my reason, I am conscious of a law requiring me "to impart to the sensuous world" the form of an ideal world, "as though through my will a natural order must arise" (*KP*, 44):

> Therefore, this [moral] law must be the idea of a supersensuous nature, a nature not empirically given yet possible through freedom; to this nature we give objective reality, at least in a practical context, because we regard it as the object of our will as pure rational beings. [*KP*, 44]

2
Characteristics of the highest good

According to Kant, then, to work to realize the requirements of moral law and to work to realize the highest possible good in this world as the object of my pure practical reason are not two different projects. This is because, as has just been shown, both the concept of the highest good "and the idea of its existence as possible through [my] practical reason" (*KP*, 110) are defined by reference to the commands of moral law. The highest good is, according to Kant, the state of affairs that moral law commands us to bring forth, were our determination to obey moral law "accompanied by sufficient physical capacities" (*KP*, 43). Thus the concept of the highest good can be thought of as being itself "the determining ground of the pure will" (*KP*, 110), so long as it is kept in mind that it is the command of moral law, and not the attraction of some good independent of that law, that actually determines the will: "the moral law commands us to make the highest possible good in a world the final object of all our conduct" (*KP*, 129).

However, even though the highest good is defined as being "the final object" of all our moral conduct, the idea of the highest good contains, necessarily, a concept independent of the idea of morality: the concept of human happiness. To make the highest possible good in this world the final object of all my conduct must mean, among other things, to make the fulfillment of my and other human beings desire for happiness the object of my conduct. For a state of affairs in which the universal desire of all human beings to achieve happiness was not fulfilled could not plausibly be called "the highest possible good in a world." Kant's idea of the highest good, therefore, is a synthesis of the "heterogeneous" concepts of morality and happiness:

> Happiness and morality are two specifically different elements of the highest good and therefore their combination cannot be known analytically (as if a person who sought his happiness found himself virtuous merely through solving his problem, or one who followed virtue found himself *ipso facto* happy in the consciousness of this conduct). The highest good is a *synthesis* of concepts. [*KP*, 113]

> It is clear . . . that the maxims of virtue and those of one's own happiness are wholly heterogeneous and far removed from being at one in respect to their supreme practical principle; and even though they belong to a highest good, which they jointly make possible, they strongly limit and check each other in the same [human] subject. [*KP*, 113]

The ideas of morality and happiness "jointly make possible," through a synthesis of "wholly heterogeneous" concepts, the idea of the highest good as the object of pure practical reason. The moral law, Kant has said, is that "unconditional condition," knowledge of which satisfies our demand for a first, or "highest," cause of action in the world (*KP*, 110). And the idea of this law is obviously central to Kant's notion of the highest good as that state of affairs whose realization is commanded by moral law. But the fact that the characteristic of respectful obedience to the command of moral law—or what Kant calls "virtue"—is the "unconditional condition" of all that is good "does not imply that virtue is [itself] the entire and perfect good as the object of the faculty of desire of rational finite beings":

> For this [entire and perfect good], happiness is also required, and indeed not merely in the partial eyes of a person who makes himself his end but even in the judgment of an impartial reason, which impartially regards persons in the world as ends-in-themselves. For to be in need of happiness and also worthy of it and yet not to partake of it could not be in accordance with the complete volition of an omnipotent rational being, if we assume such only for the sake of the argument. [*KP*, 110]

As has been previously shown, Kant's view of moral law requires of me that I impartially universalize my selfish maxim to realize my own happiness so that my maxim is transformed into a commitment to realize the happiness of all beings, myself included. Another way of phrasing this moral requirement is that instead of focusing with "partial eyes" upon myself as the sole end of my actions, I should impartially look upon all beings in the world (myself included) as "ends-in-themselves." My viewing the world from this perspective requires that I never treat another being as a means toward realizing my own ends but rather that I treat her or him just as I do myself—in effect, making her or his ends my own.

And, of course, just as transforming my selfish maxims into the form of universal laws results in the elimination of egoism as the determining ground for my actions in the world, so widening the "partial" end of my own individual happiness until it turns into the impartial end of universal happiness likewise produces this same result. To adopt the highest good as the necessary object of all my conduct in the world is thus, simultaneously, to eliminate egocentricity as an obstacle to the realization of the commands of moral law.

(c)
In defense of thesis Z2: interpreting the object of Suzuki's Bodhisattva vow as Kant's highest good in the world

"Our practice," Suzuki has said above, "is to help people, and how to help people is to practice our way in each moment. That is how to live in this world and how to practice *zazen*." How to practice *zazen* correctly, according to Suzuki, is thus "to practice our way in each moment" for the sole purpose of helping people:

> Always being with them, without any idea of discrimination, we can help others in its true sense, without giving anything, any special teaching or materials. This is actually the Bodhisattva way. When you practice zazen in this way, you have the point of zazen and the point of practice. [*WB*, IX, Fall-Winter 1970–71: 9]

The object of the Bodhisattva vow, as Suzuki has said, is "to save all sentient beings." And the "point"—the sole, motivating intention—of Zen practice, according to Suzuki, is to realize the requirements of this vow by achieving its object. Similarly, the "final object" of the requirements of moral law, as Kant has said, is "the achievement of the highest good in the world." Thus, if I can show that Suzuki's phrase "to save all sentient beings" is equivalent in meaning to Kant's phrase "to achieve the highest good in the world," then I will have demonstrated that realizing the object of the Bodhisattva vow is indeed equivalent to realizing what Kant considers to be the final object of the requirements of moral law. And thus I will have demonstrated the truth of thesis Z2: *In order to practice* zazen *correctly, according to Suzuki, my sole intention in performing that practice must be that of realizing the requirements of moral law, as Kant understands these requirements.*

Here is an outline of the argument I wish to make:

(0) In order to practice *zazen* correctly, according to Suzuki, my sole intention in performing that practice must be that of saving all sentient beings
[Suzuki's account of the Bodhisattva vow]

(1) To practice *zazen* with the sole intention of saving all sentient beings means to practice *zazen* with the sole intention of helping all people (a) realize happiness, and (b) cultivate virtue in the sense of cultivating a perfect moral character
[proposed definition of "saving all sentient beings"]

(2) To practice *zazen* with the sole intention of helping all people realize happiness and cultivate virtue is to practice with the sole intention of realizing what Kant understands to be the highest possible good in this world
[Kant's account of the "Dialectic of Pure Practical Reason"]

(3) To practice *zazen* with the sole intention of realizing the highest possible good in this world is to practice with the sole intention of realizing the requirements of morality, as Kant understands these requirements
[Kant's account of the "Dialectic of Pure Practical Reason"]

Z2 In order to practice *zazen* correctly, according to Suzuki, my sole intention in performing that practice must be that of realizing the requirements of morality, as Kant understands these requirements
[0 through 3 above]

As arguments in support of theses (0) and (3) have already been provided in subsections *a* and *b* above, I will complete chapter 4 of this study—and my defense of thesis Z2—by attempting to demonstrate the truth of theses (1) and (2).

1
To practice zazen *with the sole intention of saving all sentient beings means to practice* zazen *with the sole intention of helping people (a) realize happiness, and (b) cultivate virtue in the sense of cultivating a perfect moral character*

To save all sentient beings, Suzuki has said, means to "help others in its true sense." And the Buddhist idea of helping others "in its true sense" is, he says, that of providing the kind of compassionate help a parent might give its child:

> The "Compassionate mind" is the affectionate mind of parents. Parents always think of the growth and welfare of their children, even to the neglect of their own circumstances. Our scriptures say "Buddha Mind is the mind of the great compassion." [*WB*, IX, Winter 1970: 3]

Of course, parents want to help their children obtain happiness in this life. Thus it can be assumed that by "helping others" Suzuki certainly means "helping others find happiness." But if human happiness can be defined as the satisfaction of all one's desires, it is clear that the compassionate mind of parenthood will be concerned with more than simply helping a child satisfy all its desires. In a rare case or circumstance—that of the perfectly good child—everything a child desires will coincide with everything that is conducive, as Suzuki says above, to proper growth and welfare. In such a case, the compassionate mind of parenthood might indeed express itself through helping the child satisfy all such healthy and rational desires. But in most cases and circumstances, parents—that is, Bodhisattvas—will be faced with the problem of helping children—that is, sentient beings—whose desires are not all healthy and rational. For people's desires often lead to injury and suffering rather than to growth and welfare. Thus the help provided such people must be of a different nature from that provided the perfectly good person:

> So in the relationship between good person and you, the relationship will be to encourage . . . to give joy. . . . And for the person who is suffering, you should suffer with him. That is called *jihi* . . . . *Jihi* is usually translated "love." But love means—love has two sides. One is to give joy. And the other is to eliminate—to suffer with them. . . . To make his suffering less, we suffer with him. We share their suffering. [*SL*, III, 13]

So the compassionate mission of a Bodhisattva involves helping human beings attain happiness by two different methods. The direct method is to help people attain happiness by helping them satisfy their desires. And the indirect method is to help people attain happiness by reducing their suffering: "to make his suffering less, we suffer with him. We share their suffering":

> If he is very good we can enjoy joy of practice with him by giving good cushion, good zendo [meditation room], something like this. But actually, [for the person] who is suffering, zendo doesn't mean anything. Whatever you give him he will not accept it: "No, I don't need. I suffer a lot. I don't know why. Right now, to get out of suffering is most important point. Nothing can help me. You cannot help me," he may say. When you hear this, like Avalokiteśvara Bodhisattva you should be someone, you should be like someone who is suffering, and you should suffer as he suffers. Actually you will feel in that way. If you see someone who is suffer[ing], you will suffer too. That is because of your love, because of your inate love, your instinct, you share the suffering. That is love in its true sense. [*SL*, III, 13]

Thus "to save all sentient beings,"according to Suzuki, means to attend compassionately to the growth and welfare of all people, as if they were one's own children. And to attend to the growth and welfare of all beings means both to encourage people when things are going well for them and to be with people and suffer with them when things are not going so well. And thus the Bodhisattva way of life is rightly described as the way of helping all beings attain happiness—as long as the elimination or alleviation of others' suffering is understood as contributing to their attainment of happiness.

In addition to being concerned with helping all sentient beings find happiness, the Bodhisattva is also concerned with helping all beings find the way to live a virtuous, or morally excellent, life. To practice the way of Zen life, Suzuki says, "means to encourage people to have a more spiritual and adequate way of life as human beings" (*ZM*, 136). Thus, as Suzuki has been quoted earlier in this essay, the purpose of Zen practice is that of studying how to live one's daily life:

> How to sit is how to act. We study how to act by sitting, and this is the most basic activity for us. That is why we practice zazen in this way. . . . Buddha taught us how to act through our practice; that is why we sit. [*ZM*, 126]

As has been argued above, Suzuki views Buddha nature—which is universal to all beings—as the foundation of all virtuous behavior. According to Suzuki, it is both necessary and sufficient for living a virtuous life in accordance with the requirements of morality to cultivate and keep, through constant *zazen* practice, one's "original" Buddha nature (*ZM*, 22). Thus to practice *zazen* is to cultivate virtue itself. "If originally we have Buddha nature," Suzuki says, "the reason we practice *zazen* is that we must behave like Buddha" (*ZM*, 56).

It is clear that Suzuki views the purpose of the historical Buddha's religious practice as that of cultivating a virtuous character, which would be universally beneficial to all beings, including himself:

> Buddha was not interested in the elements comprising human beings, nor in metaphysical theories of existence. He was more concerned about how he himself existed in this moment. That was his point. Bread is made from flour. How flour becomes bread when put in the oven was for Buddha the most important thing. How we become enlightened was his main interest. The enlightened person is some perfect, desirable character, for himself and for others. Buddha want-

> ed to find out how human beings develop this ideal character—how various sages in the past became sages. In order to find out how dough became perfect bread, he made it over and over again, until he became quite successful. That was his practice. [*ZM*, 56]

And it is likewise clear that Suzuki views the purpose of a religious practice organized around the command of the Bodhisattva vow as that of helping all human beings cultivate their own virtuous character through religious practice:

> How we find the way in each moment is to think about how to help people practice a religious way. If you don't forget this point, you will find out how to treat people, how to treat things, how to behave yourself; and that is at the same time the so-called Bodhisattva way. [*WB*, IX, Fall-Winter 1970–71: 47]

In thinking "about how to help people practice a religious way," the Zen practicer is thinking with the same compassionate mind of Buddha, who "appeared in this world because of his vow to save all human beings" (*WB*, VIII, Spring 1969:9). And Buddha's way of life culminated, Suzuki says, in his teaching of the way to enlightenment—the way, that is, to attain "some perfect, desirable character, for [one]self and for others":

> Buddha took Nirvana because he had given people the chance to attain enlightenment; he had completed giving the full teaching for attaining enlightenment so there was no need for him to live anymore. That is why he took Nirvana, and his disciples understood his death in this way. [*WB*, VIII, Spring 1969: 9]

Therefore, according to Suzuki, the so-called Bodhisattva way—the way of making the vow of saving all sentient beings the determining ground of all one's actions—involves both helping human beings find happiness *and* helping them develop perfect virtue—or what Suzuki calls an "ideal character"—through giving them "the full teaching for attaining enlightenment."

2

To practice zazen *with the sole intention of helping people realize happiness and cultivate virtue is to practice* zazen *with the sole intention of realizing what Kant understands to be the highest possible good in this world.*

If the intention informing *zazen* practice, according to Suzuki, is to realize the object of the Bodhisattva vow—which is that of helping all sentient beings (including oneself) to attain happiness and a "perfect, desirable character"—then the object of the Bodhisattva vow, as understood by Suzuki, is the same as that which Kant considers to be the object of a will subject to the requirements of moral law: that is, the realization of the highest possible good in this world. For to work to realize the highest possible good in this world is, for Kant, to work to realize universal happiness consonant with universal *worthiness* of happiness, or virtue:

> Virtue and happiness together constitute the possession of the highest good for one person, and happiness in exact proportion to morality (the worth of a person and his worthiness to be happy) constitutes [the highest good] of a possible world. [*KP*, 111]
>
> In the highest good which is practical for us, i.e., one which is to be made real by our will, virtue and happiness are thought of as necessarily combined, so that the one cannot be assumed by a practical reason without the other belonging to it. [*KP*, 111]

Thus it can be plausibly claimed that to practice *zazen* according to Suzuki's understanding of that practice is, indeed, to practice with the sole intention of realizing what Kant understands to be the highest possible good in this world.

Further evidence of similarity between the Bodhisattva vow and Kant's moral requirement to realize the highest possible good in the world is presented in the following paragraphs.

According to Kant's idea of the highest good as a synthesis of the heterogeneous concepts of moral virtue and happiness, the connection between virtue and happiness must be understood as being what Kant calls a "real connection . . . according to the law of causality"—as opposed to a "logical connection . . . according to the law of identity" (*KP*, 111). The synthesis of virtue and happiness, that is to say, must be understood as an *effect* produced by some causal activity in the world. This is because the idea of the highest good "concerns a practical good, i.e., one that is possible through action" (*KP*, 113). It is a combination which must be practically *made*—because it is not born out of logical necessity. Thus, Kant maintains, the synthesis of virtue and happiness must be thought of "as the connection of cause and effect" (*KP*, 113).

If the combination of virtue and happiness is to be conceived in terms of "the connection of cause and effect," then—so Kant assumes—one must be thought of as being a necessary effect of the other's causal activity:

> Therefore, [either] the desire for happiness must be the motive to maxims of virtue, or the maxim of virtue must be the efficient cause of happiness. [*KP*, 113]

Because, however, my selfish desire for happiness is the very archetype of all those "egoistic ideas" that Suzuki views as the root of "karmic life" (*ZM*, 100)—and, thus, as the very antithesis of a life lived according to the selfless vow to save all sentient beings (see *WB*, VIII, Spring 1969:17)—the desire for happiness could never be thought of by Suzuki as the motivating cause of that overarching "maxim of virtue," the Bodhisattva vow. Similarly, Kant insists that "maxims which put the determining ground of the will in the desire for one's happiness are not moral at all and can serve as ground for no virtue" (*KP*, 113). Therefore, the efficient cause in the formation of the "synthetic" unity of happiness and virtue in the world—whether such a unity be viewed as "the highest good in the world" or as "the salvation (i.e., the perfection of happiness and character) of all sentient beings"—must, according to both Kant and Suzuki, be thought of as being a maxim of virtue. This is consistent with Kant's concept of a virtuous life—a life lived in accordance with moral maxims—as the "unconditional condition of all that is good" (*KP*, 110). And it is also consistent with Suzuki's view that a life lived in accordance with the Bodhisattva vow—a life lived, that is, according to the maxim, "I will help all beings realize happiness and a perfect, desirable character for [themselves] and for others" (see *ZM*, 56)—is indeed an efficient cause of (happiness-producing) good in the world:

> Even though all human beings in the city are busy, there is no reason why they cannot practice our way. If all join our practice of being a Bodhisattva, the result will be great. [*WB*, IX, Fall-winter 1970–71:11]

Just as Kant believes that one can realize the highest good in the world only through renouncing "incentives of inclinations" as "determining grounds influencing an action done as a duty" (*KP*, 160), and deciding instead to live acording to "maxims of virtue," so Suzuki believes that one can perfect the happiness and virtue of all living beings only through (a) renouncing those "egoistic ideas" in the thrall of which human beings are "creating and being driven by karma" (*ZM*, 100), and (b) deciding "instead of living by karma [to] live by the vow to help people who live in karma" (*WB*, VIII, Spring 1969: 9). Thus, important evidence of the similarity between the Buddhist moral requirement to save all sentient beings from suffering and the Kantian moral requirement "to make the highest possible good in a world the final object of all our conduct" (*KP*, 129) is that (1) both Suzuki and Kant view the synthesis of virtue and happiness as the final object of their respective, overarching moral requirements, and (2) both Suzuki and Kant view the synthetic relation between virtue and happiness as a *causal* one in which the practice and attainment of virtue is understood to be—in some mysterious way—the efficient cause both of universal and of individual happiness.

Suzuki's reliance upon the causal efficacy of the cultivation of virtue through *zazen* practice as a means of helping all beings realize happiness is so complete that it may feel mystical and alienating to Westerners:

> To help others and to help ourselves is the same thing; to realize the truth myself and to make you realize it, too, is the

> same thing. . . . Only when we have this view, when we stand on our own legs, can we help others. Before this, when you observe yourself with ideas like "Who am I?" "Have I attained enlightenment or not?" "Am I able to help others?" you cannot help others. When you become just you yourself, without comparing yourself to others, just "I am I," "I am here," and when you have difficulty, just "I can manage pretty well," that is Buddha. . . .
>
> Buddha is, figuratively speaking, like the sun; instead of observing things objectively, he understands his Buddha Nature in activity within himself. So, like the sun, although he is not trying to shine on everything objectively, to illuminate everything objectively, he is actually illuminating everything; he is actually helping others without trying to help. . . . So, for Buddha, to save others and to be enlightened himself is the same thing. To help others and to help himself is the same thing. For him there is nothing without. [*WB*, VIII, spring 1969:11–12]

It must be acknowledged, however, that Kant himself (to the consternation of his utilitarian critics, who believe that the primary concern of ethics should be with achieving the end of human happiness, rather than with the moral purity of the actions taken to achieve that end) is committed to placing complete reliance upon the causal efficacy of an inward condition—that of a virtuous state of mind in which "no incentives of inclinations are the determining grounds influencing an action done as a duty"—as the sole means through which happiness in the world must be realized:

> Virtue (as the worthiness to be happy) is the supreme condition of whatever appears to us to be desirable and thus of all our pursuit of happiness. [*KP*, 110]

> One is worthy of possessing a thing or a state when his possession is harmonious with the highest good. We can easily see now that all worthiness is a matter of moral conduct, because this constitutes the condition of everything else (which belongs to one's state) in the concept of the highest good, i.e., participation in happiness. [*KP*, 130]

Thus Kant, too, is open to criticism from practical, action-oriented people who might well ask how cultivating a virtuous character informed by respect for and obedience to moral law can possibly make one causally effective in practically *bringing about* that universal happiness essential to the idea of the highest possible good in this world.

Despite the mystical tone of his statement, "There is nothing without," Suzuki also acknowledges that there is something incredible, and unacceptable, about the notion that I can save all sentient beings simply by enlightening myself—that is, simply by perfecting my own moral character through *zazen* practice. He addresses this problem of credibility by distinguishing between two different kinds of effort involved in trying to bring about the salvation of everyone:

> In the East the main effort we make to solve problems and to help society is to work inside ourselves. But here in the West we try to solve problems actively, by action outside ourselves. The real way to help others should be a combination of the so-called Eastern and Western ways. [*WB*, IX, Fall-Winter 1970–71:16]

These two ways—the so-called Eastern way of helping human beings through one's attainment, manifestation, and transmission of supreme, perfect enlightenment and the so-called Western way of helping people through involvement in practical action in the world—are personified in Suzuki's Mahāyāna Buddhism by the figures of the Buddha and the Bodhisattva, respectively. The one who chooses to live by the great vow to save all sentient beings, Suzuki says, is best seen not as an individual person but as an *incarnation* or the spirit of that vow, an incarnation that skillfully takes on various forms and manifests itself through two different kinds of effort, so as to best serve those numberless beings in need of help:

> By a vow he appears in this world, and practices the Bodhisattva's Way, and attains enlightenment as Buddha did, to save all human beings. He is called an incarnated body. He changes his form in various ways—sometimes he's a Bod-

> hisattva, sometimes a Buddha; to help people, he takes various forms. [*WB*, VIII, Spring 1969:17]

Thus, as discussed in section *ii* of this chapter, as *Bodhisattvas* Buddhist practicers will be "like a white bird in the snow." Indistinguishable in the practice of their spiritual vocation from other human beings, they will be totally involved in the practical activity of the world. And as *Buddhas* these same practicers will be, "figuratively speaking, like the sun." Totally involved in the practice of *zazen*, they will understand their Buddha nature not in phenomenal but in noumenal terms, as activity within themselves:

> As . . . Buddha we should know our own nature, and we should realize that there is no "I" and no "you," that all is one being. When we realize this universal nature, we can help others without trying to help others because whatever we do, that is our helping activity.
>
> When you practice zazen there is no "you" and no "others," your practice includes everything. You are a part of me, and I am a part of you. When we reach this kind of understanding we are . . . Buddha. Everything then takes place within yourself. [*WB*, VIII, Spring 1969:13]

The terms 'Buddha' and 'Bodhisattva' refer to two different aspects, or manifestations, of the same life lived according to the great vow to save all sentient beings. As Suzuki describes a person living such a life: "sometimes he's a Bodhisattva, sometimes a Buddha; to help people, he takes various forms." As a Bodhisattva, when this person "wants to save ladies he takes the form of a lady; for boys he takes the form of a boy; for fishermen he becomes a fisherman" (*WB*, IX, Fall-Winter 1970–71:9). But as a Buddha, this person understands ladies, boys, fishermen, and other sentient beings all as part of himself—as appearances in his "Big Mind which includes everything" (*SL*, V, 10). Suzuki's concept of "big mind," as has been shown in chapter 3, section *iii*, is virtually identical to Kant's noumenal subject, the transcendental ground of all appearances in consciousness. It is the concept of a subject utterly empty of egoistic ideas and utterly beyond the phenomenal conditions of space and time. This is Buddha: "the Perpetual One, who exists from beginningless beginning to endless end. . . . He is Truth itself" (*WB*, VIII, Spring 1969:16).

And, as has been argued both in chapter 3 and in this section of chapter 4, the freedom of activity that Bodhisattvas enjoy in the phenomenal world—the freedom to engage wholeheartedly, with utter "softness of mind," in an endless succession of helping human activities; the freedom to be a first cause of benevolent actions in the world—can only be derived from their noumenally based consciousness of freedom as emptiness. And again: this noumenally based consciousness—this "original mind" that, "like the sun," is sufficient unto itself—is itself the enlightened mind of Buddha, which exists as the background and the support of the Bodhisattva's helping activities:

> So . . . before a Bodhisattva appears to save others, there must be . . . Buddha as a background. Bodhisattvas . . . and their activity of helping others come from this source, from this origin in . . . Buddha, who is Truth itself. [*WB*, VIII, Spring 1969:10]

Like Suzuki, Kant recognizes that there is something both incredible, even unacceptable about the idea that the practice of virtue can be an efficient cause of the attainment of universal happiness in this world. And, like Suzuki, Kant tries to resolve this problem of credibility—which he refers to as the "antinomy of practical reason" (*KP*, 117ff.)—first by differentiating the idea of noumenal causality from that of phenomenal causality, and then by establishing the prior status of the former as a first, unconditioned cause of action for good in the world. Thus both Kant and Suzuki posit the same causal relationship between so-called Eastern (or noumenally based) "work inside ourselves" and so-called Western (or phenomenally based) "actions outside ourselves."

I will conclude this section, and chapter 4, with a two-part discussion of Kant's resolution of the antinomy of practical reason as it relates to Suzuki's understanding of the realization of the requirements of the Bodhisattva vow. After first explaining the nature of the problem posed by the antinomy of pure practical reason and presenting Kant's general solution to this problem, I will then go on to address the important topic of Kant's *postulates* of pure practical reason, both as they contribute to his resolution of the antinomy of pure practical reason, and as they relate to similar assumptions made by Suzuki in his account of Zen practice.

The notion that a maxim of virtue can be the efficient cause of happiness is incredible, Kant says:

> Since every practical connection of causes and effects in the world, as a result of the determination of the will, is dependent not on the moral intentions of the will but on knowledge of natural laws and the physical capacity of using them to its purposes; consequently, no necessary connection, sufficient to the highest good, between happiness and virtue in the world can be expected from the most meticulous observance of the moral law. [*KP*, 113]

Even by the most meticulous observance of the requirements of moral law, I cannot rationally expect to attain—solely by the means of such observance—happiness for myself, let alone happiness for all beings. This is so for the following reasons. First of all, the attainment of happiness for myself and others depends upon what Kant calls "practical connection[s] of causes and effects in the world" (for example, a necessary means of helping a child suffering from starvation to attain happiness will be, practically, to cause food to be provided for it). Secondly, such "practical connections" depend not entirely upon my moral intention of realizing the highest possible good in the world, but also upon my mental and physical capacity to do what needs to be done in order to effect such realization (for example, in order to help a starving child, I need to be *able*, as well as willing, to cause food to be provided). Thus, because my mental and physical capacity to realize the highest good in the world is contingent upon a variety of conditions beyond my control, "no necessary connection, sufficient to the highest good, between happiness and virtue in the world can be expected."

So long as the realization of human happiness through the practice of virtue is understood as being contingent upon conditions other than the perfection of that practice, then—in defiance of Kant—it would seem that the realization of the highest good in the world cannot be thought of as the practically necessary final object of the requirements of moral law. For to say "it is *necessary* that I realize a good that is beyond my power to realize," is to state an absurdity. And, therefore, Kant's moral requirement that I work to realize the highest possible good in the world must itself be considered absurd, unless it can be demonstrated that there is what Kant calls a "real connection" between virtue and happiness. This "real connection," Kant has said, can only be the connection of cause and effect in which, just as lowering the temperature of water below its freezing point is understood as a necessary and sufficient condition for that water to become ice, so realizing perfect virtue is understood as a necessary and sufficient condition for human beings to become happy.

The unity of virtue with happiness, Kant has said, "must be thought synthetically . . . as the connection of cause and effect, for it concerns a practical good, i.e., one that is possible through action" (*KP*, 113). Yet, to think of virtuous actions as practically efficient causes of happiness in this world is, seemingly, to indulge in pure fantasy (*KP*, 114). However, if one recalls the critical distinction between phenomenal causality (causal relations among appearances in the empirical world of sense) and noumenal causality ("a pure intellectual determining ground of my causality in the sensuous world" (*KP*, 114–15), as evidenced by the existence of the practically necessary requirements of moral law) then, Kant says, it is at least not *impossible* "that the morality of intention should have a [practically] necessary relation as cause to happiness as an effect in the sensuous world" (*KP*, 115). It is not impossible for maxims of virtue to be efficient causes of happiness in the world, because, first of all, "the actions which are devoted to realizing the highest good, do belong to this world" (*KP*, 119)—that is, they are, or have the possibility of being, practically effective. And secondly, these actions proceed directly from a maxim of virtue (the maxim, "I will work to realize the highest possible good in this world") as their *intelligible cause*. Thus, because the existence of moral laws provides incontrovertible evidence of the practical activity of an intelligible causality in this world, the attainment of happiness as a necessary effect of such an intelligible causality "may be thought at least possible, though it is by no means known or understood" (*KP*, 119).

Although the existence of moral law forces me to acknowledge the possibility of there being a causal relationship between the practice of virtue and the attainment of happiness, still, *there is no way for me to know or understand* how my meticulous observance of moral maxims can actually function as an efficient cause (a) of my own and others' happiness in this world, and hence (b) of the realization of the highest good in the world. This is because "the possibility of such a connection of the conditioned [universal happiness] with its condition [the practice of virtue] belongs wholly to the supersensuous relations of things and cannot be given under the laws of the world of sense" (*KP*, 119). As Kant points out in his "Critical Resolution" of the antinomy of practical reason, "I am justified in thinking of my existence as that of a noumenon in an intelligible world" (*KP*, 114). But my noumenal existence, and "the supersensuous relations of things" in general, can never be objects of knowledge for me—as, for instance, my phenomenal existence and those natural laws describing the relations of things in the world of sense, *can* be objects of knowledge.

The causal relation between my lowering the temperature of a cup of water below its freezing point and that water's turning into ice can indeed be an object of knowledge for me, for it concerns the relation of things (appearances) in my field of sensibility. But the causal relation between (a) my respect for and obedience to maxims of virtue and (b) my and others attainment of happiness can never be such an object of knowledge. This is because the notion of my freedom to act according to my idea of moral law is the notion of an intelligible, or supersensuous, causality, which has nothing to do with my knowledge of the causal relation of things as they appear to me through my senses. Thus the efficacy of maxims of virtue as a cause of happiness in this world must remain an enigma for me. My consciousness of my freedom to follow such maxims, regardless of the causal relations of things as they appear through my senses, can never be more than what has been called in chapter 3 a *consciousness of emptiness*. For, as Kant has insisted, "the domain that lies out beyond the sphere of appearances is for us empty":

> That is to say, we have an understanding which problematically extends further, but we have no intuition, indeed not

> even the concept of a possible intuition, through which objects outside the field of sensibility can be given, and through which the understanding can be employed *assertorically* beyond that field. [*KV*, B310]

Kant's "Critical Resolution" of the antinomy of practical reason thus relies upon the problematic (see *KV*, B310) concept of an "empty" noumenal subject as the causal ground of appearances in the world of sense, just as Suzuki's explanation of the causal connection between the cultivation of an enlightened character through *zazen* practice and the happiness of all sentient beings relies upon the concept of an empty, noumenal subject—Buddha—who, in some incomprehensible way, is an efficient cause of happiness and salvation in the world.

In Kant's moral philosophy, three "postulates of pure practical reason"—freedom, the immortality of the soul, and the existence of God—are utilized in a hypothetical manner to fill, so to speak, the noumenal emptiness that is thought of as an intelligible ground of causality in the world of sense (*KP*, 122–34). Kant defends his use of these postulates by arguing as follows. Because all requirements of moral law are practically necessary (they are binding upon my actions), and because the realization of the highest possible good in the world is a requirement of moral law, therefore it is practically necessary for me to work to realize the highest possible good in this world. But, if it is in truth practically necessary for me to work to realize the highest possible good in this world, then it must be practically *possible* for me to achieve this goal. Therefore, Kant concludes, I am justified in postulating the existence of that which would make possible the realization of the highest possible good in this world, even if I have no empirical or theoretical grounds on which to justify such a postulation.

Of course, as has been argued in chapter 3, realization of the requirements of moral law, including the realization of the highest possible good in this world, would be impossible without the existence of freedom as the transcendental, noumenally based cause of actions in the phenomenal world. Thus the existence of freedom is an essential postulate of a "pure"—that is, purely rational, rather than sensuously influenced—practical reason. But my ability to realize the synthesis of virtue and happiness in the world by means of my practice and perfection of moral virtue depends not just upon the existence of freedom (as a potential cause of good in the world) but also upon my ability to perfectly realize this freedom by cultivating a disposition of "negative perfection . . . indicating that no incentives of inclinations are the determining grounds influencing an action done as a duty" (*KP*, 160). Thus, Kant says, because:

> the complete fitness of intentions to the moral law is the supreme condition of the highest good . . . this fitness, therefore, must be just as possible as its object [the highest good], because it is contained in the command that requires us to promote the latter. [*KP*, 122]

"Complete fitness to the moral law," Kant points out, is nothing less than holiness, "which is a perfection of which no rational being in the world of sense is capable" (*KP*, 122). Thus, in order to ensure the possibility of the realization of the highest good, it is necessary to postulate the possibility of what Kant calls "an endless progress" toward realization of a state of complete fitness to the moral law—a postulation that involves "the presupposition of an infinitely enduring existence and personality of the same rational being" (*KP*, 122). This is the postulate of the immortality of the soul:

> Thus the highest good is practically possible only on the supposition of the immortality of the soul, and the latter, as inseparably bound to the moral law, is a postulate of pure practical reason. [*KP*, 122]

As Kant also acknowledges, there is a contradiction, or "antinomy," between (a) my knowledge of a necessary moral requirement that virtue, as my practice of respectful obedience to moral law, be an efficient cause of happiness in the world and (b) my knowledge that "the acting rational being in the world is not at the same time the cause of the world and of nature itself" (*KP*, 124):

> Hence, there is not the slightest ground in the moral law for a necessary connection between the morality and [the] proportionate happiness of a being which belongs to the world as one of its parts and as thus dependent on it. Not being nature's cause, his will cannot by its own strength bring nature, as it touches on his happiness, into complete harmony with his practical principles. [*KP*, 124]

The postulates, or hypotheses, of freedom and immortality of the soul, by themselves, cannot resolve this antinomy between the practical necessity of the moral requirement to realize the highest good in the world and the practical impossibility of that requirement. Thus, Kant says, because "we *should* seek to further the highest good (which therefore must be at least possible)," therefore:

> also the existence is postulated of a cause of the whole of nature, itself distinct from nature, which contains the ground of the exact coincidence of happiness with morality. . . . Therefore, the highest good is possible in the world only on the supposition of a supreme cause of nature which has a causality corresponding to the moral intention. [*KP*, 125]

And thus the final postulate of pure practical reason is that of the existence of God as "a supreme cause of nature which has a causality corresponding to the moral intention."

It is important to keep in mind that Kant's postulates of freedom, immortality of the soul, and the existence of God are put forth as unverifiable assumptions—they are not presented as hypotheses, in the scientific sense, which might be proven true or false. Kant does, however, believe it is *necessary* for anyone who is respectfully obedient to the command of moral law to assume the truth of these postulates. This is because, in order to assent to the overarching command of moral law to work to realize the highest good in this world, I must assume (a) my freedom to make this command the intelligible cause of my actions in the world, (b) my capacity to realize that "unconditional condition" of the highest good, the perfection of virtue, and (c) the existence of a causal agency in nature through which my subjective intent to realize universal happiness through the practice and perfection of virtue is somehow translated into personal and societal reality.

But my need to make these assumptions is a purely subjective one. "It . . . springs," as Kant says, "from the moral disposition itself" (*KP*, 146). My belief in freedom, immortality, and a supreme causality in nature corresponding to my moral intention reflects my subjective need to resolve what has been referred to above as the "dialectical" tension between my awareness of the empirically conditioned, natural world of my senses and my simultaneous awareness of an ideal, moral counterpart to that world, which would be nature under the beneficent rule of moral law. Thus Kant's postulates of pure practical reason have no basis in empirical fact. My feeling that it is necessary to believe in the truth of these postulates reflects only:

> a subjective condition of reason . . . which is the only way in which it is theoretically possible for it [reason] to conceive of the exact harmony of the realm of nature with the realm of morals as the condition of the possibility of the highest good. [*KP*, 145]

I will conclude this discussion of Kant's resolution of the antinomy of pure practical reason by indicating how Suzuki relies upon postulates similar to those of Kant in order to provide for the possibility of realizing the requirements of the Bodhisattva vow. Evidence of Suzuki's belief in freedom as a causal ground of actions in the world has already been presented. Therefore, I will now show how the requirements of the Bodhisattva vow lead Suzuki to assume both a form of immortality of the soul, and the existence of a supreme cause of nature "which has a causality corresponding to the moral intention."

A particularly strong affirmation of the existence of what Kant calls "a subjective condition of reason"—a need to try to harmonize the realm of human nature "with the realm of morals as the condition of the possibility of the highest good"—is evidenced in the following statement by Suzuki, which is part of a lecture explaining the purpose of the Buddhist bow:

> Each bow expresses one of the four Buddhist vows. These vows are: "Although sentient beings are innumerable, we

> vow to save them. Although our evil desires are limitless, we vow to be rid of them. Although the teaching is limitless, we vow to learn it all. Although Buddhism is unattainable, we vow to attain it." If it is unattainable, how can we attain it? But we should! That is Buddhism.
>
> To think, "Because it is possible we will do it," is not Buddhism. Even though it is impossible, we have to do it because our true nature wants us to. But actually, whether or not it is possible is not the point. If it is our inmost desire to get rid of our self-centered ideas, we have to do it. [*ZM*, 45–46]

In explaining the rationale behind the Zen practice of bowing, Suzuki indicates that the perfection of virtue mandated by "our inmost desire" is not an object that can be attained in a limited period of time. Thus, he says, there is no end to our efforts to improve ourselves:

> Bowing helps to eliminate our self-centered ideas. This is not so easy. It is difficult to get rid of these ideas, and bowing is a very valuable practice. The result is not the point; it is the effort to improve ourselves that is valuable. There is no end to this practice. [*ZM*, 45]

Kant's postulate of immortality—of "an endless progress" toward the perfection of virtue (*KP*, 122)—is thus clearly reflected in Suzuki's belief that the "effort to improve ourselves" through Zen practice is mandated by some inner, subjective condition and must be thought of as continuing without end. Other statements in *Zen Mind, Beginner's Mind* reflect this belief:

> Our purpose is to keep this practice forever. This practice started from beginningless time, and it will continue into an endless future. [*ZM*, 47]

> We should try to continue our effort forever. [*ZM*, 37]

In accordance with the traditional Buddhist doctrine of *anātman*, or no–self, Suzuki does not subscribe to the view that individual human souls are immortal. But, in accordance with the

Buddha's traditional refusal to involve himself in unresolvable metaphysical disputes, Suzuki also refuses to subscribe to the opposing view, that individual human souls are *not* immortal:

> After some years we will die. If we just think that it is the end of our life, this will be the wrong understanding. But, on the other hand, if we think that we do not die, this is also wrong. We die, and we do not die. This is the right understanding. Some people may say that our mind or soul exists forever, and it is only our physical body which dies. But this is not exactly right, because both mind and body have their end. But at the same time it is also true that they exist eternally. [*ZM*, 22]

Like Kant, Suzuki is aware of the lack of any empirical evidence—and the lack of any possibility of such evidence—for the claim that "our mind or soul exists forever." However, also like Kant, he is aware of the lack of any empirical evidence—as well as the lack of any possibility of providing such evidence—for the counterclaim that our mind or soul does *not* exist forever. Thus Suzuki manages both to avoid making unsupportable metaphysical assertions and, at the same time, to acknowledge and address the subjectively conditioned human need to believe in the possibility of an endless progress toward the perfection of virtue. He does this by encouraging his students to identify not with a transitory, phenomenal self, which changes from day to day and grows old and passes away, but with that empty, noumenal ground of everything that appears in consciousness (including my phenomenal self), which he calls "big mind":

> Before we were born we had no feeling; we were one with the universe. This is called "mind-only," or "essence of mind," or "big mind." After we are separated by birth from this oneness, as the water falling from the waterfall is separated by the wind and rocks, then we have feeling. . . . When you do not realize that you are one with the river, or one with the universe, you have fear. [But] Whether it is separated into drops or not, water is water. Our life and death are the same thing. [*ZM*, 93–94]

The "big mind" that is the noumenal subject of my consciousness and the ground of my freedom in the world is not identifiable, in empirical terms, as a particular human personality or self—nor is it identifiable, in a spatial/temporal context, as something that has a beginning and an end. My empirically identifiable self, on the other hand—as Kant himself argues in his criticism of rational psychology (see *KV*, B407–28)—can hardly be thought of as an enduring (let alone immortal!) subject of consciousness, for it does not retain the same empirical characteristics for even one minute. Here is how Suzuki describes the empirically observable self:

> Within this moment, this temporal existence does not change, does not move, and is always independent from other existences. In the next moment another existence arises; we may change to something else. Strictly speaking, there is no connection between I myself yesterday and I myself in this moment; there is no connection whatsoever. . . . Today I am sitting in Los Altos. Tomorrow morning I shall be in San Francisco. There is no connection between the "I" in Los Altos and the "I" in San Francisco. They are quite different beings. Here we have the freedom of existence. [*ZM*, 106]

Thus, through carefully observing my constantly changing empirical self, Suzuki says, I can cultivate awareness of the empty and unchanging "big mind" that is the noumenal ground of my empirical self and the source of "the freedom of existence." And thus, Suzuki says elsewhere, "to live in the [empty] realm of Buddha nature means to die as a small [empirically identifiable] being, moment after moment" (*ZM*, 31). But "to die as a small being" does not mean to pass away or disappear: it means to awaken to consciousness of freedom as emptiness. Therefore, Suzuki says, "to pass away" is not a very adequate expression for this kind of death: "Perhaps 'to pass on,' or 'to go on,' or 'to join' would be better" (*ZM*, 94). In dying as a small being, moment by moment, I constantly "go on," endlessly progressing in my effort to express the "big mind" of Buddha—a mind that, as Suzuki has said, instead of being egotistically centered upon the ever-changing desires of the empirical self, is informed by the selfless vow to save all sentient beings. Thus, through distinguishing between the concepts of a transitory phenomenal self and an eternal noumenal subject, Suzuki introduces the postulate of immortality into his account of Zen practice.

A Buddhist teacher's account of Zen practice might seem an unpromising place to look for evidence of a belief in Kant's final postulate of pure practical reason, the existence of God. But the idea of the Bodhisattva vow, like the idea of Kant's highest good, is the idea of *causing* beneficial change in the world through the practice and perfection of virtue. Thus the vow requires, for its realization, that there be an efficient causal force in the natural world corresponding to my moral intention to realize universal happiness through the practice and perfection of virtue. And this requirement leads Suzuki, just as it leads Kant, to postulate the existence of some superhuman causal agency.

It is obvious to Suzuki, as well as to Kant, that my morally mandated efforts as an individual to realize universal happiness through the practice and perfection of virtue are, by any rational standard, hopelessly inadequate. This tension between my sense of what is morally required of me by the Bodhisattva vow and my sense of the hopelessness, or impossibility, of fulfilling these requirements is reflected in the words of the four Buddhist vows quoted above:

> Although sentient beings are innumerable, we vow to save them.
> Although our evil desires are limitless, we vow to be rid of them.
> Although the teaching is limitless, we vow to learn it all.
> Although Buddhism is unattainable, we vow to attain it.

The final object of Buddhism, the salvation of all sentient beings, is obviously unattainable through my day by day efforts and activities in the world. Nevertheless, as Suzuki has said, "even though it is impossible, we have to do it because our true nature wants us to" (*ZM*, 45). Thus, according to Suzuki as well as Kant, due to a subjective condition of my reason it is *necessary* for me to believe in the existence of a causality in nature, which corresponds to my moral intention to work for the happiness of all beings. And thus Suzuki, like Kant, finds it necessary to postulate the existence of a supreme causal agent that both transcends and supports my human effort to realize, in the form of practical results in the world, my maxim to help all human beings attain happiness.

Christianity, Suzuki says, correctly puts emphasis upon God, rather than upon egocentric human effort, as the true causal source of beneficent activity and creation in the world of nature:

> According to Christianity, every existence in nature is something which was created for or given to us by God. . . . But if you think that God created man, and that you are somehow separate from God, you are liable to think you have the ability to create something separate, something not given by Him. For instance, we create airplanes and highways. And when we repeat, "I create, I create, I create," soon we forget who is actually the "I" which creates the various things; we soon forget about God. [*ZM*, 66]

It is true, Suzuki says, that as individual human beings, "moment after moment we are creating something, and this is the joy of our life" (*ZM*, 65):

> But this "I" which is creating and always giving out something is not the "small I"; it is the "big I." Even though you do not realize the oneness of this "big I" with everything, when you give something you feel good, because at that time you feel at one with what you are giving. [*ZM*, 65]

From the two passages just quoted it can be seen that Suzuki identifies helping activity having its source in the "big I" or "big mind" (which, as the noumenal ground of all the phenomena appearing in consciousness, is one with everything) with helping activity having its source in God (who, when understood as the causal ground of "every existence in nature," might likewise be said to be one with everything). And the great "danger of human culture," Suzuki goes on to say, is to "forget about God"—to lose touch with the "big I" that is one with the causal ground of all creation:

> Actually, to create with the "big I" is to give [that is, is to give out what has been created by God]; we cannot create and own what we create for ourselves since everything was created by God. This point should not be forgotten. But because we do forget who is doing the creating and the reason for the creation, we become attached to the material or exchange value. This has no value in comparison to the absolute value of something as God's creation. [*ZM*, 66]

For Suzuki, as a Zen teacher, the way to maintain awareness of the existence of that noumenally based "big I" or "big mind" that is one with God as the supreme causal activity in nature is to practice *zazen*—to cultivate, that is to say (using the terminology developed in chapter 3, section *iii*), *Ri*, or consciousness of freedom as emptiness. Beginning with that basic activity—perhaps comparable with the activity of prayer in Kant's Christian tradition—Suzuki goes on to distinguish three stages of causal, or creative, activity relevant to the realization of the Bodhisattva vow to work for the happiness of all sentient beings. The first stage, he says, involves our recognition that the entire world of nature emerges miraculously "from nothing"—that is, emerges miraculously from a transcendent causal ground unknowable to us:

> When we sit in the cross-legged posture, we resume our fundamental activity of creation. There are perhaps three kinds of creation. The first is to be aware of ourselves after we finish zazen. When we sit we are nothing, we do not even realize what we are; we just sit. But when we stand up, we are there! This is the first step in creation. When you are there, everything else is there; everything is created all at once. When we emerge from nothing, when everything emerges from nothing, we see it all as a fresh new creation. [*ZM*, 67]

To sit *zazen*, as has been argued in chapter 3, is to cultivate awareness of the noumenal self that transcends all spatial/temporal conditions and is sufficient to itself. This, using Suzuki's terminology, is to cultivate awareness of *Ri* or emptiness. Thus, in the effort, through *zazen* practice, to "go beyond the subjective and objective world which is *Ji* . . . you are not thinking anything, you are not watching anything" (*SL*, IV, 1). So "the first step in creation," according to Suzuki, proceeds from that empty awareness cultivated through *zazen* practice; it proceeds, that is, from my unconceptualized awareness of an unknowable, transcendent, causal ground of the world of experience that appears to me through my senses. And thus, "when we emerge from nothing, when everything emerges from nothing, we see it all as a fresh new creation." We understand and participate in the world, that is to say, as "something which was created for or given to us by God."

The second and third steps of creation—in which human beings themselves become efficient causes of events in the world—proceed in turn, according to Suzuki, from this all-important first step:

> The second kind of creation is when you act, or produce or prepare something like food or tea. The third kind is to create something within yourself, such as education, or culture, or art, or some system for our society. So there are three kinds of creation. But if you forget the first, the most important one, the other two will be like children who have lost their parents; their creation will mean nothing. [*ZM*, 67]

If God, or the "big I," is not recognized as the supreme causal ground of all that occurs in the world of nature, then we human beings become separated from the true source of our own causal activity in the world—our lives become disoriented, "like children who have lost their parents." Thus it is necessary, according to Suzuki, to cultivate faith in and awareness of God as the true causal source of our power to act practically in the world. But the only way to cultivate such faith and awareness, Suzuki repeats, is by transcending the egocentric confines of the empirically defined "small I" through *zazen* practice, and in this way—through identifying with my "big I," my empty, noumenal self—actually realizing God's activity in my own human existence:

Usually everyone forgets about zazen. Everyone forgets about God. They work very hard at the second and third kinds of creation, but God does not help the activity. How is it possible for Him to help when He does not realize who He is? That is why we have so many problems in this world. When we forget the fundamental source of our creating, we are like children who do not know what to do when they lose their parents. [*ZM*, 67]

5

Conclusion

Just as Kant has argued (see chapter 4, section *iii (c)*, above) that religious belief is crucially important to a person's ability to live according to the command of moral laws, so he has also argued that philosophical inquiry is crucially important to a person's ability to sustain moral and religious convictions in the face of self-doubt and confusion. Through the practice of such inquiry, he says:

> we shall avoid the error of a crude and unpracticed judgment and (which is far more important) the extravagances of genius, by which, as by the adepts of the philosopher's stone, visionary treasures are promised and real treasures are squandered. [*KP*, 163]

"Innocence is a splendid thing," Kant writes in the *Groundwork of the Metaphysic of Morals*, "only it has the misfortune not to keep very well and to be easily misled" (*GW*, 22). Thus, even supposing there is a "fact of reason," or an "original nature," through which human beings are empowered to know what they should and should not do, there remains the possibility that people will be misled. Such people, as Suzuki says, may lose their "original self-sufficient mind," and thereby "lose all precepts" (*ZM*, 22). On this account, Kant concludes:

> even wisdom—which in itself consists more in doing and not doing than in knowing—does require science as well, not in order to learn from it [science], but in order to win acceptance and durability for its [that is, wisdom's] own prescriptions. [*GW*, 22]

Original practical wisdom, which "consists more in doing and not doing than in knowing," requires the support of methodical, scientific thinking, Kant says, not because I have something new to learn from such thinking, but because I need to struggle within myself to "win acceptance and durability" for my ideas of what I should and should not do. The power of moral ideas to practically influence what I do, and do not do, is, Kant says, constantly in danger of being undermined by specious thinking. For:

> Man feels in himself a powerful counterweight to all the commands of duty presented to him by reason as so worthy of esteem—the counterweight of his needs and inclinations, whose total satisfaction he grasps under the name of 'happiness.' [*GW*, 23]

And from the struggle between the egocentric demands of "needs and inclinations" and the selfless commands of duty arises what Kant calls a "natural dialectic":

> that is, a disposition to quibble with these strict laws of duty, to throw doubt on their validity or at least on their purity and strictness, and to make them, where possible, more adapted to our wishes and inclinations; that is, to pervert their very foundations and destroy their whole dignity—a result which in the end even ordinary human reason is unable to approve. [*GW*, 23]

If Suzuki's account of Zen practice is interpreted from the viewpoint that Kant advances in these statements, then it will be apparent why Suzuki (see chapter 4, section *iii*) says that "ego-centered ideas"—whose total satisfaction might well be said to be grasped under the name "happiness"—"are delusion, covering our Buddha nature":

> We are always creating and following them, and in repeating this process over and over, our life becomes completely occupied by ego-centered ideas. This is called karmic life, or karma. The Buddhist life should not be karmic life. The purpose of our practice is to cut off the karmic spinning mind. [*ZM*, 100]

It is clear that Suzuki views "ego-centered ideas" to be what Kant calls "a powerful counterweight" to the Buddhist way of life. And it is also clear that Suzuki views the purpose of Zen practice—the purpose of what he has called "the rules and way of Zen life"—to be that of cutting off such ideas. For, Suzuki says, "egoistic ideas are delusion, covering our original Buddha nature." Thus once a Zen practicer's life "becomes completely occupied by ego-centered ideas," these ideas, by obscuring the practicer's original Buddha nature, are indeed likely to adversely affect the practicer's attitude toward the precepts of Zen practice—a result that, multiplied among many members of a Buddhist community, might indeed pervert the foundation of the precepts of Zen practice and, as Kant says, "destroy their whole dignity."

In bringing this study to a close I would like to discuss briefly, from the Kantian viewpoint just developed, the two examples presented in chapter 1 as evidence of an "American temptation" to separate the practice of *zazen* from the practice of respectfully observing the commands of moral precepts. These examples are *(a)* certain statements in Alan Watts's essay "Beat Zen, Square Zen, and Zen," and *(b)* Rick Fields's anecdote about the Buddhist teacher who "had slept with one or more of his students."

(a)

In contrasting himself with advocates of a strict, "boarding school style" of Zen, Watts once described his attitude toward Zen practice as "easy and free-floating."[1] Perhaps because of his informal and at times iconoclastic approach to Buddhist religious practice, Watts has been called "in many ways more of a Taoist than a Buddhist."[2] Taoism, Watts has written elsewhere, "constantly makes fun of Confucian solemnity, of the seriousness with which it is supposed that the right and the wrong can be defined and society put in permanent order."[3] To prove his point, Watts translates the great Taoist philosopher, Chuang-tzŭ:

> Talk of charity and duty to one's neighbor drives me nearly crazy. Sir, strive to keep the world to its own original simplicity. And as the wind bloweth where it listeth, so let virtue establish itself. . . . The heron is white without a daily bath. The raven is black without daily coloring itself.[4]

In his book *Beat Zen, Square Zen, and Zen*, Watts expresses the view that the true roots of Zen are to be found "in the old Chinese masters steeped in Taoism."[5] However, the historical thesis that Zen Buddhism is a product of a synthesis of Indian Buddhism and Chinese Taoism is one that is sharply rejected by Suzuki, as it was by Dōgen many centuries earlier.[6] In lecturing to his Tassajara students, Suzuki distinguishes the way of Taoism from that of Buddhism:

> And what is the difference between Taoism and Buddhism. . . . Do you know?. . . . Very similar. If you read it as a book it is maybe the same, but the way we read is different. When Buddhist read it that is Buddhist book. When Taoist read it that is Taoism. It is rather . . . it is actually same vegetable . . . same vegetable, but if Buddhist eat it that is Buddhist food, and if ordinary people . . . vegetarian people eat it [that is] vegetarian food . . . just food. [*SL*, I, 4]

In *Beat Zen, Square Zen, and Zen*, Watts quotes the Chinese Zen master, Lin-chi, as an example of the Taoist spirit of Zen:

> Just be ordinary and nothing special. Eat your food, move your bowels, pass water, and when you're tired go and lie down. The ignorant will laugh at me but the wise will understand.[7]

These words, Suzuki says, will be Taoist when read by a Taoist—but they will be Buddhist when read by a Buddhist. For example, in regard to the way a Buddhist eats food, Suzuki says:

> The way we eat food is not just because the vegetable . . . has some particular nourishment. You know, yang or acid or alkaline. To eat food is part of our practice. That is the difference. We—for sake of practice we eat food, not just to take nourishment. To help our way, to practice Buddha's way we eat food. Not just to support ourselves as a human being or [as] a kind of animal, like fish. [*SL*,I, 4]

So, according to Suzuki, it is for the sole purpose of practicing the Buddha's way that a Buddhist should eat food. If the Buddha's way can be rightly described as the way of realizing the Bodhisattva's vow to help all sentient beings realize happiness and attain perfection of character, then a Buddhist will, in Lin-chi's words, eat food, move the bowels, pass water, and sleep all for the sole purpose of realizing the object of that vow. Taoists, on the other hand, will not have this idea of "living by vow" in mind when they eat, move their bowels, pass water, or sleep:

> To eat food or to understand food or things as . . . something which exists with . . . not much relationship or not much contact with practice is Taoist way. And Buddhist way is [this]: "to practice our way, we eat food." So it includes always our mind, our practice. [*SL*, I, 4]

From the interpretive viewpoint developed in this study, it is the presence, in the mind of the Buddhist, of the moral command to work selflessly for the salvation of all sentient beings that distinguishes true Buddhist practice from what Suzuki sees as being the essentially amoral way of Taoism—the way described by Chuang-tzŭ as that of letting virtue establish itself, just "as the wind bloweth where it listeth." Obviously, the words of Lin-chi quoted by Watts—as well as a great many other statements in the literature of Zen—could be read either way: either as Buddhist in Suzuki's strictly moral sense, or as Taoist according to Suzuki's interpretation of Taoism as an essentially amoral religious practice. It does appear, however, that Suzuki's view of the Buddhist life as one that is lived solely by vow, solely as a means to the end of realizing the requirements of a moral law to work for the salvation of all beings, conflicts in spirit with what Watts calls his "easy and free-floating attitude" toward Zen practice.

This appearance is, nonetheless, deceiving. For Watts's personal reluctance to embrace the traditional "boarding school" style of monastic Zen practice has deep roots in Buddhist history, going back to the birth of Mahāyāna Buddhism, when the focus of Buddhist spiritual practice widened to recognize laypersons as well as monks as capable of following the way of supreme enlightenment.[8] The path of realizing the Bodhisattva vow by renouncing monastic life and "living in the world" has been attractively presented in the popular "ox-herding" pictures and poems, various versions of which have appeared during the last several centuries of Zen practice. These drawings and poems, illustrating progressive stages in the life of a Zen practicer, were first composed by a twelfth-century Chinese Buddhist artist who (to acknowledge the partial truth of Watts's thesis regarding the Taoist origins of Zen) based his work on earlier Taoist drawings and poems.[9] The final poem in one version of the series states:

> Barefooted and naked of breast, I mingle with the people of the world. My clothes are ragged and dust-laden and I am ever blissful. . . . I go to the market place with my wine bottle and return home with my staff. I visit the wine shop and the market, and everyone I look upon becomes enlightened.[10]

It has been shown in chapter 4, section *iii*, of this essay that Suzuki himself endorses the tradition of practicing Buddhism by living in the world, rather than by remaining cloistered in a monastery. For he instructed his students to realize the Bodhisattva's vow of saving all sentient beings by becoming "like a white bird in the snow":

> When people are like snow, we should be like snow. When people become black, we should be black. And always being with them, without any idea of discrimination, we can help others in its true sense, without giving anything, any special teaching or materials. This is actually the Bodhisattva way. [*WB*, IX/Fall-Winter 1970–71: 9]

Thus Suzuki, while sharply distinguishing between the Taoist and the Buddhist attitudes toward religious practice, obviously does not equate the way of Buddhism with monastic practice. While expressing concern that a Zen student's religious practice be informed by the Bodhisattva spirit of selfless compassion, he specifically denies that his students should cling to any specifically "Buddhist" teachings or materials in practicing the Bodhisattva way. "This is actually the Bodhisattva way," he says: to always be with others without discrimination, to be indistinguishable from them either in one's appearance or in one's private thoughts, and thus to help people "in its true sense," simply by living as a friend with them in the midst of their world.

And thus, as Watts suggests in his essay, even the practice of hopping freights or "digging" jazz music[11] might be Zen practice—might be the practice of realizing the object of the Bodhisattva's vow through being "like a white bird in the snow." Whether such practices are or are not Buddhist in nature will depend upon the kind of relationship—selfless or ego-centric—that practicers have with those sentient beings with whom they are living and practicing. If I join the society of those who hop freights, I should—if I am Suzuki's kind of Buddhist—live with them utterly without discrimination, being black when they are black, being covered with snow when they are covered with snow, and in general trying my best to be a good friend to them without any idea of giving them some special teaching or materials. The key point will not be what specific rules of conduct I am observing but whether or not I live "by vow instead of by karma" (see *WB*, VIII, Spring 1969: 9). The key point, that is to say, is whether or not I am doing what I am doing for the sole purpose of realizing the moral requirement to work for the salvation of all sentient beings.

Therefore, it may well be correct, from Suzuki's standpoint, for Zen students to turn their back on traditional Buddhist monastic practice and go out, as the ox-herding poem says, to "mingle with the people of the world." As Suzuki says:

> The most important thing is not rules but to find out the true source of the teaching with your eyes, with your ears—wherever you are is how you understand the source of the teaching. That is more direct way to know the source of the teach-

> ing—without trying to establish some particular way for yourself. So if you stick to words, and if you do not see true way by your eyes, by your nose, ears or tongue—sticking to some rules, and ignoring actually direct experience of everyday life—[then] even though you practice zazen it doesn't work. [*SL*, XII, 8]

Regarding the phrase, "source of the teaching," Suzuki says we should not try to figure out intellectually what this source is:

> "Source of the teaching" is not something which you can understand by words, but something which you . . . have when you do things quite naturally and intuitively. . . . Time is always going on and on. We have not much time to say, "Good or bad." Moment after moment we should follow the flow of the time. You should go [where] the time goes. We don't have time to say, "This way or that way." When we became tired of doing something you might say, "This way or that way," just to kill time, but actually when you see the vegetables in the garden which are almost dried up in the hot weather, you have not much time to say what will be the appropriate thing to do for today. [*SL*, XII, 7]

From the point of view expressed in these last statements, the spirit of Chuang-tzŭ's words—"as the wind bloweth where it listeth, so let virtue establish itself"—does not seem so different, after all, from the spirit of Suzuki's teaching that "moment after moment, we should follow the flow of the time." Just as "the heron is white without a daily bath," and "the raven is black without daily coloring itself," so Zen students should not drive themselves and other people crazy with "talk of charity and duty to one's neighbor," but instead realize that the source of the teaching of charity and duty "is not something which you can understand by words, but something which you . . . have when you do things quite naturally and intuitively."

Thus, although the Buddhist life is, according to Suzuki, a life lived by vow instead of by ego-centered ideas, or karma (*ZM*, 100; *WB*, VIII/Spring 1969: 9), to live one's life by vow does not necessarily mean to talk—or even to think—about ideas like "charity" or "duty" or even "saving all sentient beings." In order to understand this point, it is helpful to recall Suzuki's distinction (discussed in chapter 4, section *iii (c),* 2) between Buddha understood as a human being acting in history—that is, Buddha understood as what we have called in this study a "Bodhisattva"—and Buddha understood as truth itself:

> For the Buddhist, Buddha is not just an historical person, he is truth itself. An historical Buddha cannot be perfect, but the background of the historical Buddha should be truth and, if so, truth itself should be the real Buddha for us. Without this kind of background, Buddha would not have been remembered by human beings for such a long time. When Buddha is acknowledged as truth itself, then, as long as truth exists, and as long as we care for the truth, we can remain as Buddhists. This Buddha is the Sambhogakāya Buddha. [*WB*, VIII/Spring 1969:10]

The "Sambhogakāya" Buddha—the Buddha whose name is synonymous with the word "truth"—is, as Suzuki has pointed out, the true source and foundation of the historical—or "Nirmānakāya"—Buddha's ability to help others:

> The true Buddha is the Sambhogakāya Buddha, and when the Sambhogakāya Buddha takes some activity, or is observed by someone, he may be called the Nirmānakāya Buddha. So before the Nirmānakāya Buddha there must be the Sambhogakāya Buddha, and before a Bodhisattva appears to save others, there must be the Sambhogakāya Buddha as a background. Bodhisattvas, and Buddhas, and their activity of helping others come from this source, from this origin in Sambhogakāya Buddha, who is truth itself. [*WB*, VIII/Spring 1969:10]

Thus, Suzuki says, "Buddha's teaching is not the written teaching, or something told by the historical Buddha" (*WB*, VIII/Spring 1969:10). The source of Buddha's teaching is truth itself, and one comes to know it through "direct experience of everyday life"—through experience of a life in which, "moment after moment we should follow the flow of the time." It is the ever-changing world of nature itself that teaches us our duty. For as Suzuki has said (in chapter 4, section *i*, above):

> Things are going on in a very strict way. There is no exception. Wherever there is something, there is some rule, some truth behind it, which is going on strictly, controlling things without exception. [*WB*, XII 1973: 50]

And similarly, the source of the historical activity of Bodhisattvas in helping others—and the source of the Bodhisattva vow itself—is not, ultimately, some written or spoken teaching regarding notions of charity or duty or saving all beings. Rather, Suzuki says, "wherever you are is how you understand the source of the teaching." According to Suzuki, it is the Bodhisattva's direct awareness of the world of nature—including, of course, her awareness of what Suzuki calls "true nature" as the noumenal ground of all natural phenomena appearing in consciousness (chapter 4, section *ii*, *a*)—that empowers her in her work to realize the vow of saving all beings. This means that as a person practicing the Bodhisattva way I can help others solely through my practice of *zazen*—my practice of seeing form as emptiness and emptiness as form—without entertaining any specific idea of helping:

> When you practice zazen there is no "you" and no "others," your practice includes everything. You are a part of me, and I am a part of you. When we reach this kind of understanding we are the Sambhogakāya Buddha. Everything then takes place within yourself. For one with this understanding there is no objective world anymore. Without trying to help others, we will help others anyway; that is the Sambhogakāya Buddha, and that is the way to help others, the way to preserve our teaching, the way to practice Buddhism. [*WB*, VIII/Spring 1969:13]

Thus the iconclastic words of Chuang-tzŭ—and Alan Watts—which challenge the connection between religious practice and any specific body of transmitted rules and teachings, do not necessarily indicate the absence of a spirit and an insight that are truly Buddhist in Suzuki's sense. For in order to "understand the true source of the teaching transmitted from Buddha"—in order to understand the true source of the teaching of living by vow instead of by karma—Suzuki insists that "to have direct experience of everyday life is the most important thing." So, even though with our words we may distinguish between the Buddhist way and the Taoist way—or between the rules of the monastery and the rules of hopping freights—we should not forget that the true source of Buddha's teaching is to be understood directly "by your eyes, by your nose, ears, or tongue."

And therefore, because "truth itself should be the real Buddha for us," to have direct experience of our everyday life—and, as has been argued in this study, through this direct experience of form, or phenomena, to recognize the truth of emptiness, or what Kant calls the noumenal world—is actually to have direct experience of the Buddha's way, whether one calls oneself a Buddhist, a Taoist, or a simple tramp. And so the true way, Suzuki says, can be understood through my encounter with a stick or a stone—or even, in the spirit of Lin-chi's words above, with the toilet paper I use after moving my bowels:

> So True Way could be a stick. True Way, the original way of the Buddha, could be a stone. Like Ummon said, "It may be toilet paper." (Laughing). . . . It is just instead of Buddha we say, "toilet paper." Anyway, even though you say, "Buddha," it doesn't make much sense. (Laughing) So it may be much better to say, "toilet paper," or "three pounds of hemp," as Tōzan said. [*SL*, XII, 9]

(b)

If you are a teacher you should behave like a teacher.
*[*WB, *VII/Summer 1968:18]*

If a Zen student can practice Zen by hopping freights, or listening to jazz—or using toilet paper—then it might seem that a Zen teacher and a Zen student could both likewise practice Zen while engaging in sexual intercourse together. In the spirit of Lin-chi, such a view of Zen practice might be expressed this way:

> Just be ordinary and nothing special. Eat your food, move your bowels, pass water, and, when you're sexually aroused, go and lie down together.

According to Suzuki, a "Taoist" interpretation of this paraphrase of Lin-chi's words would treat an act of casual sexual intercourse—like the acts of eating, moving one's bowels, and passing water—as something that is done for its own sake, "with . . . not much relationship or not much contact with practice." (*SL*, I, 4). A Buddhist interpretation of these words, on the other hand, would have to treat casual acts of sexual intercourse—just like acts of eating or passing water—as "part of our practice" (*SL*, I, 4). Paraphrasing Suzuki's Buddhist interpretation of the act of eating, I can formulate this possible Buddhist interpretation of the act of intercourse:

> To have sexual intercourse with our teacher and other students is part of our practice . . . for the sake of practice we have sex, not just to enjoy the release of orgasm. To help our way, to practice Buddha's way we have sexual intercourse. [compare *SL*, I, 4]

Such a "Buddhist" interpretation of casual sex, however, hardly seems plausible in the context of the interpretation of Suzuki's account of *zazen* that has been presented in this book. In regard to Suzuki's story of the two Zen monks meeting a woman at the river (chapter 3, section *iii, c*), it is clear that, although Suzuki praised the monk who violated the *letter* of the precepts by carrying the woman across the stream in his arms, he nevertheless was not advocating—or envisioning the possibility of—sexual intercourse with the woman as a part of that monk's practice of the Bodhisattva way. On the contrary, Suzuki praised the monk for *not* thinking about the woman as a sexual object—contrasting the behavior with that of his companion who, while abstaining from the act of physically holding the woman in his arms, continued mentally to "carry" sexual thoughts about her. "To think about it," Suzuki says, "is actually violating the precepts" (*SL*, VIII, 8).

In this same lecture, Suzuki discusses "how we keep our precepts." In the course of the discussion he contrasts our normal way of understanding, in which we dualistically perceive other human beings as objects of desire, with the effort made in *zazen* practice to "see things as they are":

> Usually, why people become attached to the objective world, or to something they see, is because they understand things in only one way: "Here is something very good, very sweet—I have to eat." And we think that something exists here without us—whether we try to eat it or not, we think the cake exists. That is the normal way of understanding. [*SL*, VIII, 3]

But the true understanding of the cake, Suzuki goes on to say, is that "cake becomes cake because we want to eat it." So it is Suzuki's view that "*we make cake.* There is no cake, actually, without us." And once we understand that the cake—the object of our desire—is something we ourselves create, then, "when we understand in that way, we are seeing cake, but we are not seeing cake. And this is how we keep our precepts." [*SL*, VII, 3]

Thus, the Buddhist attitude toward a piece of cake—or toward an object of sexual desire—is not, as Lin-chi's words might suggest, simply to move toward it and eat—or copulate with—it. Eating food in a Buddhist way, Suzuki says, "includes always our mind, our practice (not small mind. . . . Big mind which includes things)":

> And if we think this is just vegetable that is not our way. We must treat things as a part of ourselves which exist in our practice or in our Big Mind. Do you understand this point? . . . small mind means mind which is under limitation of desires or some particular emotional understanding or discrimination. . . . So actually, even though you think you are observing things as it is, actually you are not. [*SL*, I, 5]

To see a person as an object of my sexual desire is not to see her as she is—as a being independent of me and of my act of observing her. So, Suzuki says, "because of our discrimination, or because of our desires we are not observing things as it is. So Buddhist way is trying very hard . . . to eliminate this kind of emotional discrimination or prejudice . . . to see things as it is" (*SL*, I, 5). And "seeing things as it is" means, Suzuki has said, to take into account the influence that the powerful counterweight of desire exerts upon our perceptions and thoughts:

> So when we say "things as it is," it means to practice hard to get rid of our desires. . . . Not to get rid of . . . [but] to count our desires, to calculate. . . . Usually we don't count our desires. Without reflecting on our selfish judgment we say, "He is good . . . bad." [But] Someone who is bad to *me* is not always bad. To someone else he may be a good person. In this way we see things as it is. So when we understand the mind transmitted from Buddha to us we can see things as it is. This is Buddha Mind. [*SL*, 5]

To see the woman as she is, means to practice *not seeing*—not seeing things darkly, as it were, through the stained glass of desire. Thus Suzuki describes the practice of *zazen*:

> The mind we have when we practice zazen is the great mind in which we don't try to see anything. We stop thinking; we stop emotional activity; we just sit. Whatever happens to us we just sit. If something happens we are not bothered by it. It is like something in the great sky. The sky doesn't care . . . whatever happens in the sky . . . even the atomic bomb . . . it doesn't care. That is the mind transmitted from Buddha to us. [*SL*, I, 5]

Thus, from the statements of Suzuki that have been presented in this study, it would appear that Suzuki does not in any way encourage, as a part of Zen practice, either attachment to or pursuit of objects of sexual desire. On the contrary, in describing *zazen* as a practice in which thinking and emotional activity are stopped, in which a kind of profound detachment from "whatever happens to us" is cultivated, in which one realizes the Buddhist vow to help others by making a specific effort *not* to see them as objects of sexual desire, Suzuki would appear to reject the view of Zen practice expressed in my paraphrase of Lin-chi's words: "when you're sexually aroused, go and lie down together."

On the other hand, Suzuki was certainly not puritanical in his attitude toward sexuality. As the abbot of the first Zen training monastery in the United States, he instituted a sexual revolution of sorts in monastic practice by allowing male and female Zen students to live and train together.[12] The fact that Suzuki, a Japanese, not only tolerated the liberal sexual standards of American youth in the late 1960s but actually institutionalized these standards in creating what was possibly the first coeducational training monastery in the history of Buddhism, indicates that he saw no holy alliance between the precepts of Zen practice and the conventional morality of the past. Thus what Rick Fields refers to as "the freedom of American women"[13]—and men as well—to lead sexual lives unsanctioned by matrimony was not seen by Suzuki as an obstacle to Zen training.

The true significance of Fields's example of the sexually promiscuous Zen teacher lies, I believe, not so much in the area of sexual morality as in that of the ethics of the teacher/disciple relationship. The question I want to raise in regard to the example is this: Regardless of the kind of sexual morality prevailing among a particular group of human beings practicing *zazen* together, can a Zen teacher's multiple sexual affairs with his or her students ever be plausibly explained—from the point of view of Zen practice developed in this study—as being, in Suzuki's sense, a part of Buddhist practice?

Of course, any explanation seeking to expand the boundaries of the traditional master/disciple relationship in Zen Buddhism so as to include the practice of sexual intercourse between them would naturally be suspect from a Kantian viewpoint as a possible example of a "natural dialectic":

> That is, a disposition to quibble with . . . strict laws of duty, to throw doubt on their validity or at least on their purity and strictness, and to make them, where possible, more adapted to our wishes and inclinations. [*GW*, 23]

Because modern Buddhist monks and nuns have no "strict laws of duty" proscribing sexual love and marriage, the "natural dialectic" that one might imagine occuring in the mind of a Zen monk or nun who wished to rationalize his or her sexual affairs with students would probably not occur in a situation in which, say, a nun fell in love with one of her students and went on to have a long-term relationship or a marriage with him. For the pursuit and cultivation of a mutually satisfying sexual and emotional relationship with another person cannot, from Suzuki's viewpoint, be plausibly interpreted as a breach of duty.

In the example described by Fields, however, the monk's sexual relations with his students were clearly impulsive, casual affairs. "Fresh from the monastery and used to the conventional morality of Japan," he "had been swept off his feet by the freedom of American women."[14] And in respect to impulsive, casual sexual relationships, it does seem possible there are Buddhist duties that such a monk might be tempted to quibble with, if he were to try to rationalize this behavior. Such duties would not, of course, be expressed by (nonexistent) Buddhist precepts prohibiting falling in love or having a sexual affair with someone. Rather, it seems more likely that they would be rules or guidelines applying to relationships between human beings in general, and the relationship between a teacher and his or her students in particular.

Of course, the overarching Buddhist rule or guideline regarding human relationships is given in the Bodhisattva vow to devote one's life to helping other people realize the universally held goals of happiness and perfection of character. And in the particular case of a teacher's relationship to her or his students, this vow would seemingly require the teacher to make the best possible use of her relationship with her students for the purpose of helping them attain these same universally held goals. So the critical question to ask of a Zen teacher who engages in casual—and perhaps the clearest definition of casual would be "multiple"—sexual affairs with his or her students, is this: How do you explain your sexual relationships with your students as an expression of your vow to work for the salvation of all sentient beings?

In the case of the Zen monk referred to by Fields, if he indeed felt "swept off his feet" by a combination of the absence of familiar moral conventions and the presence of willing sexual partners, one would expect that he might, in all honesty, decline to explain his conduct in respect to the Bodhisattva vow. Probably he would simply acknowledge that he had become carried away by sexual desire—perhaps going on to blame his actions on the freedom of American women! Such an acknowledgment, while it might reflect unfavorably upon the Zen teacher's personal character, would not, as Kant says, "throw doubt on the validity" of what must be considered—at least in many cases—a strict law of duty for a teacher:

the duty not to allow sexuality to insert itself into the teacher-student relationship.

This view of a teacher's duty is universally held in cases where the teacher-student relationship involves students who may be, for various reasons, especially vulnerable to sexual abuse—children and mentally disturbed or retarded individuals. However, as differences between a teacher's and a student's age and mental and physical capacities diminish, the view that there is a general duty, applicable to all possible types of teacher-student relationships, that prohibits a teacher from engaging in multiple sexual relations with his or her students becomes less plausible. Clearly, the case of an unmarried ski instructor who, during a single ski season, has successive affairs with several of her vacationing bachelor pupils is worlds apart from the case of a teacher of mentally retarded children who forces his young students to participate in sexual activities.

The case of a religious teacher who becomes sexually involved with several of his or her students obviously lies somewhere between these two extremes. On the one hand, a person who joins a religious sect is usually either an adult or someone near the age of adulthood. Thus it might seem that, like the ski instructor, a religious teacher does not have the same duty to abstain from entering into sexual relations with his adult students as he might have if those students were either children or childlike in their mental or physical capacities. However, as Suzuki's disciple and successor, Richard Baker, has pointed out, "the student-teacher relationship [in Zen practice], lacking specific definition or tradition, shifts easily—especially when stressed—into spousal and parental relationships."[15] This would mean that, according to Baker's observations, there is a tendency for some Zen students to *become childlike* in their relationship with their teacher, confusing this relationship both with what he calls "the intimate, committed, usually sexual relationship" of a wife to her husband, and the loving, but at the same time utterly dependent, relationship of a child to its parent.[16]

Baker's observations about the childlike behavior of Zen students in their relations with their teacher bring to mind Freud's observations about the phenomenon of transference which occurs almost universally in patients undergoing psychotherapy:

> The patient is not satisfied with regarding the analyst in the light of reality as a helper and adviser who, moreover, is remunerated for the trouble he takes and who would himself be content with some such role as that of a guide on a difficult mountain climb. On the contrary, the patient sees in him the return, the reincarnation, of some important figure out of his childhood or past, and consequently transfers on to him feelings and reactions which undoubtedly applied to this prototype. This fact of transference soon proves to be a factor of undreamt-of importance, on the one hand an instrument of irreplaceable value and on the other hand a source of serious dangers.[17]

Alan Watts has suggested that in Buddhism and certain other Eastern religions, "we do not find either philosophy or religion as these are understood in the West. We find something more nearly resembling psychotherapy."[18] The main resemblance between an Eastern religious practice like Zen Buddhism and Western psychotherapy, Watts says, is "in the concern of both with bringing about changes of consciousness, changes in our ways of feeling our own existence and our relation to human society and the natural world."[19] If Watts is correct—as I believe he is—in viewing Zen Buddhism as a kind of psychotherapy because it is concerned "with bringing about changes of consciousness" in the Buddhist practicer, then it would not be at all surprising if something similar to the psychotherapeutic phenomenon of transference should occur in the context of the emotionally charged relationship between a Zen student and his or her teacher. While objectively acknowledging his relationship with his teacher to be a limited one—"as that of a guide on a difficult mountain climb"—it is clear that subjectively a Zen student might well be tempted to "see in him the return, the reincarnation, of some important figure out of his childhood or past, and consequently [transfer] on to him feelings and reactions which undoubtedly applied to this prototype."

The following description of the traditional Zen master/disciple relationship by Watts lends support to the view that this relationship provides fertile ground for the growth of transference:

> When at last the applicant gains admission to the master, he finds himself confronted by a very formidable figure—usually a much older man, superbly self-confident and at ease, completely present and undistracted, and with the kind of twinkle in his eyes which indicates that he sees through the student like glass. In Chinese and Japanese culture the Zen master is, furthermore, a great authority figure, far more so than father or grandfather, and the student meets with him in the most formal circumstances—the master enthroned in his inner sanctum, and the student bowing most humbly before him. Everything is done, in short, to impress the student that in being admitted he has received the greatest condescension from a personage who has attained heights of wisdom far beyond his ken.[20]

Richard Baker, commenting on his early years as a Zen teacher, remarks "how great a problem was the seemingly enormous power I had in other people's lives. I didn't realize then how much power they assumed and gave me in their lives."[21] Thus, what is being called "transference" in the Zen student/teacher relationship can obviously create problems for both teacher and student. Describing what can happen to a person experiencing the transference phenomenon, Freud says:

> He behaves like a child who has no power of judgment of his own but blindly believes anyone whom he loves and no one who is a stranger to him. The danger of these states of transference evidently lies in the patient's misunderstanding their nature and taking them for fresh real experiences instead of reflections of the past. If he (or she) becomes aware of the strong erotic desire that lies concealed behind the . . . transference, he believes that he has fallen passionately in love; if the transference changes over, then he feels insulted and neglected.[22]

The task of the psychotherapist—and, to follow Watts in the association of Zen practice with psychotherapy, the task of the Zen teacher—in helping people deal with emotional problems arising out of the psychological state of transference is, Freud says:

> Constantly to tear the patient out of his menacing illusion and to show him again and again that what he takes to be new

> real life is a reflection of the past. And lest he should fall into a state in which he is inaccessible to all evidence, the analyst takes care that neither the love nor the hostility reach an extreme height. This is effected by preparing him in good time for these possibilities and by not overlooking the first signs of them. Careful handling of the transference on these lines is as a rule richly rewarded.[23]

Freud also issues a warning to psychotherapists—a warning that seems applicable to Zen teachers as well—that they themselves are not immune to the powerful effects of transference. He cautions therapists "against misusing this new influence," gained through transference, whereby the therapist/teacher becomes an object of intense love and admiration:

> However much the analyst may be tempted to become a teacher, model, and ideal for other people and to create men in his own image, he should not forget that that is not his task in the analytic relationship, and indeed that he will be disloyal to his task if he allows himself to be led on by his inclinations. If he does, he will only be repeating a mistake of the parents who crushed their child's independence by their influence, and he will only be replacing the patient's earlier dependence by a new one. In all his attempts at improving and educating the patient the analyst should respect his individuality.[24]

If the task of a Zen teacher is correctly described by Watts as being similar to the task of the psychotherapist in that both try to help people bring about major, unsettling "changes in consciousness, changes in our ways of feeling our own existence and our relation to human society and the natural world," then like a psychotherapist, a Zen teacher will be, as Freud says, "disloyal to his task" of helping his students if in his relationships with them "he allows himself to be led on by his inclinations." This means that just as it is the teacher/therapist's duty, according to Freud, "constantly to tear the patient out of his menacing illusion and to show him again and again that what he takes to be new real life is a reflection of the past," so it is also his duty constantly to tear *himself* out of that menacing illusion—referred to in psychotherapeutic language as "counter-transference"—whereby he is "tempted to become a teacher, model, and ideal for other people and to create men in his own image."

From this view of a Zen teacher's duty, Fields's case of the Zen monk who slept with one or more of his students might justifiably be treated as an example of a violation of the ethics of the master/disciple relationship. For, from the psychotherapeutic perspective just developed—and from Richard Baker's observations of the behavior of his students—Zen students might be considered highly likely to develop a transference-type relationship with their teacher, wherein they idealize and fall in love with her or him, mistaking for "new real life" feelings that are but a reflection of the effects of past parental relationships. And—certainly from a psychotherapeutic perspective, but also, it would seem, from the perspective of the Buddhist vow to help all beings in their efforts to realize happiness and perfect their character—it is clearly a Zen teacher's *duty* in the context of the student/teacher relationship to take care, in Freud's words, "that neither the love nor the hostility [in the transference relationship] reach an extreme height." This duty will be discharged, Freud goes on to say, by preparing the student "in good time for these possibilities and by not overlooking the first signs of them." But Zen teachers will be negligent in their duty if they overlook the signs of transference in their students, and doubly negligent if they compound this mistake by succumbing to the temptation of the counter-transference—succumbing, that is, to their inclination to become "a teacher, model, and ideal" for their students.

Baker acknowledges the problems that arose in his own teaching experience when he "took it for granted that Zen Center students understood that the teacher-student relationship was neither parental or spousal."[25] For, by not realizing "how much power they assumed and gave me in their lives," Baker was indeed, it seems, guilty of having overlooked the first signs of transference in his students, thus failing to prepare them, as Freud says, "in good time for these possibilities." As Baker himself puts it, "I could have shed the projections better."[26]

Of course, as Freud acknowledges, the transference phenomenon is "an instrument of irreplaceable value" in psychotherapy, as well as "a source of serious dangers." For the patient's childlike attachment to the therapist as a wise and compassionate parent provides what Freud calls "an opportunity for a sort of *after-education*" of the patient: "it can correct mistakes for which his parents were responsible in educating him."[27] Similarly, if Zen training is thought of as a form of growth-inducing psychotherapy, it can be seen how the childlike love and respect that a Zen student often has for her or his Zen teacher can provide an opportunity for a kind of reliving and restructuring of an earlier period of growing up under the guidance of one's actual parents.

Again, however, the constant danger in the transference situation is that the person playing the role of the idealized parent figure will succumb to the heady effects of the counter-transference and forget the fact that he or she is playing the role of "model and ideal" for the sole purpose of aiding the student in psychological growth and development. Psychotherapists are specifically trained to be aware of this danger, but Zen teachers—so it would appear from Richard Baker's comments—are not. It is in this context that I would suggest the case of the Zen monk "fresh from the monastery" should be understood. Not recognizing the manifestation of transference in a student's expression of passionate love for him, the monk mistook this "reflection of the past" for "new real life." And "led on by his inclinations" to be loved and admired, the monk allowed the Zen teacher/student relationship to "shift easily," as Baker puts it, into a spousal (sexual) and parental relationship.

One might feel some pity for Zen teachers who mistake their students' delusory attachment to a prototype from the past for "new real" love for themselves. Nevertheless, according to the interpretation of Zen practice developed in this study, it is clear that the Zen teacher—as a person who has vowed to work selflessly for the salvation of all beings—has a responsibility to help each student understand and break free from the delusory and compulsive effects of attachment—attachment that, in the transference situation, is conditioned and determined by ghostly manifestations of the past. And it is not just Freud's view, but the view of Suzuki and Kant as well, that those whose vocation it is to help others by various skillful means—including the irreplaceable but dangerous means of the transference—will be disloyal to their task if they allow themselves to be led on by their inclinations, instead of making the fulfillment of their duty to others (and to themselves) the sole, guiding reason for their actions.

Appendix: Dōgen and Kant

A Kantian interpretation of Dōgen's writings on Zen practice would obviously require a book in itself. In this appendix I will limit myself to discussing the compatibility of the interpretation of Zen practice developed in this study with views expressed in three contemporary studies of Dōgen, each of which treats the ethical dimension in his account of Zen practice. These three studies are Masanobu Takahashi's *The Essence of Dōgen*,[1] Thomas P. Kasulis's *Zen Action/Zen Person*,[2] and Francis Cook's essay, "Dōgen's View of Authentic Selfhood and its Socio-ethical implications."[3] I will argue that the two major theses of the Kantian interpretation of Zen practice developed above are to a significant degree compatible with views expressed in all three of these studies. My arguments will necessarily be brief, but I hope nonetheless to convince a doubtful reader that there is no reason to reject summarily the possibility of interpreting Dōgen's writings from a Kantian perspective.

I will first attempt to demonstrate that thesis Z1 of the present study—zazen *practice is a necessary means for realizing the requirements of moral law, as Kant understands these requirements*—does not conflict with Dōgen's view of the relationship between *zazen* practice and ethical conduct, as this view is interpreted by Takahashi and Kasulis. Both these authors, I shall argue, understand Dōgen to be advancing the view that the state of purity of mind necessary for fully realizing the requirements of moral precepts is a product of the insight into emptiness that is cultivated in *zazen*. And such an understanding of the role of *zazen* as a necessary means for fully realizing the requirements of moral law parallels Kant's view—as it has been presented in this study—of the necessary role that a discipline of the speculative restriction of reason plays in cultivating that consciousness of freedom as emptiness, which is itself the pure, noumenally grounded mind of morality.

Secondly, I shall try to demonstrate that Dōgen, like Kant, understands the primary purpose of religious practice to be ethical in nature. That is, following the arguments developed by Takahashi, Kasulis, and Cook as they relate to the arguments developed in this study, I shall try to show that, for Dōgen, attainment of insight into emptiness through *zazen* practice is never an end in itself for the practicer, but rather a *means* by which the practicer can become like Buddha and act with unselfish compassion in the world for the benefit of all beings. In the course of this second demonstration I will first argue that for Dōgen, as for Kant, the relationship between *zazen* (or the practice of a discipline of the speculative restriction of reason) and the fulfillment of the requirements of moral precepts is truly reciprocal, in that, just as Dōgen believes the cultivation of insight into emptiness to be necessary for the realization of moral precepts, so he also believes the practice of respectful obedience to the requirements of moral precepts to be necessary for attaining insight into emptiness. Then I will argue that thesis Z2 of the present study is not in conflict with Dōgen's account of Zen practice, as presented by Takahashi and Cook, by showing how these two authors affirm the view that for Dōgen the Bodhisattva vow to save all sentient beings must be the primary motivating intention behind the practice of *zazen*.

i: Thesis Z1 Tentatively Applied to Dōgen: Zazen *Practice, According to Dōgen, Is a Necessary Means for Realizing the Requirements of Moral Law, as Kant Understands these Requirements.*

In a footnote to the first chapter of *The Essence of Dōgen*, Masanobu Takahashi compares Dōgen's notion of *shikan-taza* or "*zazen* for *zazen's* sake" (*ED*, 4)[4] with Kant's notion that morality should be practiced for the sake of the moral law alone:

> Kant insists that morality should be based upon a pure objective criterion, not upon concrete reality such as personal happiness in one's daily life. The moral will of the individual ought to be pure. We find the same philosophical bias in Dōgen's idea of *"zazen for zazen."* [*ED*, 83]

The difference between Kant and Dōgen, Takahashi goes on to argue, is "that Dōgen tries to locate this purity of the moral will in the practice of *zazen.* He does not posit a theoretical explanation of it" (*ED*, 83). But, as has been argued in chapter 4, section *ii (a)* of this study, the capacity to practice morality for the sake of the moral law is not, for Kant, dependent upon any theoretical explanation or understanding:

> There is no need of science or philosophy for knowing what a person has to do in order to be honest and good, and indeed to be wise and virtuous. It might even be surmised in advance that acquaintance with what everyone is obliged to do, and so also to know, will be the affair of every person, even the most ordinary. [*GW*, 403–4][5]

Moreover, Kant views the purity of the moral will as a condition of "negative perfection" (*KP*, 160), or "moral apathy" (*MM*, 407). As has been argued in chapter 3, section *iii (c)* above, this mental condition can be fully realized and maintained only through the practice of a discipline of the *restriction* of theoretical understanding. Thus it has been claimed in this study that Kant's discipline of the speculative restriction of reason, when viewed in its practical context as an expression of the human effort to cultivate moral purity, performs precisely the same function as *zazen.* For the practical function of Kant's Critical discipline is to awaken in the practicer a consciousness of freedom from "the impetuous importunity of the inclinations" based on insight into the emptiness of both theoretical understanding and empirical knowledge when applied to the self.[6] Therefore, if Dōgen, as Takahashi suggests, locates the purity of the moral will in the practice of *zazen,* then thesis Z1—zazen *practice is a necessary means for realizing the requirements of moral law*—can indeed be tentatively applied to Dōgen's account of *zazen,* provided that (a) Dōgen understands the condition of purity of mind cultivated in *zazen* to be a necessary condition for acting in a morally praiseworthy way, and (b) Dōgen's view of *zazen* practice is compatible with the view of *zazen* as a discipline of the speculative restriction of reason, as developed in this study.

That Dōgen does understand the condition of purity of will cultivated in *shikan-taza*, or "*zazen* for *zazen's* sake," to be essential for acting in a morally praiseworthy way is indicated both by Takahashi's discussion of Dōgen's ethics in *The Essence of Dōgen* and by Thomas P. Kasulis in *Zen Action/Zen Person.* According to Kasulis, full realization of the conventional moral command "do no evil" means, for Dōgen, to cultivate through *zazen* practice a state of mind in which evil is no longer produced (*ZA*, 94–95).[7] And attaining this state of mind of "nonproduction" is in itself both necessary and sufficient to fully realize the commands of morality (*ZA*, 99, 102). Similarly, Takahashi makes the claim that for Dōgen the practice of insight into emptiness through *zazen* is "inclusive" of the practice of observing moral precepts:

> Inclusiveness means that all the commandments of Buddha are included in *zazen* itself. Thus *zazen* is practiced for its own sake, because all the rules and commandments of Buddha can be observed by adhering to it alone. [*ED*, 4–5]

Moreover, Dōgen's own words demonstrate that he does indeed consider *zazen* practice as the essential means for keeping moral precepts:

> When it says to recite the preceptual scripture day and night and to wholeheartedly keep the precepts, it means that one should follow the practice of the Ancients and concentrate only on sitting. When sitting in meditation, what precept is not maintained? What merit is not produced?[8]

Thus neither of these Dōgen scholars, nor Dōgen himself, contests the view advanced in thesis Z1 that *zazen* practice is a necessary means for fully realizing the requirements of moral law—where "fully realizing the requirements of moral law" refers to realizing a perfectly virtuous mental state in which, as Kasulis expresses it, "the efficacy of one's spiritual cultivation is such that one is no longer capable of murder" or other evils (*ZA*, 96). Kasulis, however, like Takahashi, suggests that Kant's notion of realizing the requirements of moral law can be distinguished from Dōgen's notion of cultivating a state of moral purity through *zazen* practice because Kant adopts a theoretical or *thinking* approach to morality (*ZA*, 98). Kant's "thinking" approach, Kasulis says, is incompatible with Dōgen's view that "without-thinking" is "in itself the essential art of *zazen*" (*ZA*, 71).[9] In what follows I shall argue that Dōgen's description of *zazen* as the practice of "without-thinking" is in fact compatible with the Kantian interpretation of *zazen* developed in this study.

Kasulis distinguishes Dōgen's notion of 'without–thinking,' or *hishiryo* from his notions of 'thinking' (*shiryo*) and 'not–thinking' (*fushiryo*). 'Thinking' includes most of what we typically regard as consciousness (*ZA*, 73), while 'not–thinking' is the conscious effort a person sometimes makes "to blank his mind and break off all trains of thought" (*ZA*, 74). 'Without–thinking,' Kasulis says, is a third, more fundamental mode of consciousness, which is "prereflective" (*ZA*, 75–76). That is to say, 'without-thinking' is the natural, spontaneous experience of being conscious in the world before we begin self-consciously to reflect upon that experience or to attempt to block such reflection. And for Dōgen, *zazen* practice "is the epitome of without-thinking" (*ZA*, 77).

Kasulis's explanation of Dōgen's view of *zazen* practice is based on a phenomenological interpretation of Dōgen's writings, which, in some important ways, is philosophically incompatible with the Kantian approach adopted in the present study.[10] However, in reference to Kasulis's explanation of Dōgen's three modes of consciousness, it can be shown convincingly that neither consciousness of the commands of moral law nor the practice of a discipline of the speculative restriction of reason are, for Kant, accurately described as "a thinking mode" of consciousness (see *ZA*, 98). Awareness of the command of moral law is not, for Kant, derived from any thinking process, because, as has been shown above in chapter 4, section *ii (a)*, the fundamental law of pure practical reason is a principle *originally present* as a "fact" of human consciousness (*KP*, 31, 47). Awareness of this fundamental principle, Kant says, "forces itself upon us" a priori, and is not generated by analytical thinking or by reflection on experience (*KP*, 31):

> Thus the objective reality of the moral law can be proved through no deduction, through no exertion of the theoretical, speculative, or empirically supported reason; and, even if one were willing to renounce its apodictic certainty, it could not be confirmed by any experience and thus proved a posteriori. Nevertheless it is firmly established of itself. [*KP*, 47]

Therefore, because the moral efficacy of Kant's fundamental principle of pure practical reason is dependent upon "no exertion of the theoretical, speculative, or empirically supported reason," Kant's moral theory is not, I believe, accurately characterized as "a thinking mode" of morality.

Still less plausibly can Kant's approach to morality be interpreted as a "thinking" approach when one considers his notion of the noumenal self as the transcendental ground of freedom. As discussed above in chapter 3, section *i*, by use of the complementary concepts of phenomenon and noumenon I can think of myself both in terms of how I appear to myself as an object of my sense experience and in terms of who I am *independently* of how I appear to myself. It is only in terms of this latter way of thinking about myself, Kant argues, that the ideas of freedom and morality make any sense (*KV*, Bxxix). But this latter way of thinking about myself is really a form of 'without-thinking' (*hishyiro*), as Kasulis explains Dōgen's use of this term. 'Without-thinking' Kasulis writes, "neither affirms nor denies, accepts nor rejects, believes nor disbelieves. In fact, it does not objectify either implicitly or explicitly" (*ZA*, 75). Similarly, Kant insists that the notion of a noumenal self, correctly used, never signifies, either implicitly or explictly, an objective reality. Rather, it signifies the emptiness that marks the limits of all conceptual forms of knowledge:

> The concept of a noumenon is necessary, to prevent sensible intuition from being extended to things in themselves, and thus to limit the objective validity of sensible knowledge. The remaining things, to which it [sensible knowledge] does not apply, are entitled noumena, in order to show that this knowledge cannot extend its domain over everything which the understanding thinks. But none the less we are unable to comprehend how such noumena can be possible, and the

> domain that lies out beyond the sphere of appearances is for us empty. [*KV*, B3111]

Kant says that the concept 'noumenon' is "a *limiting concept*, the function of which is to curb the pretensions of sensibility; and it is therefore only of negative employment" (*KV*, B311). However, this purely negative use of the concept 'noumenon' does not mean that by practicing Kant's discipline of the speculative restriction of reason, whereby I critically perceive the flux of appearances in my consciousness as the "sensible sign" (*KV*, B574) of noumenal emptiness, I am practicing a kind of 'not–thinking' (*fushiryo*). For as Kant indicates in his chapter on the paralogisms of pure reason, to refuse to succumb to the temptation to flesh out my notion of myself as noumenon is not to *stop* my thinking but rather to *divert* it "from fruitless and extravagant speculation to fruitful practical employment . . . directed always to objects of experience only" (*KV*, B21). Thus the function of the thought of an empty noumenal self in the practice of Kant's Critical discipline is not that of stopping the mind but rather that of purifying it of delusory thinking based on a falsely objectified view of the self. In refusing to objectify appearances in consciousness as things in themselves while refusing, at the same time, to affirm or deny the existence of a domain beyond these appearances, the practicer of Kant's Critical discipline truly does engage in a form of 'without–thinking' similar to that insight into emptiness cultivated in *zazen* practice. And the mental state cultivated through this discipline might well be termed, phenomenological implications aside, "a nonconceptual or prereflective mode of consciousness" (*ZA*, 75).

To the extent that Kasulis's concept of a "prereflective" mode of consciousness reflects the phenomenological orientation of his interpretation of Dōgen, this concept cannot properly be applied to Kant without acknowledging the fundamental differences between Kant's critical philosophy and Husserl's phenomenology—differences that, as Husserl himself maintained, "are not incompatible . . . with an inner affinity."[11] A discussion of such differences is beyond the scope of this book. However, I hope that in pointing out those aspects of Kant's moral theory that relate to a state of consciousness purified of the delusory effects of conceptualization and objectification I have shown that there is indeed an "inner affinity" between a Kantian and a phenomenological interpretation of the mode of consciousness cultivated through *zazen* practice.

It is by setting ourselves free from self, Takahashi says in his explanation of the place of selflessness, or *muga*, in Dōgen's ethics, that "we can acquire that basic strength with which to reject *evil* and choose *good*" (*ED*, 29). Thus Dōgen, according to Takahashi, sees the cultivation of a radical state of selflessness as a necessary means to the end of realizing the requirements of conventional morality. And like Takahashi, Kasulis also understands the elimination of selfishness to be the necessary means by which ethical ideals are realized according to Dōgen's view of Zen practice. This is shown in Kasulis's discussion of the ethical import of Dōgen's statement in *Shōbōgenzō*, "Genjō-kōan"—"to study the self is to forget the self":[12]

> Zen . . . eliminates selfishness by modeling oneself after oneself and, therefore, forgetting oneself. For Zen, compassion and intuitive wisdom are the same because both radiate from the pre-ego mode of without-thinking. Only if the ego has been extirpated can there be compassion without distinctions and wisdom without presuppositions. [*ZA*, 98]

The arguments advanced in the present study in support of thesis Z1—zazen *practice . . . is a necessary means for realizing the requirements of moral law, as Kant understands these requirements*—would thus appear applicable to Dōgen's view of *zazen* as well as to Suzuki's. For the practice of Kant's discipline of the speculative restriction of reason—just like the practice of Dōgen's *zazen* of 'without-thinking'—produces in the practicer a state of mind transcending selfishness, a state of mind in which practicers indeed forget, or discard, their belief in an objectively real, empirical self in order to "model" themselves after an empty noumenal self that can be the subject of free, moral action. Furthermore, like Kasulis's interpretation of Dōgen's "Genjō-kōan," Takahashi's interpretation of Dōgen's practice of *kū*, or emptiness, lends support to the claim that there is a close resemblance between the Kantian view of selflessness as the *product* of insight into the empty, noumenal nature of the self, and Dōgen's view of selflessness as the practical product of insight into *kū*, or emptiness. For Dōgen, as Takahashi interprets him, *muga* (no–self) is fully realized only through the practice of *kū*, whereby the concept of emptiness is applied to "every physical phenomenon and the various physical actions proceeding from the human spirit" (*ED*, 29, 33).

One important reason why complete selflessness in our human conduct is realized only through the practice of emptiness is that, as Takahashi explains:

> Even in [practicing] altruism, without *kū* we shall not be able to live in accord with such an ideal because our keen interest in the result of our altruistic deeds is likely to have the adverse effect of egoism. We should practice altruistic deeds and yet still transcend them, in other words, should turn them into *kū* so that they may become true in themselves. [*ED*, 34]

Takahashi then goes on to remark, in a footnote comment, that Dōgen's notion of *kū*, or emptiness, "is exactly the same as Kant" when Kant speaks of a duty to promote another's happiness "without hoping for something in return" (*ED*, 84). Thus, the transcendence of self-centeredness that is both the practical result of the practice of the Critical discipline and the identifying feature of a truly moral act for Kant, is seen by Takahashi as similar to the nonegotistic manifestation of empty self-nature cultivated in Zen practice.

However, Takahashi sees a tension between what he calls "the pure abstract quality of Kant's ethical theory" and the fact that "in practice what is expected in our daily lives is not an abstract type of morality but, real results from it" (*ED*, 84). This tension, Takahashi claims, leads Kant to abandon at times the abstract purity of his ethics in the interest of focusing on real results. Thus, for example, in Part II of *The Metaphysic of Morals* Kant seems to reduce his ethics to a form of utilitarianism in speaking of a duty to promote happiness (*ED*, 84). In contrast to Kant, Takahashi concludes, Dōgen's notion of *kū*, "takes the real very much into consideration, and yet it dares to transcend it":

> *Kū* sets much value on the real way of morality, but at the same time it tries to transcend it so that worldly matters such as fame or profit are quite foreign to it. It aims at, in a sense, a purity which transcends purity itself. [*ED*, 85]

Takahashi is correct in associating Kant's promulgation of a duty to promote happiness with a concern that the practice of morality be relevant to the reality of daily life. However, I believe he is wrong in viewing this concern of Kant as a "contradiction in his ethical position of deontology" (*ED*, 85). In chapter 4, section *iii (b)* of this study it has been argued that the attainment of universal happiness is, for Kant, an inseparable part of that highest good which *morality requires* us to strive to realize through our actions in this world. Thus, for Kant, it is the moral law—and not the worldly, utilitarian concern for human happiness—that remains at the heart of our duty to promote the happiness of others. On the other hand, the fact that Kant's ethical theory recognizes the promotion of human happiness as a moral duty is sufficient, it seems to me, to rebut Takahashi's charge that "Kant's formative ethics is likely to lay so much stress on purity, that it may disregard the real facts" of human life (*ED*, 85).

Takahashi observes that Kant's insistence that actions of an ethical nature be performed for the sake of duty alone—and not for the sake of satisfying our inclinations—is related to Dōgen's instruction in the *Shōbōgenzō Zuimonki* that "the primary requisite for the followers of Buddha is to leave self-centeredness" (*ED*, 85). However, he warns:

> [Kant's] theory of duty as an act of pure will may sometimes go against natural inclination. A charitable act from pure duty may possibly disregard the heart of the object of such charity and even turn out to be harmful [*ED*, 85]

In contrast to the practicer of "Kant's pure ethics," Takahashi goes on to say, "the practicer of *kū* wishes happiness to some wretched person out of real sympathy and will share joy with him when it is attained. This is true charity" (*ED*, 85).

Takahashi's criticism suggests that Kant's insight into noumenal emptiness may, in its practical, ethical expression, produce different results from the practice of *kū* because the Kantian practice involves an unnatural preoccupation with obedience to duty alone and "may sometimes go against natural inclination." Takahashi contrasts Kant's ethics with the ethical expression of Dōgen's Zen, which he sees as being intimately connected with the expression of human emotions such as sympathy and joy. His criticism raises the issue of how Dōgen and Kant each view the relationship between duty and natural inclination. But this issue—because it relates to the discussions in chapter 4, sections *i* and *ii*, concerning the reciprocal relationship between *zazen* practice and respectful obedience to duty—is best discussed in connection with the second major thesis of the present study as it might be applied to Dōgen's account of Zen practice.

ii: Thesis Z2 Tentatively Applied to Dōgen: In order to Practice Zazen *Correctly, According to Dōgen, My Sole Intention in Performing that Practice Should Be that of Realizing the Requirements of Moral Law, As Kant Understands these Requirements.*

(a)

In defense of the view that Dōgen affirms a reciprocally supportive relationship between respectful obedience to unconditional rules, or precepts, and cultivation of the enlightened mind of Zen practice

It is certainly true, as Takahashi suggests in the footnote passage discussed above, that Kant, while he acknowledges the rightness and amiability of actions based upon emotions such as sympathy and joy (*GW*, 398), emphasizes that actions performed due to the influence of such emotions "stand on the same footing as . . . inclinations"—that is, they may deserve "praise and encouragement, but not esteem" (*GW*, 398). The most esteemed type of action for Kant—the type of action that alone has "moral content" (*GW*, 398)—is, as Takahashi indicates, an act done from pure duty. And the characteristic feature of a charitable act performed from pure duty is, Kant says, that even if every human emotion and inclination prompting one to act charitably to another person were absent as a motivating influence, still in that apathetic condition a person could nonetheless act charitably solely for the reason that to act in such a manner is the way of duty (*GW*, 398). Only in performing an action for the sole reason that it is the way of duty, Kant says, is that state of selfless purity achieved that confers upon an action true moral worth (*GW*, 398).

However, while Takahashi correctly depicts Kant's ethics as grounded on respectful obedience to the way of duty, rather than to the "way" of natural inclinations and human emotions, I think that this aspect of Kant's thought, far from distancing him from Dōgen, actually draws him closer in spirit to Dōgen's view that Zen practice involves the abandonment of self-centeredness. For in the *Shōbōgenzō Zuimonki* Dōgen says explicitly, "people who study the Way must abandon human emotions. What is called abandonment of human emotions is to go in accord with the Way of Buddhas" (*SZ*, 30–31).[13] And again, further on in the same passage, Dōgen says:

> One must only first abandon worldly emotions and enter into the Way of Buddhas. To enter into the Way of Buddhas is to abandon the act of distinguishing good and bad in your own mind. . . . What you think in your own mind to be good, or what people of the world think is good, is not necessarily good. Therefore, forget the views of others, abandon even your own mind, and follow the Teachings of Buddha. . . . Even though you think a certain thing may be good and should be in accord with the Way of Buddhas, though you wish to perform and carry it out, if it is something not included in the practice of the Buddhas and Patriarchs, you should not do it. [*SZ*, 31]

I understand Dōgen to be saying in this passage that leaving self-centeredness through entering into the way of the Buddhas may involve sometimes going "against natural inclination," as Takahashi critically describes the practice of Kant's ethics of pure duty. Thus, far from counseling practicers of Zen to allow the human emotions of sympathy and joy to guide their conduct, Dōgen would appear to be saying that "even though you think a certain thing [for instance, performing a charitable act] may be good," you should nonetheless "abandon even your own mind and follow the Teachings of Buddha." I do not think Dōgen is implying that the teachings of Buddha might, in some conceivable situation, forbid the performance of charitable acts. But I do think he is saying, in a truly Kantian manner, that even in the performance of charitable acts, the Buddhist trainee should learn to base such actions on respectful obedience to the Buddhist *teaching* to act charitably, rather than on one's own human emotions or natural inclinations.

Many of Dōgen's statements in the *Shōbōgenzō Zuimonki* express a truly Kantian view of the role of duty in religious practice:

> Although one carries out difficult and painful practices without anxiety for his body, as long as his mind has not entered the Way of Buddhas and he refuses to do what is contrary to his own inclinations, even though it be the Way of Buddhas, he has not abandoned his mind. [*SZ*, 22–23]

> Without retaining your own subjective appreciation, you should follow the community and act in accord with the behavior of the ancients. [*SZ*, 3]

> Students of recent times cling to their own emotive views and base themselves on their own opinions . . . as long as they are wandering in delusion seeking something which resembles their own emotional judgments, most of them make no progress on the Buddha Way. [*SZ*, 12]

> It is when you carry on without any quest from your own mind, even as to fulfilling the Way or obtaining the result, that you would be in conformity with the principle that you should not seek outwardly. [*SZ*, 47]

> The Buddhist Teaching should be studied only for its own sake. The basic reality of this is that one must cast off his own body and mind, retaining nothing, and give it over to the vast ocean of the Buddhist Teaching. After that, without being concerned with any right or wrong, without maintaining personal attitudes, even if it be something that one insistently wants to do, whatever would not accord with the principle of the Buddhist Teaching should be abandoned. . . . Once hav-

> ing gone over to the Way of Buddhahood, think no more of yourself, but just continue to act in accordance with the rules of the Buddhist Teaching, and do not harbor personal prejudices. . . . When the heart seeks nothing, it is at peace. [*SZ*, 89]

> The attitude needed to study the Path is that even if they go against one's own ideas, if they are the words of one's teacher, or the stated principles of the Sage's Teachings, one should follow them completely, and abandon one's original personal opinions. This mind is the foremost requirement of the study of the Way. [*SZ*, 100]

Thus Kant's view that moral purity is attained by selfless obedience to the way of duty would appear to be closely related in spirit to Dōgen's view that the pure mind of Zen practice is attained by transcending the mind ruled by natural inclinations and human emotions through the practice of selfless obedience to the "rules of the Buddhist teaching." Moreover, Dōgen, like Kant, would likewise seem vulnerable to the criticism that he at times appears willing to carry his principle of selfless obedience to extremes that, as Takahashi has warned, may "even turn out to be harmful." Thus he offers the following counsel to a Zen student struggling with the difficult decision whether to join the monastic community or stay home and care for his aged mother who depends upon him for support:

> Once you have given up your life to enter the Way of Buddhas, even if your old mother should starve to death, would not the virtue of having allowed her only son to enter the Way be a good help to her attainment of the Way? [*SZ*, 67][14]

Just as Kant says that one should perform one's action for the sake of duty alone, so Dōgen, in his essay "Points to Watch in Buddhist Training," tells his students that "you should train for the sake of Buddhism alone":[15]

> The various Buddhas do not show deep compassion for all sentient beings for either their own or others' sake. . . . Simply practice Buddhism for the sake of Buddhism; this is the true Way.[16]

As Takahashi notes, Dōgen advises his Buddhist trainees not to perform acts of compassion "for either their own or others' sake" because, "the primary requisite for the followers of Buddha is to leave self-centeredness" (*ED*, 84)[17] and "our keen interest in the result of our altruistic deeds is likely to have the adverse effect of egoism" (*ED*, 34). Thus, performing an action solely for the sake of Buddhism—that is, solely for the sake of (Buddhist) duty—has the effect, for Dōgen, of fulfilling the "primary requisite for the followers of Buddha"—to abandon self-centeredness. And the abandonment of self-centeredness is, as Takahashi interprets Dōgen's teaching, simultaneously the realization of insight into *kū*, or emptiness.

Takahashi relates the notion of *muga*, or selflessness, to the broader notion of *kū* by saying "*kū* is what *muga* is to be" (*ED*, 29). Thus the strength of a Buddhist trainee's insight into emptiness, Takahashi says, can be traced to his or her freedom from self-attachment (*goga-ridatsu*) (*ED*, 30). This would suggest that the discipline of observing Buddhist precepts and other teachings "for the sake of Buddhism alone" not only has the effect of purifying the trainee's actions from the taint of egotism, but also has the effect of opening the trainee's mind to insight into *kū*, or emptiness. And thus Dōgen, like Kant, would seem to affirm a reciprocally supportive relationship between the practice of insight into emptiness (through the practice of *zazen*, or a discipline of the speculative restriction of reason) and the practice of selfless obedience to apodictic rules of conduct. By giving his trainees this admonition—"just continue to act in accordance with the rules of the Buddhist teaching, and do not harbor personal prejudices"—Dōgen is, from Takahashi's viewpoint, actually showing them the gateway to the practice of Buddhist wisdom.

Support can be found in *Zen Action/Zen Person* as well for the view that "the presence of Buddhist realization" is cultivated through one's earnest efforts to obey the Buddhist precepts (*ZA*, 97). Simply by accepting a moral imperative, such as "thou shalt not kill," Kasulis says, "one undertakes a religiously moral life" (*ZA*, 98). And from that point on, if spiritual cultivation is continued, its efficacy will become "such that one is no longer capable of murder" (*ZA*, 98). That is to say, by the practice of earnestly obeying moral laws the Buddhist trainee comes to realize a state of the *nonproduction* of evil within oneself—a state that, Kasulis argues, is not different from the state of 'without-thinking,' of which *zazen* is the epitome (*ZA*, 77, 95). Thus respectful obedience to moral imperatives like the phrase "Thou shalt not kill" is seen by Dōgen as an important means of realizing the enlightened mind of Zen practice. "As Dōgen would put it," Kasulis says, "to say that one supersedes such phrases would be 'a teaching of Mara [the devil]' " (*ZA*, 96).

Dōgen himself states clearly that acceptance of, and obedience to, moral precepts are necessary means to the attainment of enlightenment. If the Buddhas and patriarchs of the past had not unfailingly received and observed the Buddhist precepts, he says, in the passage from *Shōbōgenzō*, "Jukai" quoted in the introductory chapter of this study, "it would have been impossible for them to become Buddhas or patriarchs."[18] And in the *Shushō-gi* ("The Meaning of Practice-Enlightenment")—a compilation of key passages from Dōgen's writings—the role of receiving and observing moral precepts as a means for attaining the enlightened mind of Zen practice is affirmed unequivocally:

> By receiving these precepts one realizes the supreme Bodhi-wisdom, the adamantine, indestructible enlightenment of the various Buddhas. . . . The Bhagavat [honorific title for the Buddha] has clearly shown to all sentient beings that when they receive the Buddha's precepts, they enter into the realm of the various Buddhas—truly becoming their children and realizing the same great enlightenment.[19]

(b)

In defense of the view that, for Dōgen, the effort to fulfill the requirements of moral law—as Kant understands such requirements—represents not merely a means to the attainment of enlightenment, but also the end of Zen practice itself: that end being to realize the Bodhisattva vow to save all sentient beings

To argue that Dōgen assigns a religious *function* to the practice of respectfully obeying moral precepts is not, of course, to argue that Dōgen, like Kant, views the realization of such precepts as the ultimate *end* of religious practice. However, if one accepts

Kant's view of what it means to fully realize the requirements of morality—the view that to fully realize the requirements of moral law is to work to realize the highest good in this world—then the arguments advanced in the present study in support of thesis Z2 do indeed apply to Dōgen, just as they apply to Suzuki. For Dōgen, like Suzuki, clearly views the end of Buddhist religious practice to be the realization of the "Bodhisattva vow" to save all sentient beings. In this concluding section of the appendix I will not repeat my arguments, set forth in chapter 4, section *iii*, above, which attempt to demonstrate an affinity between Kant's notion of realizing the highest good in the world and the Buddhist notion of realizing the Bodhisattva vow to save all sentient beings. I will only attempt to show how, for Dōgen—as he is interpreted both by Takahashi and by Francis Cook—the sole, motivating intention informing the practice of *zazen* must be the realization of this vow.

The second chapter of Dōgen's great treatise on Zen practice, *Shōbōgenzō*, focuses upon the *Prajñāpāramitā Hridaya Sūtra*, or the *Hannya Haramitsu Shingyō* as it is called in Japanese. Takahashi describes the meaning of the terms *hannya* and *haramitsu* in Dōgen's thought as follows: *hannya* (i.e., *prajñā*) is "the wisdom through which one knows the truth of *kū*" (emptiness), while *haramitsu* means "salvation from actual suffering" (*ED*, 34). Therefore:

> The meaning of *hannya-haramitsu* is that we can both be saved and save others by achieving *satori* through the experience of *kū*. Moreover, it should not be forgotten that this teaching is expounded as *Bosatsu-dō* [the way of the Bodhisattva]. As long as *haramitsu* is interpreted as "to save one's own self" it is bound to be confined to the theoretical grounds of Hīnayāna Buddhism. It will not develop into *Bosatsu-dō* as Mahāyāna Buddhism until it entertains the altruistic action of saving others. [*ED*, 34)[20]

"The definitive aim of *zazen* practice," as Takahashi interprets Dōgen's thought on this subject, "is to make us conduct even the four cardinal modes of behavior: walking, standing still, sitting and lying down—according to the truth of *kū*.. . . . Thus we can bring the practice of *kū* into full play even in our daily lives and with it the wisdom of *hannya* will become activated" (*ED*, 34). But according to Takahashi's interpretation of Dōgen, *zazen* as the practice of *kū* and the bringing "into full play . . . the wisdom of *hannya*" will be incomplete—will not be the manifestation of the Bodhisattva way—if it takes place in isolation from the effort to save other beings:

> Without the practice of altruism or at least the willingness to practice it, not only shall we not be able to step into the world of *Bosatsu-dō*, but also we will not be able to make our own world complete. . . . To understand the truth of *kū* by the means of the wisdom of *hannya* is in reality to become Buddha. But simply remaining in this state is not what Buddha should be. The truth of Buddha becomes realized through the practice of altruism by *jihi* [mercy]. . . . Thus the wisdom of *hannya* within the context of the *haramitsu* [salvation from suffering] by *jihi* marks the essence of Buddha. [*ED*, 34–35]

Jihi, Takahashi says, is the essence of *gangyō*—the Bodhisattva's "prayer for the salvation of all those who people the world" (*ED*, 36). The Bodhisattva "who cherishes this prayer most strongly and works the hardest for universal salvation through *jihi*" is Avalokiteśvara Bodhisattva, whose practice of *kū,* or emptiness, is the subject of the *Prajñāpāramitā Hridaya Sūtra (ED*, 36). And it is in following the example of Avalokiteśvara, or *Kannon-Bosatsu*, by working one's hardest for universal salvation through the practice of *jihi*, that Dōgen, according to Takahashi's interpretation, envisions the realization of the true end of Zen practice:

> Wisdom and *jihi*, these two qualities are of the essence of Buddha. . . . But both are not juxtaposed as being of equal value. This wisdom of *kū* has its import only as it functions effectually to bring *jihi* to its full perfection. On the other hand, it is in *jihi* that Buddha reveals his true nature. . . . *Kannon-Bosatsu* is in the process of actualizing this great *jihi*; for that great aim, he practices *kū*. Dōgen wrote the chapter, *Maka-Hannya-Haramitsu* in conformity with the above doctrine of [the *Hannya-haramitsu] Shingyō*. This fact implies how

> strongly Dōgen urges individuals to imbibe the spirit of *Kannon* as the actualization of the *kōan* [i.e., the actualization of Zen teaching]. Indeed, *Kannon* must be the highest, most ideal form of the *Bosatsu-dō* that the believer could follow. [*ED*, 36–37]

Like Takahashi, Francis Cook in his essay "Dōgen's View of Authentic Selfhood and its Socio-ethical Implications" argues that Dōgen took "most seriously" the Mahāyāna teaching that the cultivation of enlightenment through Zen practice "is but a means, albeit a necessary means, to the end of liberating all sentient beings" (*DV*, 140–41).[21] Evidence of the importance Dōgen assigned to the Bodhisattva vow to liberate all beings is indicated in part, Cook says, by the fact that two separate essays in the *Shōbōgenzō* are devoted to the subject— "Hotsu Bodai Shin" [Arousing the enlightened mind] and "Hotsu Mujō Shin" [Arousing the supreme mind]. These two essays show, Cook says, that from Dōgen's viewpoint, concern and active work for the salvation of others are not only involved as necessary *means* in the process of attaining enlightenment (as means of eliminating delusory self-centeredness), "but are really the ultimate goal" of that process (*DV*, 140–41). For Dōgen, Cook argues, the real goal of Zen practice is "that of commitment toward all beings and sympathy with their suffering" (*DV*, 140–41). And he goes on to quote from "Hotsu Bodai Shin":

> What is called "arousing the enlightened mind" means to make a vow to liberate all sentient beings at a time when oneself is not yet liberated. If one arouses this mind, no matter how humble in appearance one is, one is the guide of all beings. [*DV*, 140–41]

Thus for Cook, as for Takahashi, the enlightenment envisioned in Dōgen's account of Zen practice is above all an enlightenment *for others*—"that is, its proper function is that of eliminating suffering and struggle in the world" (*DV*, 140–41). And thus the views of these two Dōgen scholars support the claim that the realization of the Bodhisattva vow to save all sentient beings is, for Dōgen, the true end of Zen practice.

The claim that Dōgen views altruistic action as the true end of Zen practice would appear, at first glance, to clash with Dōgen's admonition in the "Gakudō Yōjin-shū" ["Points to watch in Buddhist training"], which states explicitly that "one does not undergo Buddhist training for the sake of others."[22] However, Dōgen goes on to say, in the passage already referred to in section *ii (a)* of this appendix, that "you should train for the sake of Buddhism alone. The various Buddhas do not show deep compassion for all sentient beings for either their own or others' sakes. . . . Simply practice Buddhism for the sake of Buddhism; this is the true Way."[23]

Here Dōgen is clearly *not* denying the claim that "the various Buddhas show deep compassion for all sentient beings." That is to say, he is not denying the claim that realization of the Bodhisattva vow to save all sentient beings is the true end of Buddhist practice. Rather, in this section of the "Gakudō Yōjin-shū"—entitled "The need for selfless practice of the way"—Dōgen, like Kant, emphasizes that compassion should be practiced *selflessly*, simply because it is our duty to practice it, regardless of whether or not we happen to feel a personal inclination to help others. Such radical selflessness, or forgetting of self, as Kasulis, Takahashi, and Cook all point out in their work on Dōgen, cannot be realized apart from the practice of *zazen* as "the epitome of without-thinking" (*ZA*, 77), as "the practice of *kū*" (*ED*, 34), as the realization of an emptiness that, Cook suggests, is perhaps better translated a "boundless openness" (*DV*, 139). But to hold that the realization of a subjective state of radical selflessness through the practice of *zazen* is, for Dōgen, an end in itself would be, from the perspectives of Takahashi's and Cook's studies, both to place Dōgen outside the Mahāyāna tradition of compassionate action in the world and to ignore his own writings on the importance of arousing the enlightened mind by the vow to liberate all beings.

Notes

Preface

1. Sigmund Freud, "Observations on 'Wild' Psycho-analysis," in *Collected Papers*, ed. Joan Riviere (New York: Basic Books, 1959), 2:298.

2. Ibid., 303.

3. Freud, *An Outline of Psycho-Analysis*, trans. James Strachey, rev. ed. (New York: Norton, 1969), 32.

4. Masao Abe, *Zen and Western Thought*, ed. William La Fleur (London: Macmillan, 1985), 114.

5. See, e.g., *ZM*, 99ff., *ZM*, 113ff., and the entire series of *Sandōkai* lectures.

6. See, e.g., Rick Fields, *How the Swans Came to the Lake* (Boulder: Shambhala, 1981), 258–60, 272.

7. See ibid., 258.

Chapter 1

1. In the text cited, Kant speaks only about the validity of religious *beliefs* (specifically, the belief in God). However, in applying Kant's thesis to the practice of Zen I will be extending the thesis to include religious *practices* (such as *zazen*) as well. This extension, of course, reflects my

own interpretation of Kant, which I hope will be vindicated in the course of this study.

2. See T.R.V. Murti, *The Central Philosophy of Buddhism* (London: George Allen & Unwin, 1955), 212.

3. Alan W. Watts, *Beat Zen, Square Zen, and Zen* (San Francisco: City Lights Books, 1959), 5.

4. Fields, *The Swans*, 246.

5. See, e.g., Eihei Dōgen, *Zen Master Dōgen: an Introduction with Selected Writings*, trans. Yūhō Yokoi and Daizen Victoria (New York: John Weatherhill, 1976), 84–87 ("The admonition 'receiving the precepts of a Bodhisattva is the first step to becoming a Buddhist' is something of which all trainees of the Way should be aware").

6. Ibid., 84.

7. Jiyu Kennett, *Selling Water by the River: A Manual of Zen Training* (New York: Vintage Books, 1972), 250.

8. Ibid., 212–14.

9. Ibid. The version of the third specific precept translated by Kennett is that of Dōgen's influential descendent, Keizan, and reads as follows: "*Do not covet.* The doer, the doing and that which has the doing done to it are immaculate; therefore there is no desire. It is the same doing as that of the Buddhas." In Dōgen's essay, "Receiving the Precepts," the third prohibitory precept appears simply as "do not engage in sexual relations." See Dōgen, *Zen Master Dōgen*, 86.

10. Dōgen, *Zen Master Dōgen*, 85.

Chapter 2

1. See *Webster's New World Dictionary*, 2d college ed., s.v. "autonomy."

2. Ibid., s.v. "heteronomy."

3. That methodologies expounded in language similar to Kant's have had disastrous effects when applied in child rearing is convincingly argued by Alice Miller in *For Your Own Good*, 2d ed. (New York: Farrar, Straus, Giroux, 1984). Applying Miller's critique of "poisonous pedagogy" to the writings of Kant demands and deserves a study in itself. It cannot be

denied that the language of Kant's "methodology"—which argues that duty, rather than inclination, should be the dominant influence on personal choice—is dangerously similar in tone to many of the (predominantly German) child rearing treatises referred to by Miller. However, Kant's response to a letter from Professor J.G. Sulzer—a writer on ethics whose "Essay on the Education and Instruction of Children" is one of the treatises quoted and discussed at length by Miller—illustrates how differently these two thinkers approached the subject of moral education. Sulzer, who observed it was "not very easy . . . to implant obedience in children" (Miller, *For Your Own Good*, 13), advised the use of "force and compulsion" (ibid.) in the early years of childhood: "If their wills can be broken at this time," he wrote, "they will never remember afterwards that they had a will" (ibid.). In a note to the text of the second edition of his *Groundwork of the Metaphysic of Morals*, Kant reveals that he had received a letter from "the late distinguished Professor [J.G.] Sultzer" asking, "what it is that makes moral instruction so ineffective, however convincing it may be in the eyes of reason?" (*GW*, 411). In his reply, Kant argues that teachers of morality "try to do too well by hunting everywhere for inducements to be moral—they spoil their medicine altogether by their very attempt to make it really powerful." As an alternative to the methodology of force and compulsion in moral instruction, Kant suggests that morality is best taught by example rather than by inducement. "Even children of a moderate age," Kant says, are impressed by a good example, "and duties should never be presented to them in any other way" (ibid.). Kant's deep regard for human freedom—and his respect for human beings as "ends in themselves" see e.g., *GW*, 428–29)—distinguish his writings from the horrifying examples of "poisonous pedagogy" presented by Miller (see *For Your Own Good*, 3–102, and compare Kant's own suggestions for educating children by "practical questions" and the discussion of examples. at *KP*, 155–57).

Chapter 3

1. For a discussion of Kant's concept of intellectual intuition as it relates to certain topics in Buddhist philosophy, see the author's paper, "Prajñāpāramitā and Intellectual Intuition," *Journal of Buddhist Philosophy* 1 (1983), 47.

2. Edward Conze, trans., *Buddhist Wisdom Books: The Diamond Sutra, The Heart Sutra* (London: George Allen & Unwin, 1958), 89.

3. Ibid., 79–81.

4. Ibid.

5. This reading of the text of the "Methodology of Pure Practical Reason" finds support in the *Metaphysic of Morals*, where Kant writes that an important foundation for "inner freedom" is "the duty of apathy"—"moral apathy," he calls it—which precludes a person's "letting himself be ruled by his feelings and inclinations" (*MM*, 407).

Chapter 4

1. Fields, *How the Swans Came to the Lake*, 230–31.

2. John Stuart Mill, *Utilitarianism* (Indianapolis: Bobbs-Merrill, 1957), 6.

3. Fields, *The Swans*, 231.

4. Suzuki, lecture on monastic rules, January 18, 1970. The source of this quotation, as well as that of other similarly noted references in this subsection, is a notebook of handwritten transcriptions of lectures by Suzuki, made by the author of this study between December 20, 1969, and July 28, 1970. The lectures were transcribed from memory shortly after Suzuki delivered them. Because there are no page numbers on the transcriptions, the references refer only to the date of the lecture from which the quotation is taken.

5. In the continuation of the above quotation, Suzuki says that the rules that concern him are "not necessarily written rules or rules set up by the management of the monastery to help them manage the daily affairs without interference from students—not these kind of rules necessarily but the kind which often are unwritten" (*PO*, 1/18/70).

6. Conze, *Buddhist Wisdom Books*, 78.

7. Edward Conze, *Buddhist Thought in India* (London: George Allen & Unwin, 1962), 211.

8. Conze, *Buddhist Wisdom Books*, 78.

9. My analysis of the role of "the highest good" in Kant's moral theory is influenced by Viggo Rossvaer, *Kant's Moral Philosophy: An Interpretation of the Categorical Imperative* (Oslo: Universitetsforlaget, 1979).

Chapter 5

1. Watts, quoted in Fields, *The Swans*, 221.

2. Ibid.

3. Alan Watts, *Psychotherapy East and West* (New York: Pantheon, 1961), 73.

4. Ibid., 74–75.

5. Watts, quoted in Fields, *The Swans*, 221.

6. See *Zen Master Dōgen*, "A Monk at the Fourth Stage of Meditation" (*Shōbōgenzō Shi-zen Biku*), 159–67. In the course of a lengthy refutation of the view that the practice of Buddhism has anything to do with the practice of either Confucianism or Taoism, Dōgen quotes with approval the great sixth-century teacher Chih-i, a patriarch of the T'ien-tai sect of Buddhism, who observed that the then current practice of combining the Taoist teachings of Chuang-tzŭ and Lao-tzŭ with the teachings of Buddhism resulted in "a mixture of these various teachings that confuses beginners, preventing them from deciding what is true and what is false" (*Zen Master Dōgen*, 163). Dōgen specifically criticizes Chuang-tzŭ's statement—"High and low station in life, pleasure and pain, right and wrong, gain and loss all occur spontaneously"—as a demonstration of its author's willful ignorance of the strict laws of cause and effect (karma) (*Zen Master Dōgen*, 162).

7. Watts, quoted in Fields, *The Swans*, 221.

8. See Richard H. Robinson and Willard L. Johnson, *The Buddhist Religion*, 2nd ed. (North Scituate: Duxbury Press, 1977), 86: "The Mahāyāna innovation was to proclaim that the bodhisattva course is open to all." Robinson and Johnson point out, however, that even in the most "libertarian" Mahāyāna texts, such as the *Vimalakīrti-Nirdeśa Sūtra*, the layperson's path to enlightenment is considered "a second-best for those unable to take the yellow robe" (96).

9. Paul Reps, comp., *Zen Flesh, Zen Bones* (Middlesex: Pelican Books, 1971), 135.

10. Ibid., 147.

11. Watts, *Beat Zen, Square Zen and Zen*, 25.

12. Fields, *The Swans*, 261.

13. Ibid., 246.

14. Ibid., 248.

15. Richard Baker, "A Zen-American Tale," interview in *The Vajradhatu Sun* (official publication of Vajradhatu and the Nalanda Foundation, Boulder, Colo.), August-September, 1985: 6.

16. Ibid.

17. Sigmund Freud, *An Outline of Psychoanalysis*, trans. James Strachey, rev. ed. (New York: Norton, 1949), 31–32.

18. Watts, *Psychotherapy East and West*, 3.

19. Ibid.

20. Ibid., 134–35.

21. Baker, "A Zen-American Tale," 6.

22. Freud, *An Outline of Psychoanalysis*, 33.

23. Ibid., 34.

24. Ibid., 32.

25. Baker, "A Zen-American Tale," 6.

26. Ibid.

27. Freud, *An Outline of Psychoanalysis*, 32.

Appendix

1. Masanobu Takahashi, *The Essence of Dōgen*, trans. Yuzuru Nobuoka (London: Kegan Paul International, 1983).

2. Thomas P. Kasulis, *Zen Action/Zen Person* (Honolulu: University of Hawaii Press, 1981).

3. *Dōgen Studies*, ed. William LaFleur (Honolulu: University of Hawaii Press, 1985).

4. Quotations from Masanobu Takahashi's *The Essence of Dōgen* are cited in this text using the abbreviation *ED*.

5. A slight change in Kant's original language has been made in this passage, the words "person" and "everyone" having been substituted for the words "man" and "every man."

6. The problematic nature of this reading of Kant's "Methodology of Pure Practical Reason" is acknowledged at the beginning of argument (*c*) in subsection *iii* of chapter 3.

7. Quotations from Thomas P. Kasulis's *Zen Action/Zen Person* are cited in this text using the abbreviation *ZA*.

8. Eihei Dōgen, *Record of Things Heard from the Treasury of the Eye of the True Teaching: A Translation of the* Shōbōgenzō-zuimonki, trans. Thomas Cleary (Boulder: Prajñā Press, 1980), 3.

9. Kasulis is quoting from Dōgen's *Shōbōgenzō*, "Zazengi."

10. See the comments on Husserl and Kant, below.

11. Edmund Husserl, *Ideas*, trans. W.R. Boyce Gibson (New York: Macmillan, 1952), 70. It is unfortunate that, despite this acknowledged "inner affinity," Husserl developed his phenomenology largely without reference to Kant. The conspicuous absence of all but the briefest references to Kant in the *Ideas*—a work that investigates so much of the same philosophical terrain first explored in the *Critique of Pure Reason*—calls to mind the statement, attributed to Hölderlin, that "the work of Kant stands as an unconquered fortress behind the advancing front lines of modern thought."

12. See, e.g., Dōgen, *Moon in a Dewdrop: Writings of Zen Master Dōgen*, ed. Kazuaki Tanahashi (San Francisco: North Point Press, 1985), 70.

13. Quotations from Dōgen's *Shōbōgenzō Zuimonki*, using the Thomas Cleary translation noted above, will henceforth be cited in this text using the abbrevation *SZ*.

14. Dōgen is, however, also careful to tell the monk that this decision "is a difficult matter; it is not for anyone else to decide. You must just think it over thoroughly on your own" (*SZ*, 67).

15. Dōgen, "Points to Watch in Buddhist Training" ("Gakudō Yōjinshū"), part 4 ("The need for selfless practice of the way"), in *Zen Master Dōgen*, 51.

16. Ibid.

17. Quoting Dōgen in *Shōbōgenzō Zuimonki.*

18. Dōgen, *Shōbōgenzō*, "Jukai," in *Zen Master Dōgen*, 85.

19. Dōgen, "Shushō-gi," in *Zen Master Dōgen*, 61.

20. Hīnayāna, or Theravāda ("Way of the Elders"), and Mahāyāna are the two main branches of Buddhism. Theravāda Buddhism might be said to focus on the path of individual liberation, while Mahāyāna Buddhism emphasizes the path of the Bodhisattva, as discussed in chapter 4, section *iii (a)* of this study. See, e.g., Robinson and Johnson, *The Buddhist Religion*, 86–88.

21. Quotations from Francis Cook's essay, "Dōgen's View of Authentic Selfhood and its Socio-ethical Implications," as it appears in the book *Dōgen Studies*, are cited in this text using the abbreviation *DV*.

22. Dōgen, *Zen Master Dōgen*, 51.

23. Ibid.

Works Cited

Abe, Masao. *Zen and Western Thought.* Ed. William La Fleur. London: Macmillan, 1985.

Baker, Richard. "A Zen-American Tale." Interview in *The Vajradhatu Sun* (official publication of Vajradhatu and the Nalanda Foundation, Boulder, Colo.), August-September 1985: 6.

Conze, Edward, *Buddhist Thought in India.* London: George Allen & Unwin, 1962.

———. trans. *Buddhist Wisdom Books: The Diamond Sutra, The Heart Sutra.* London: George Allen & Unwin, 1958.

Cook, Francis. "Dōgen's View of Authentic Selfhood and its Socio-ethical Implications." In *Dōgen Studies,* ed. William LaFleur. Honolulu: University of Hawaii Press, 1985.

Dōgen, Eihei. *Moon in a Dewdrop: Writings of Zen Master Dōgen.* Ed. Kazuaki Tanahashi. San Francisco: North Point Press, 1985.

———. *Record of Things Heard from the Treasury of the Eye of the True Teaching: A Translation of the* Shōbōgenzō-zuimonki. Translated by Thomas Cleary. Boulder: Prajñā Press, 1980.

———. *Zen Master Dōgen: An Introduction with Selected Writings,* trans. Yūhō Yokoi and Daizen Victoria. New York: John Weatherhill, 1976.

Fields, Rick. *How the Swans Came to the Lake.* Boulder: Shambhala, 1981.

Freud, Sigmund. "Observations on 'Wild' Psychoanalysis." In *Collected Papers*, ed. Joan Riviere. New York: Basic Books, 1959.

———. *An Outline of Psycho-Analysis.* Rev. ed. Translated by James Strachey. New York: Norton, 1969.

Husserl, Edmund. *Ideas.* Translated by W.R. Boyce Gibson. New York: Macmillan, 1952.

Kant, Immanuel. *Critique of Practical Reason.* Translated by Lewis White Beck. Indianapolis: Bobbs-Merrill, 1956.

———. *Critique of Pure Reason.* Translated by Norman Kemp Smith. New York: St. Martin's Press, 1965.

———. *The Doctrine of Virtue: Part II of The Metaphysic of Morals.* Translated by Mary J. Gregor. New York: Harper & Row, 1964.

———. *Groundwork of the Metaphysic of Morals.* Translated by H.J. Paton. New York: Harper & Row, 1964.

Kasulis, Thomas P. *Zen Action/Zen Person.* Honolulu: University of Hawaii Press, 1981.

Kennett, Jiyu. *Selling Water by the River: A Manual of Zen Training.* New York: Vintage Books, 1972.

Mill, John Stuart. *Utilitarianism.* Indianapolis: Bobbs-Merrill, 1957.

Miller, Alice. *For Your Own Good.* 2d ed. New York: Farrar, Straus, Giroux, 1984.

Murti, T.R.V. *The Central Philosophy of Buddhism.* London: George Allen & Unwin, 1955.

Olson, Phillip. "Prajñāpāramitā and Intellectual Intuition," *Journal of Buddhist Philosophy* 1 (1983): 47–68.

Reps, Paul, comp. *Zen Flesh, Zen Bones.* Middlesex: Pelican Books, 1971.

Robinson, Richard H., and Willard L. Johnson. *The Buddhist Religion.* 2nd ed. North Scituate: Duxbury Press, 1977.

Rossvaer, Viggo. *Kant's Moral Philosophy: An Interpretation of the Categorical Imperative.* Oslo: Universitetsforlaget, 1979.

Suzuki, Shunryu. "City Practice." *Wind Bell* IX (Fall-Winter 1970–71): 4–46.

———. "First *Sandokai* Lecture." *Wind Bell* XII (1973): 45–50.

———. Lecture on monastic rules. Transcription by author made from memory shortly after delivery of lecture. January 18, 1970.

———. Lecture on the relationship between rituals, rules and precepts. Transcription by author made from memory shortly after delivery of lecture. July 28, 1970.

———. *Sandōkai* Lectures. Thirteen lectures on the Zen Buddhist text, *Sandōkai*, delivered at Tassajara Zen Mountain Center, May 27–July 6, 1970. Zen Mountain Center Library, Tassajara, California. Photocopy.

———. "*Sandōkai* Lecture V." *Wind Bell* XVI (Winter 1978–79): 28–31.

———. "Teacher and Disciple." *Wind Bell* XIII (1974): 3–5.

———. "The Trikāya." *Wind Bell* VIII (Spring 1969): 4–18.

———. *Zen Mind, Beginner's Mind.* Ed. Trudy Dixon. New York: John Weatherhill, 1970.

Takahashi, Masanobu. *The Essence of Dōgen.* Translated by Yuzuru Nobuoka. London: Kegan Paul International, 1983.

Watts, Alan. *Beat Zen, Square Zen and Zen.* San Francisco: City Lights Books, 1959.

———. *Psychotherapy East and West.* New York: Pantheon, 1961.

Index

D

E

O

P

T